The Eclectic Guitar Lesson Collection

VRENY VAN ELSLANDE

© ZOT Zin Publishing 2020

All rights reserved. No part of this publication may be reproduced, distributed, or transmitted in any form or by any means, including photocopying, recording, or other electronic or mechanical methods, without the prior written permission of the publisher.

1st edition

www.zotzinmusic.com

Ordering information: For details, contact the publisher at the web address above.

Editor: Dr. Angela Blewitt, Dylan Garity

Page design: Ljiljana Pavkov
Cover design: Andrey Poletskiy

This cover has been designed using resources from Freepik.com.

Cataloging-in-Publication Data

Van Elslande, Vreny.
Guitar essentials: the eclectic guitar lesson collection / Vreny Van Elslande.

Los Angeles, Calif. : ZOT Zin Publishing, 2020.

ix, 194 p. : ill.

ISBN 978-1-7353571-2-6

Guitar — Instruction and study. 2. Guitar — Methods — Self-instruction. 3. Guitar — Studies and exercises. I. Title.

Finally a book that pays just as much attention to the why as it does to the how! With so many books that offer only licks and styles, this book dives into the theory a guitarist needs to apply those licks. A much needed resource for guitarists at any skill level.

CARL VERHEYEN
(Solo artist, band leader & Member of Supertramp since 1985)
CarlVerheyen.com

I met Vreny in 2002, and started lessons with him more or less as a beginner. My time learning with Vreny gave me the clarity and organization I was after, and within only a couple years of starting lessons, I was touring internationally in bands and teaching guitar full-time on my own. Without a doubt, Vreny's teaching methods are the cornerstone of my musical education and my career as a teacher and touring musician. Few teachers in my life could transform the passion I had for learning so efficiently into real understanding and musical ability.

MICHAEL BEACH
Melbourne, 2020
michaelbeach.org

TABLE OF CONTENTS

Introduction ix

Chapter 1: Maximum Results Practice 1
   Focus 2
   Short Drills 3
   Alternate Between Cerebral and Physical Activity 4
   Use A Metronome 4
   Slower is Better 5
   Make Practice Lists and Schedules 6
   Track Your Results 7
   Be Resourceful 8
   Listen Intently 9

Chapter 2: Learn The Fret Board 10

Chapter 3: The Major Scale 15
   What is a Scale? 15
   What Do You Use a Scale For? 15
   The Major Scale 16
   Accidentals 18

Chapter 4: Single-String Soloing 20
   Linear vs. In Position 21
   Single-String Soloing Explained in a Nutshell 23
   Here's Why Singing Solfeggio Will Bring You Better Results 26
   Common Single-String Soloing Mistakes and Some Pointers 28

Chapter 5: The Minor Pentatonic Scale 32
   Fingerings 33
   Some Quick Pentatonic Scale Theory 33
   How to Learn and Practice These Five Scale Shapes 34
   Soloing in Major Keys With Minor Pentatonic 35

Chapter 6: The Hindustan Scale 36

Chapter 7: Pentatonic Substitution 39
   Over a C Chord 39
   Over a Dm Chord 40
   Over Altered Chords 41
   Minor Pent. Substitution Over a II - V - I Chord Progression 42

Chapter 8: Creative Pentatonic Chord Progressions 44
   Pentatonic Substitution Chords 44
   Chords Taken from Blues 45
   The Dom7alt Chord Pentatonic Substitution 45
   Cool Chord Progressions for the A Minor Pentatonic Scale 46

Chapter 9: Key Signatures ... 48
   The Key Signature Theory ... 48
   Each Key Signature Signifies a Specific Major Scale ... 49
   The Order of Sharps and the Order of Flats ... 50
   What Does This Mean: "The Order of..."? ... 50
   Which Scales Have ♭'s and Which Have ♯'s? ... 51
   How to Apply This to Learn All Major Scales ... 51
   How to Practice Key Signatures ... 56

Chapter 10: The Circle of 4ths and 5ths ... 58

Chapter 11: The Modes ... 59
   Ionian ... 59
   Dorian ... 59
   Phrygian ... 60
   Lydian ... 60
   Mixolydian ... 60
   Aeolian ... 61
   Locrian ... 61
   Modes: What's the Big Deal? ... 62

Chapter 12: In-Position Scale Fingerings ... 66

Chapter 13: Improvisation over IVm Modal Interchange ... 67

Chapter 14: Improvisation over ♭VImaj7 Modal Interchange ... 68

Chapter 15: Key and Scale ... 69

Chapter 16: The Whole Tone Scale ... 70
   Chords in the Whole Tone Scale ... 71
   When and Where Do You Use the Whole Tone Scale? ... 71

Chapter 17: Theory of Intervals ... 73
   Organization of Intervals ... 76

Chapter 18: 3rd Intervals ... 79
   The Minor 3rd ... 79
   The Major 3rd ... 80

Chapter 19: Chords and Inversions ... 82
   The Difference Between Major and Minor Chords ... 82
   Scale Degrees ... 84
   Bar Chords ... 86
   Inversions ... 89

Chapter 20: The Notes In All Triads ... 92

Chapter 21: All Triads in the Key of C ... 95

Chapter 22: Cycles: The Study of Voice-Leading & Composition ... 97

Chapter 23: Dm & Em Over G7 Triad Substitution ... 100

Chapter 24: The dim7 Passing Chord ... 105

Chapter 25: The Augmented Line Cliché — 108
- On the I Chord — 108
- On the V Chord — 108

Chapter 26: Writing in Different Modes — 110

Chapter 27: Chord Formulas — 112
- Some Helpful Chord Formula Logic — 113

Chapter 28: Improve Your Timing — 122

Chapter 29: Ear-Training — 124
- Using Known Songs for Leverage — 125

Chapter 30: The Four Schools of Guitar Technique Training — 128

Chapter 31: All Twenty-Four Finger-Combinations — 131
- 1. Accuracy Drill — 131
- 2. Dexterity Drill — 133

Chapter 32: Short Scalar Speed Drills — 135

Chapter 33: Comping with Guide Tones — 138
- What is Comping and What Are Guide Tones? — 138
- Comping With 3rds and 7ths — 138
- Comping With Guide Tones in Blues — 139

Chapter 34: Over Eighty Ways to Make Guitar Solos Better — 142

Chapter 35: Secondary Dominants — 176

Chapter 36: Harmony In Composition & Songwriting — 179
- I, IV, V — 179
- Chord Functions Within a Major Scale — 179
- Common Progressions — 180
- Substitutions — 180

Chapter 37: Major Blues Rhythm Styles — 182
- Honky Tonk Style — 182
- Blues Bass Lines — 183
- Blues With Approach Chords from Below — 185
- Blues With Approach Chords From Above — 186
- Blues With Sliding 9th Chords — 187

In Closing — 188

Vreny & ZOT Zin Music — 189

Free Bonus Goodies — 195

Before you continue,

get all your **free Bonus & practice materials**

on the last page!

INTRODUCTION

There is so much to learn about music, so much one can do on a guitar, so many different styles and genres to master—it's endless. My vast guitar and music curriculum has grown to many thousands of pages over the past twenty-seven years, and I have sifted through the theory, chords, knowledge, skills, and exercises to create this book of tidbits for you.

There's something for everybody in this book. Some of it is basic, some of it is a quick read, and some of it is for high intermediate or more advanced players, who will find new tricks here and there throughout. This book consists of gems gleaned from years of playing and teaching guitar, and I have organized it for maximum productivity.

The first chapter covers how to practice more efficiently. Every guitarist, no matter their level of prowess, will benefit from this chapter. Experience has taught me that even top-level guitarists didn't necessarily get there practicing in efficient ways. One can only guess how much better a guitarist could have been, or how much sooner they could have gotten that good, if only they had known about or had better applied the lessons we will cover in this chapter.

The second chapter tackles fret board knowledge. Beginner and intermediate guitarists will greatly benefit from the exercises in this chapter, but many advanced guitarists can further improve, too. I've worked with tons of great guitarists through the years who reaped great benefits taking their fret board memorization to the next level.

Chapter three covers the major scale. This is something that everybody should know, and yet it might surprise you to hear how many really great guitarists there are who get stuck when they try to explain the scale. A good test to know for sure how well you know something is to try to teach it to a six-year-old child. If the kid immediately understands what you're talking about, and you don't get stuck in your explanation, only then do you know for sure that you have mastered the material. Otherwise, you've discovered a blind spot in your musicianship.

Next, we move on to single-string soloing. While it seems obvious how complete beginners or intermediate students benefit from playing guitar solos on one string, upper-intermediate and advanced players have reported great improvement in their improvisation and broader guitar skills after spending time on this as well.

You get the idea; there's something here for everyone.

Some topics that at first glance seem more geared toward beginner students will benefit the more advanced students as well, who might find out they need to brush up on some theory knowledge. Conversely, some of the more challenging material is explained in such a way that a less experienced student can still learn from it.

This book is a precursor to a thorough, complete music theory book for guitarists that I'm writing. It will cover absolutely everything there is to know about music theory. But, in the meantime, here are some tasty tidbits of guitar essentials.

All that said, my goal in writing this book is to:

1. Give insight into some of the tricks and techniques I use to propel my students from complete beginner to full-time professional in only a couple of years.

2. Provide a selection of lessons I selected from my ZOTZinGuitarLessons curriculum.

3. Help you become a better and more confident, creative, and well-rounded musician.

Before we dive into it all, some conventions:

1. There is no generally accepted standard when it comes to depicting guitar neck diagrams. In the significant guitar book collection I have at my studio, about half of the books show guitar necks with the bass string on top, and about half with the bass string in the bottom. In this book, all guitar neck diagrams are depicted with the bass string on top and the treble string at the bottom.

    I personally have always felt that neck diagrams that have the bass string on top make more sense. After all: when you hold a guitar, your bass string is always up closer to the ceiling too. It's a closer, more accurate visual representation of what you are physically doing: as your eyes move down the neck diagram strings, your fretting hand also moves toward the floor.

    I do understand that there are strong, valid points for either system. People who are more used to seeing neck diagrams with the bass string at the bottom make the valid point that this conforms to how tablature is mapped out. However, because guitar players are notoriously less adept at sight-reading, and because tablature and guitar neck diagrams don't really have anything to do with one another, I think that the benefits you get from seeing your hand move in the same direction as the neck diagrams far outweigh the less useful benefit you get from having the neck diagram being lined up with tablature.

2. The most common symbol we use to label minor chords is the letter "m." You will also see dash (as in D-, F- etc.) used quite often, depending on the resource or the composer. Rather than opting for consistency, I use both throughout the book so you get used to seeing minor chords written both ways.

3. In some European countries, including Belgium, we use the solfeggio note name "si" for the note B. In other countries, including the US, we say "ti" instead of "si". Throughout the book, I either use si or ti or ti/si, based on the situation or context. Know that both are solfeggio names for the note B.

Let's begin!

CHAPTER 1: MAXIMUM RESULTS PRACTICE

For best results, always practice with optimal efficiency. One of the reasons why my students progress exceptionally well is that I give very focused, timed exercises that guarantee maximum results with streamlined effort.

I don't just give my students information, drills, and exercises; I also teach them how to practice the learned material effectively. This practice guidance applies principles discovered through research in the fields of psychology, productivity, learning styles, and neuroscience.

Here's a quick personal story to illustrate where my passion to help my students experience extraordinary results comes from.

When I was sixteen, a high school friend let me hold his shiny, green Ibanez. I had never touched a guitar before then. I knew, from the moment it touched my hands, that *that* was what I wanted to do for the rest of my life. It was like a light bulb went off, an epiphany. I was going to be a pro musician. I didn't even know how to properly hold the instrument, but I knew I was going to earn my income as a guitarist.

After two years of self-study and a year of mandatory military service, I started going to music school. In my first year, I told my guitar teacher about my dream of becoming a professional musician. She diplomatically told me to not get my hopes up because I had "started rather late." Top-level musicians, she told me, start at a young age. She was a very highly respected, world-class classical guitar teacher. Five years later, she told me she had been mistaken with her assessment of me. Because of my fast progress, she had come to believe I had all it took to reach my musical goals. I completed the ten-year program in only seven, graduating three years ahead of time. To my knowledge (and assuming I've been correctly informed about this), this had never happened before in any music school in Belgium.

It was my teacher's hope that I would go to conservatory to pursue a career as a classical guitarist. Instead, I applied to Berklee College of Music in Boston and immediately was accepted. I went for a dual major—"Music Production & Engineering" and "Guitar Performance"—and I finished the five-year program in about three-and-a-half years, graduating Summa Cum Laude for both my degrees.

You might wonder, "Why this story"?

I apply the same learning principles and techniques in my teaching approach that made it possible for me to graduate five years earlier than anyone else. I learned and acquired over fifteen years' worth of musical knowledge and guitar skills in a third of the time it took my classmates.

You can progress that quickly, too. You just need the right teacher, the right approach, and the right knowledge of how to do things. Would you like to acquire a vast amount of musical knowledge in no time at all? Would you like to be more efficient and learn with much less effort? If you answer yes, then I've got to tell you that the only way to make this happen is with a top-quality teacher or mentor, combined with **top-quality practice**.

After all, no matter how great the lessons or lesson materials you learn from, they're not going to make as much difference if you practice that material ineffectively. Practice makes permanent, so excellent practice matters.

That's why, before we cover anything else, we first need to discuss some important practice hints that will help you get maximum results from the upcoming lessons.

Focus

When there is no focus, then you're noodling, not practicing. Don't check emails. Shut down your computer and your phone if you have to. Your ability to keep your attention on the task at hand is what will have the greatest impact on the quality of your results. It is a skill that you can train. How do you train anything? Simple, you just do it. Correct your attention back to the task if you feel yourself getting distracted.

Moreover, when dealing with a challenging part, zoom in on the core of the challenge you are dealing with. You do this by removing all other activity or interference. For example, don't repeatedly practice an entire song if there's only one bar in it that you have a hard time executing correctly. That seems like an awful waste of valuable practice time. Only practice that one bar. I know that seems like common sense, and yet it keeps blowing my mind how often I need to bring that up or correct that in lessons.

Here's another example. When you have a certain rhythm that you can't figure out or that keeps tripping you up, don't try to cover the whole measure/rhythm all at once. Work it out in smaller sections, one beat at a time. *That* is focus.

When you have a challenging chord switch, where your fingers can't quite move adequately from chord to chord, don't strum busy rhythms. That would be a major distraction, taking brainpower away that could be allocated to the fretting hand. It's much better to strum simple quarter note down strokes only, so all your focus can be directed to the fretting hand executing the chord switches. When one hand struggles with a task, simplify what the other hand is doing, or if necessary, stop doing anything at all with it.

In other words, focus in guitar practice includes the following strategies:

1. Isolate the area of difficulty/obstacle.

2. Break things down into smaller segments.

3. Slow down a fast-paced technical passage to a tempo that makes the challenging piece of music easy to perform.

4. Repeat the action over and over again until the rough area gets easier or disappears entirely.

5. Get rid of any extraneous actions that are not necessary to get the job done:

    a. Only move fingers that need to move.

    b. Don't make extraneous, unnecessary arm motions while strumming.

      c. When your fretting hand is struggling with certain chord fingerings, don't strum rhythmically complex patterns, so you are able to direct more focus toward your fretting hand.

      d. Practice with full presence and awareness. Always ask yourself:

          i. "What is the difficulty I need to overcome here?"

          ii. "What am I trying to achieve?"

          iii. "What can I leave or weed out that is unnecessary, so I get to the core of the difficulty and get it resolved as soon as possible?"

You then slowly and attentively keep repeating the challenging action until it becomes effortless and natural. At that point, start adding whatever other elements back in—the ones you left out to simplify (your other hand, the rest of the song, more complicated strumming, and so on).

More importantly: be aware! That, too, is focus. Be present and in the moment at all times. If your mind is wandering off to something else, go do the "something else" first.

I can't even begin to tell you how very often I find myself correcting a student's hand position, only to find that student playing with that same less-good hand position again two minutes later, and the week after, and the week after, and … the week after.

Spending so much time doing something incorrectly without paying due diligence to correct and adjust it, probably has to be about the most gargantuan waste of time one could imagine.

That lack of awareness can cost you dearly in:

- ▶ Time and progress
- ▶ Results
- ▶ Money (paid for lessons, books, etc.)
- ▶ Health (injuries due to bad technique that is left uncorrected during practice time).

Life is too short and precious to waste it in a cloud or haze of thought. Be present and in the moment while you practice.

Short Drills

Researchers in the fields of neuroscience and psychology know for a fact that the brain works at its optimum when handling study material in little chunks of information repeated at regular intervals. What this means specifically is that our brain works best when we feed it smaller segments of information, and then feed it that same information on a regular basis, like for example once a day.

Unless the activity is more physical than cerebral, such as for example technique exercises, avoid practicing more than fifteen minutes at a time on anything that involves intense concentration or brain-processing. It's generally accepted in neuroscience that after about fifteen minutes, one's concentration level starts dissipating. If you practice in short ten- to fifteen-minute drills, you benefit from two major advantages:

1. **You keep your concentration at peak performance.**

   By the time your concentration is about to start losing its peak, you're already off to the next drill. In this way, you get more out of your practice time. Much better results, with much less effort, in much less time.

2. **You become a more complete musician.**

   When you practice short drills, you lift yourself up in more different areas of your musicianship in a shorter amount of time.

   As an example: when you have half-hour drills to practice, you can only do two exercises in an hour. When you have ten-minute exercises, you can fit in six drills during the course of an hour. We need this kind of efficiency because there's so much to practice on the path to becoming a really great musician: ear training, rhythm, technique, songwriting, scales, improvisation, fret board knowledge, theory, harmony, and so much more.

   When you practice short drills, you consistently become more proficient in a vast array of areas in a shorter amount of time. You don't want to be the guitarist who is only good at playing rhythm, or who only knows how to solo, or who can only play one style, or who knows a lot of theory but can't apply it, or who has amazing technique but subpar timing. There are many reasons why you don't want that. For one, guitar becomes all the more fun when you can do a little bit of everything pretty well. Jamming with people is more fun, for you *and* for them, when you can do a variety of really cool things. You get the idea—when you become a more complete musician, you gain access to experiences and levels of musical joy you'd miss out on otherwise.

Alternate Between Cerebral and Physical Activity

This is another great way to get more done and keep your concentration up. After you have practiced a couple of concentration-intense guitar exercises in a row, move on to technique exercises that train your speed, dexterity, control, or coordination.

Speed and muscle coordination exercises require a different kind of concentration that is not as mentally demanding or draining as the heavy brain-processing memorization, fret board, or music theory drills. By the same token, when you feel like your arm is about to fall off because you worked your muscles hard, go back to practicing something that requires more brain processing. This gives your hands, fingers, and arms some well-deserved rest.

Use A Metronome

The metronome is an indispensable tool for training one's rhythm and technique. You can't efficiently train your time-feel or technical ability in any other way than with a metronome (or drum machine). With this tool, top musicians spend a great deal of their practice time honing their speed and technique as well as their timing and rhythm-playing skills.

One can also use a metronome to practice sight-reading. Set the metronome at a slow, comfortable tempo; then, read the music along with the tempo of the beeps. Used that way, the metronome is a fantastic tool to track or evaluate your music-reading abilities. The higher the bpm (beats per minute, basically the tempo) at which you can read new music without making too many mistakes, the stronger your sight-reading chops are.

Slower is Better

It's remarkable how much valuable time most guitar students waste trying to tackle new material they are struggling with, at a tempo that is way above their abilities. It's even more unbelievable how many students keep persisting in this approach long after it should have been obvious that it is clearly not working, rather than shifting to an approach that does work. Einstein stated it best: "Insanity is doing the same thing over and over again, expecting different results."

When, after six or eight tries, you still have not been able to make it to the end of this one-bar rhythm you have been trying to execute, chances are you're probably trying to play it way too fast for your abilities. Nine out of the ten times, the student who practices in this inefficient way gets increasingly frustrated. Very odd! Why get frustrated yet persist in ways that don't work, when the solution is really simple? The solution is to **slow down, pace yourself, and give your brain time to put all the elements in order.**

This same principle applies to developing technical prowess on guitar. The quickest way to reach the level where you can play really fast is by first practicing the speed exercises really slowly for a longer period of time. Always figure things out or practice new things very slowly, and then gradually increase the tempo a couple of bpm at a time. The slow pace improves muscle memory and control. It gives your brain time to process information adequately, which it can't do when that information is fed to the brain at a rushed pace with a sloppy delivery. In other words: **speed** is the byproduct of **accuracy**. Someone who can shred fast, scalar lines doesn't move their fingers all that much *quicker* than you do—the person just moves their fingers *less*.

Most of all, be patient. The more you try to rush into things, the more that will hurt your progress.

It's an interesting paradox, and it might even be counterintuitive to some people, but you will progress the fastest when you do things slowly enough for long enough. At a slow pace, you're not sending confusing, mixed messages to the brain, which is what happens when you keep playing random mistakes.

Some of the benefits you gain from practicing things as slowly as is necessary:

1. You don't have to go back in time to relearn or unlearn something (a vast time-waster).
2. You don't grow bad habits that need to be fixed (another huge waste of time and talent you won't have to worry about).
3. You stay in control.
4. You practice with more awareness. It's hard to be aware when things fly by in a rush.
5. You get much better, faster, stronger results in way less time.

It's an old adage, but it also holds true in learning guitar: Slow and steady wins the race.

Make Practice Lists and Schedules

Every author who has ever written any book on productivity, goal-setting, or success, from Tony Robbins to Jack Canfield or Brian Tracy, has at least one chapter dedicated to the importance of writing down your to-do list at the start of a new day or the night before.

As it turns out, one accomplishes a lot more at a higher level and with better results when you have your goals and tasks for the day written down.

There's also something very visceral and motivating about crossing out a task you've just completed. It creates a good feeling, and it gives you energy.

Every morning at the start of my day, I type up my list of things I want to accomplish and practice that day. I print it out and immediately start tackling the items one by one. I put the most important goal or task at the very top. You want to knock that one out first. When I finish a task, I scratch through it with a red pen. It gives a great sense of satisfaction to see all the red on the page toward the end of the day. I like the color because it stands out.

Here's an example of one of my old scale practice schedules:

Melodic Minor Scale	Harmonic Minor Scale	Harmonic Major Scale
C	C	C
F	F	F
B♭	B♭	B♭
E♭	E♭	E♭
A♭	A♭	A♭
D♭	D♭	D♭
F♯	F♯	F♯
B	B	B
E	E	E
A	A	A
D	D	D
G	G	G

Microsoft Word makes it very easy to make tables like this in a jiffy. When you write down your planned items for the day, things get done.

Track Your Results

Top sports coaches, successful investors, and high-level businesspeople all track their results. They collect data and track stats to help them stay the course and to see where they can improve. You'll see in the technique chapter "Twenty-Four Finger Combinations" that I added a tracking page. I mainly use result tracking as a great motivational tool.

For example, back when I needed to lose some weight, I had a record where I kept track of my body stats: weight, BMI, waistline, arm muscle size, thigh size, chest size, and so on. Seeing those numbers move in the right direction week after a week was a great motivator to keep going. It's satisfying to know you're on the right track. It's also reassuring to know that what you are doing is working. How can you tell if you're not tracking your results?

Here are some of the areas of guitar progress I used to track:

1. **Fret board knowledge**
    - ▶ Tool: timer.
    - ▶ See how quickly you can find all the notes of a scale across the length of the guitar neck's fret board. We'll cover this in the upcoming fret board memorization chapter.

2. **Technical ability, speed**
    - ▶ Tool: metronome.
    - ▶ Before moving on to another technique drill, write down your fastest metronome setting (before it got sloppy) for the drill you just practiced.

3. **Time feel**
    - ▶ Tool: metronome.
    - ▶ Play rhythm drills designed to improve time feel, and keep a journal of how often (how many bars, how many seconds) you were perfectly on the beat.

4. **Voice leading and chord knowledge**
    - ▶ Tool: timer.
    - ▶ Voice lead through cycles with triads. Stop the timer when you hit your first chord again. We'll cover voice-leading cycles later on. I aim for less than twenty seconds to finish the cycle.

5. **Sight-reading**
    - ▶ Tool: metronome
    - ▶ Sight-read a new piece of music with the metronome set at a slow tempo. Write down your metronome setting for that piece and how often you got lost or had to stop. Sight-read different pieces every day and always jot down your tempo and the number of mistakes made. When you play these pieces again a couple of weeks later, play them five bpm faster.

6. Interval knowledge

- ▶ Tool: metronome.
- ▶ I used a backing track for this that I created in Band in a Box. Band in a Box is sequencing software where one can type in a chord progression, and the software will generate a band playing that progression. I created a track where I had an eight-bar chord progression in the key of C, then for the next eight bars the same chord progression in the key of F, going up the circle of fourths every eight bars. I call it the ninety-six-bar drill. You can change the playback tempo in the software. Choose an interval, for example 3^{rds}, then solo with that interval over the track, through all twelve keys. Pick a tempo that is challenging, yet doable. Keep track of the speed. Try to raise the bpm by three or four beats every week. Do this for all intervals. *(We'll cover how to play 3rd intervals later.)*

You can track virtually anything that needs practice.

- ▶ If you have a hard time switching chords, pick two chords and switch back and forth between them with a metronome. Switch chord on every beat. Write down at what bpm you could do this before it got sloppy. For more advanced players who can still further improve their flexibility and strength, do this with tough, stretchy chord shapes.
- ▶ If you have a hard time with the physicality of playing bar chords, play Lenny Kravitz's "Fly Away" **(||: A B C | G D :||)** with E-shape bar chords. Jot down how long you could play before your hand or forearm started feeling like it was about to fall off. Try to get a bit further in the song every time you practice this. When you can do this without your arm or hand needing rest any longer, play the song twice in a row and track how your arm is holding up.

Tip: Make sure to stretch. Stretching makes one's hands and arms stronger, and protects against possible injury.

Be Resourceful

Tony Robbins once said that people who fail to start or achieve their goals, often tend to blame a lack of resources. You've probably heard the excuses before: "I didn't have the same upbringing like these rich kids." "I didn't have the money to make the movie I always wanted to make." "I didn't have the time to start my dream business." "I didn't have the support I so needed." Robbins explains that it's not always a lack of resources that is to blame for someone's lack of success, but a lack of **resourcefulness**.

Be a problem-solver—become a solution-driven person. Steve Vai talks about this in interviews. Whenever he had something he couldn't pull off, he turned the obstacle that needed to be overcome through practice into a fun, neat little exercise that he made up. Same story goes for Steve Morse, who is one of my favorite guitar players. Morse made up exercises that contained certain picking mechanics or string changes that he had a hard time pulling off at faster speeds.

Make up your own exercises and write them down on tab paper.

There are always solutions for any problem or obstacle. You just have to actively want to find or create those solutions.

Listen Intently

The best, most accomplished guitar players listen deeply to the notes they play.

That is why they got that good. Really listen to what you play. Don't just play shapes, patterns, exercises, drills, scales, and finger movements. Don't play as if you're zoned out, on automatic pilot. Don't let it be your eyes that lead your fingers. Instead, listen deeply to every note you play.

Connect to your guitar. Connect to the sounds.

Listen not only to the sound of the notes, but to the feel of each new interval, chord, or scale you learn. Every interval, chord, or scale has a certain feel, personality, emotion, and vibe. Settle into that feel, notice it, describe it—even write down labels and analogies that capture the essence of that feel, sound, and vibe.

Certain mental pictures help facilitate this. Think of your fret board as a giant color palette. You are the painter throwing splashes of C colors, and F♯ colors, and B♭ colors against the canvas of silence into the Universe. The splashes of sound-paint you are exuding through your heart and fingers into the sky reach your listeners and touch their hearts. Feel how each sound touches and moves you. Hear the whole world that each individual note contains and exhibits. Hear its personality. Listen for hours to each note. No pressure, no intent, no "trying to"—just let the sounds come to you, and notice how they affect you.

One thing I used to do was sit for hours listening to just two notes—for example, F♯ and E♭. After a while you start hearing how each of these notes has a very distinct, recognizable personality. F♯ sounds in your face, harsh and spiky, while E♭ sounds warm and fluffy like a warm, comforting bed of feathers. It's like sound-meditation, but most importantly, it's amazing what that attention to detail and in-depth listening will do to the quality of your practice and your progress.

CHAPTER 2: LEARN THE FRET BOARD

Let's talk about fret board mastery. There are numerous major benefits to really knowing where all the notes are on the guitar neck. You learn anything new you want to learn with much greater ease when you know your fret board well. Whether you want to learn new scales, new chords, songs, or solos—it's all a breeze when you don't have to search for the notes.

First off, you want to learn the open string names. From **bass to treble** (thickest to thinnest string) the open strings are tuned to the notes **E A D G B E.**

Here's a great drill to memorize the open string names. Point at any random string and say the name of that string as fast as you can. Do two-minute sessions of this, three times a day. Do more sessions if you have the time.

I can assure you that in a few days you'll have the open string names mastered.

Once you have them memorized, memorize the following theory.

- ▶ There are only twelve notes in the music tuning system that we use in the Western world.
- ▶ These twelve notes are what we call a **half step** apart from each other. A **half step**, also called a **semitone**, is the distance from one fret to the adjacent fret. This is the smallest distance we have between two notes. Since we only have twelve notes in music, when you go up twelve consecutive half steps on one string, the thirteenth half step is the first note again.
- ▶ We use seven letters to name these twelve notes. **C D E F G A B**. Those notes are called **naturals.** Those are the white keys on a piano.
- ▶ The notes E and F are always right next to one another, on adjacent frets. There's no fret in between them.
- ▶ The notes B and C are located on adjacent frets as well.
- ▶ For all other adjacent letter distances, skip a fret, because they are a **whole step** (two frets) apart. Here are the five whole steps:
    - ▷ A to B
    - ▷ C to D
    - ▷ D to E
    - ▷ F to G
    - ▷ G to A
- ▶ The five remaining in-between notes, which you skip when playing any of these whole steps, are called **accidentals**. Those notes, played with the black keys on a piano, are named using the same seven letters, followed by the accidental symbol for sharp (♯) or flat (♭).

When you play all these seven naturals in order starting from the note C, this gives you **C D E F G A B**. This is a C major scale. We'll cover the major scale in just a bit.

Meanwhile: here's the location of every C note.

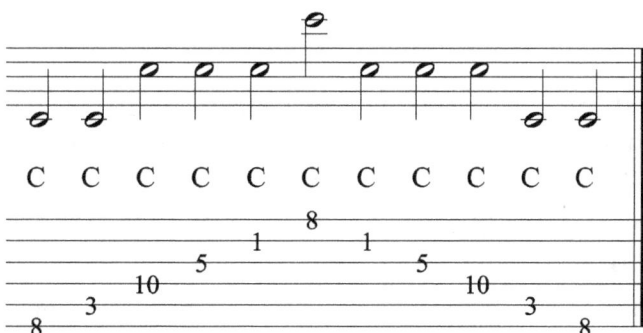

Let's outline how you should practice this for best results.

To begin, play the first C note on the low E string, then add the C on the A string.

Play only those two C notes back and forth (without looking at the above picture) until you can play them fairly quickly back-to-back and until you have them memorized.

Then, add the C note on the D string. Play these three C notes up and down the strings, over and over again (go from low E string to A string to D string to A string to low E string).

When you feel you have mastered this, add the C note on the fifth fret of the G string.

Again, play those four C notes up and down the strings, back and forth. (Play from low E string up to G string and from G string back down to low E string, without skipping strings.)

Keep going until you have covered the C note on every string.

Drill time:
Do three sessions of three minutes a day
= a 9-minute daily drill.

Once you have the C note location on every string memorized, practicing as described, you are ready to move on to the D notes. Only move on to the D notes when you are pretty comfortable and confident playing the C notes without hiccups or hesitation.

Important tip:

Focus on seeing the notes in relationship to the open strings and the twelfth fret marker.

Notice the double dot marker on the twelfth fret on the guitar neck? This indicates where your guitar neck starts over again, meaning that when you place your finger on the twelfth fret of the low E string, you are playing an E note that is up an octave from the low open E string note. In other words, all the open string names repeat on the twelfth fret. Use that knowledge to your advantage in memorizing all the C's. Don't just memorize notes by fret number locations. Instead, notice the distance relationships of notes you're trying to memorize to the open string or to the twelfth fret. Seeing such relationships will help you memorize certain notes on certain strings more quickly.

For example:

- ▶ C on the low E string is two whole steps down from the E note on the twelfth fret. E, down a whole step to D, then down a whole step to C means we have gone down four frets (two whole steps) from the twelfth fret, and this equals C on the eighth fret.
- ▶ The C note on the A string is three frets up from A, as in A (open), B (second fret), C (third fret).
- ▶ C on the D string is easy to memorize, as it is a whole step down from D on the twelfth fret. C is on the tenth fret on that string.
- ▶ C on the B string is easy to memorize, too. It's on the first fret, because as you now know, B to C is a half step.
- ▶ The notes on the treble E string are easy to memorize because they are on the same frets as the low E string; thus, you only have five strings to learn, instead of six.

Once you have all C notes mastered, go through all D notes using the exact same practice method as described above. Start with the D on the low E string. See how it is two frets down from the E on the twelfth fret. Then, figure out the D on the A string (fifth fret), and keep playing these two D notes until you feel you don't have to think anymore. At that point, add the next D, and so on. The D notes will be easier to memorize, because you already know where all the C's are. The D notes are up two frets from the C's. That right there is another relationship you can use to your advantage to speed up the learning process.

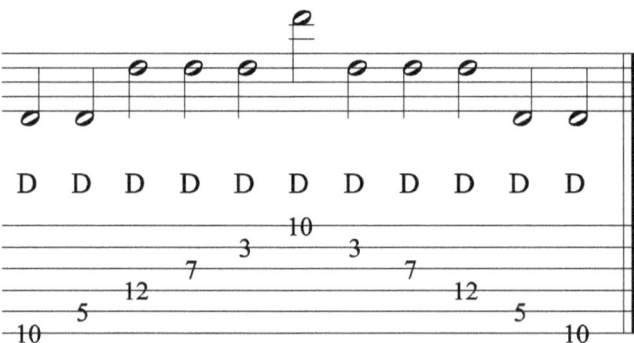

When you have all D notes down perfectly well, don't move on to the E's just yet. Instead, go back to the C notes. You will struggle a bit with those C notes for a quick minute, but they will come back to you quite fast. Once you feel you can play all C's pretty effortlessly again, do the D notes again. Keep going back and forth between all C notes up and down the neck, and then all D notes up and down the neck, until you can play all C's and all D's fairly quickly without having to think all that much anymore.

When you reach that level, move on to the E notes.

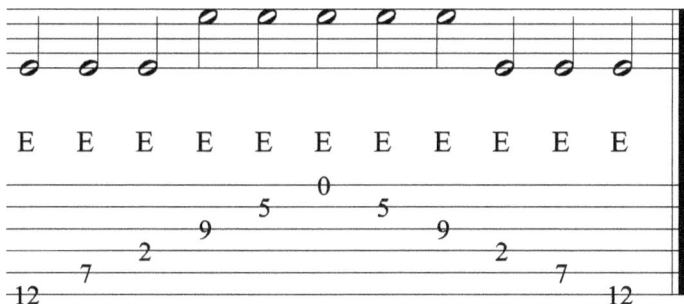

The E's are not too hard to learn, because there are two E strings, which only leaves four more E's to memorize.

Do the same drill you did with the C and D notes, now with the E notes, until mastery. When you can play all the E notes pretty quickly without having to think all that much, don't move on to the F notes just yet. Go back, once more, to the C's. These will be a little less good again, but you will get them back to your previous best level in a very short time. Once you get all C's down, move on to D's again, then when you get these back to top level, onto the E's again.

Once you can play all C's, D's and E's fairly quickly back-to-back without messing up too much, you're ready to move on to the F notes.

F is one fret above E.

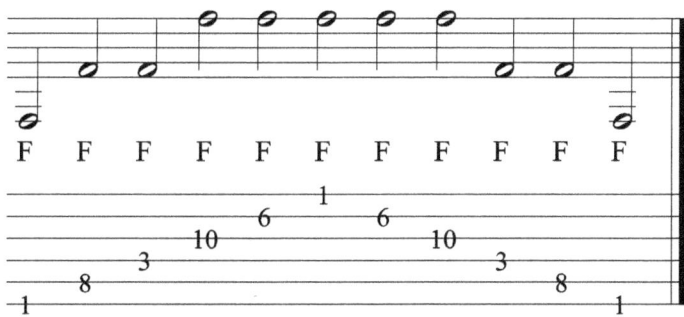

When you can play all F's fairly well, go back to C's, D's, E's and F's, back-to-back, over and over again, until you can play all of them very comfortably and without too much hesitation.

Then all G notes:

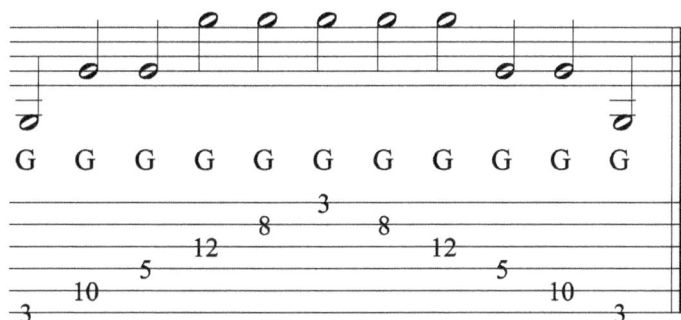

Same deal. Only move on to the A notes when you can play all C, D, E, F, and G notes up and down, back-to-back, without pause.

Then learn all A notes by applying the above practice approach.

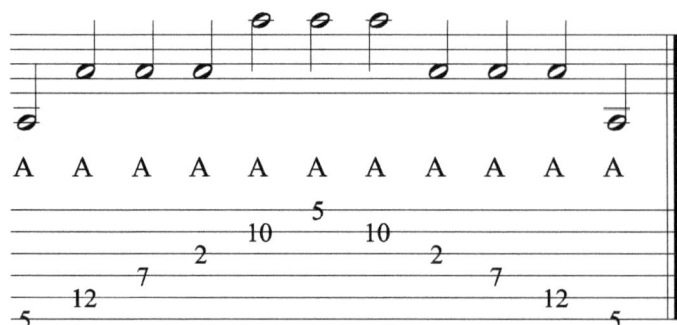

When comfortable with all of the above, finally move on to the B's, which are two frets above the A's and one fret below all the C's. Learning the B locations will be fairly easy by now, especially since you have two points of reference you can use to memorize their locations on the neck.

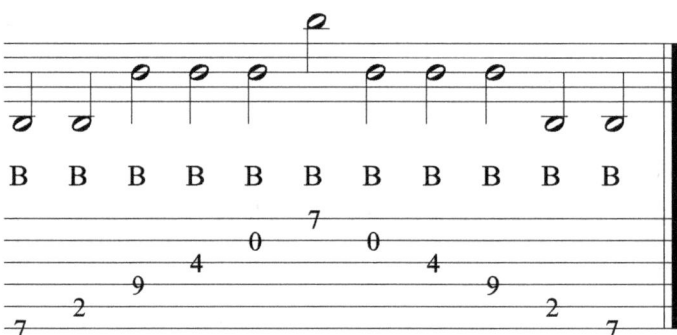

Once you have all of the above notes down, start timing yourself.

As a daily drill, start your timer and then, as fast as you can:

Play all C's up and down the guitar neck, immediately followed by all D's up and down the neck, then all E's, F's, G's, A's and B's. When you hit your last B note, stop the time and write it down. It's very motivating to see your times improve. The goal you are aiming for is to knock out all notes in less than a minute. When you can knock out all seven notes that quickly, you're a huge step closer to being able to pull off the final-level fret board mastery exercise I give my students. This above exercise is merely the introduction exercise leading up to that really challenging final-level drill, the one that makes our students *double* their fret board knowledge in the first seven days of doing the drill. In the week after that, they double their fret board knowledge again. It's the only fret board drill you will ever need.

If you want to fully master your instrument and your fret board in no time, contact me at **vreny@zotzinmusic.com** to set up a lesson so you can see yourself quadruple your fret board knowledge and your note recognition speed in less than two weeks.

CHAPTER 3: THE MAJOR SCALE

What is a Scale?

A scale is a series of sounds organized from lowest- to highest-sounding note. Most of the scales we use in the Western world's music consist of seven different notes. These notes are spaced at certain distances from one another. *(Note: There are also scales with more than or fewer than seven notes).*

These distances between sounds are called **intervals** and are expressed in **steps**.

As we discussed in the last chapter, the smallest interval between two notes is called a **half step**. Another name for half step is **semitone**. You play a half step interval when you play two adjacent keys on a piano. This corresponds to two adjacent frets on a guitar neck. You can see how this looks in the following graphic. The black dots on the two adjacent frets *(framed with a rectangle for visual reference)* show two notes a half step apart on the G and on the A string.

A **whole step** is a distance of two half steps. You play a whole step when you skip a fret (two frets' distance). For example, the notes C and D are a whole step apart.

Most scales consist of a series of sounds that follow in a succession of whole and half step distances. Each scale has its unique order and number of whole and half steps.

What Do You Use a Scale For?

A scale is used to communicate musical ideas, to talk with your guitar.

Music is communication. When you improvise guitar solos, you're talking with your instrument. When you play or write music, you're communicating with your audience and with the other musicians you play with. Songwriting is storytelling.

The definition of communication is the exchange of thoughts, ideas, concepts, and emotions with one another through language. That language can be: regular spoken language, non-verbal communication (body language, facial expressions, gestures, tapping fingers on a table, etc.) and of course, music.

Guitar Essentials

As you know, in spoken language, there's grammar. Grammar is a language's operating system, outlining the structure of that language. This structure makes it possible for everybody in the country or area where that language is spoken to communicate in an intelligible manner. Grammar defines in what order to place the words into sentences, where to put commas and periods (breaks), how to conjugate verbs (which control time), and so on.

You can think of each of the 2,048 scales that exist in music as different languages.

The grammar, or in other words the structure, of each scale, is formed by that scale's unique series of intervals. Just as authors use grammar so the reader is able to read and comprehend their stories, composers and songwriters use any of these 2,048 given scale structures so that listeners can follow and enjoy the melodies.

Musicians who are about to perform or jam with one another first of all decide upon a scale. They also all agree on one of the twelve starting points for that scale, which is called a key. After all musicians in the room have decided to jam in (for example) the key of A, they'll musically communicate with one another using the seven notes of the A major scale. In this way, they share chords and melodies all speaking the same musical language. Communication and interaction are happening.

In the Western world, the most commonly used scale is the major scale.

The Major Scale

All of our music theory books take the major scale as the starting point from which all other scales and music theory are explained.

The scale that one chooses to write with impacts the mood, atmosphere, and sound of the music one creates with it. For example, the reason Arabic music sounds so different from music in the Western world is simply that Arabic scales consist of different whole and half step configurations. Arabic scales have more half step intervals and a different structure than our major scale, and the result is that Middle Eastern music has a totally different musical sound, emotion, atmosphere, and texture than the major scale music in the Western world.

A music scale is defined by its interval structure. There are two ways musicians learn the structure and organization of the major scale:

(1) through intervallic distances from note to note, and (2) by half step locations.

1. Intervallic distances from note to note

For the major scale, the intervallic distances from note to note are:

Whole step / whole step / half step / whole step / whole step / whole step / half step

I like abbreviating this to "two whole half three whole half."

That structure is easy to see on one string, as shown below.

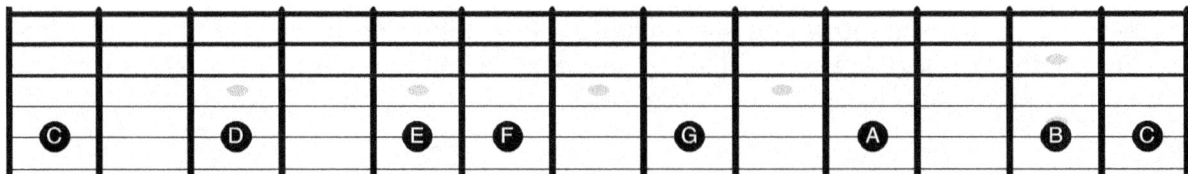

Here's that same major scale structure on a piano keyboard. Start from the note C to see the major scale structure formed by all the white keys.

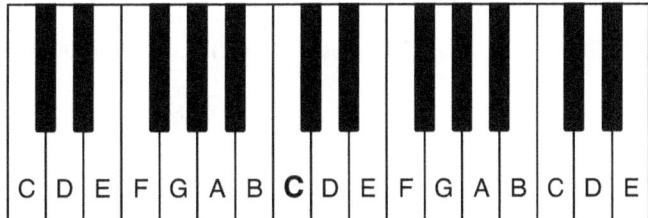

Notice how the black keys on the piano correspond to the frets that don't have a note dot on the above guitar neck. Those are the notes between the naturals. Also notice that there is no black key between E-F and B-C on the piano keyboard. Correspondingly, there's also no fret space between those notes on the guitar neck.

2. **Half step locations 3-4 & 7-8**

    The half steps are between the third and the fourth note and between the seventh and the eighth note. The previous guitar neck picture shows these notes are E-F and B-C.

    Here are the notes E-F and B-C shown on the second string without the other scale notes.

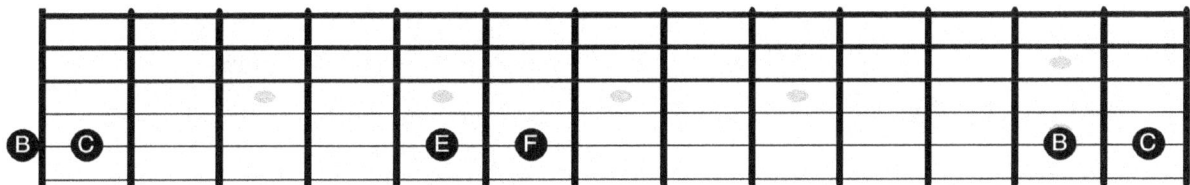

The following piano keyboard shows how E-F and B-C are adjacent keys on a keyboard. Two adjacent frets on a guitar neck = two adjacent keys on a keyboard.

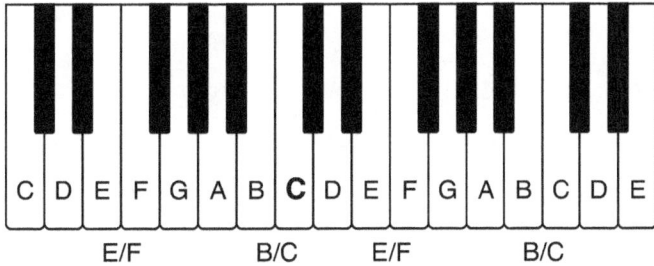

When you start this particular structure that is called a **major scale** on the note C, you happen to play all naturals, which means:

▶ White keys of the piano, or in other words

▶ Alphabet note names only, or in other words

▶ No sharps (♯) or flats (♭).

17

This scale is called **the C major scale**.

The C major scale is the only major scale that consists of white keys only, meaning that the scale does not have any sharps or flats. It's called a major scale because its structure is two whole half three whole half. It's called a **C** major scale because it starts on a C note.

Accidentals

Since there are twelve notes in our music, seven of which are naturals, this means that there are five more notes that need a name. These are the notes **in between** the naturals. They are the black keys on the piano. We use music notation symbols called **accidentals** to name those five black keys.

The accidentals are:

- ♯ This is the sharp symbol. It raises the natural up a half step
- ♭ This is the flat symbol. It lowers the natural down a half step
- ♮ This is the natural symbol. It restores a note that was previously sharped or flatted back to a natural. This symbol overrides any flats or sharps that were previously applied to that note in that bar. Every time that note reappears *(in that octave only)* for the remainder of that bar, it will be as a natural.

Notes with accidentals have two names: a "sharp" (♯) name and a "flat" (♭) name.

For example: **F♯** and **G♭**

These are the two names for the note we have on the second fret of the E-string between F and G. The different names that exist for any given note are called **enharmonics** or enharmonic note names.

You might ask yourself, "If there are two different note names for the notes with accidentals, how do you know what to name those notes?"

The short answer is that this depends on two things:

1. The direction of a melody.
   - ▶ In ascending melodies, we always use sharps: **A A♯ B C C♯ D D♯ E F F♯ G G♯**
   - ▶ In descending melodies, we always use flats: **B B♭ A A♭ G G♭ F E E♭ D D♭ C**

2. Scale-specific accidentals. There are systems in place that define whether a scale has sharps or flats. This will make sense when we cover key signatures.

There are also accidentals that raise or lower a note a whole step.

- ▶ 𝄪 This is the double sharp symbol. It raises a natural up a whole step.
- ▶ 𝄫 This is the double flat symbol. It lowers a natural down a whole step.

With no accidentals to worry about, the C major scale is typically the first scale students learn in music schools all over the world. It's the easiest scale to play on a piano.

The next page shows the notes of the C major scale mapped out on each string.

Since single-string soloing is such a great way to learn new scales, the next chapter will cover how to solo on one string at a time, in the key of C.

Students who immediately play solos with a newly learned scale, even if still a bit shaky with the scale, always master that scale much faster than students who play the scale up and down a billion times as a rote memorization drill. People who create (melodies, solos, songs) with new things they have learned always learn much more quickly and have more fun in the process. That's why right off the bat you want to solo and play music with the new scales you learn.

But before we get into all the action, let me first introduce you to a unique approach that will bring you a giant step closer to fret board and improvisation mastery:

"Linear" or **"single-string" playing.**

CHAPTER 4: SINGLE-STRING SOLOING

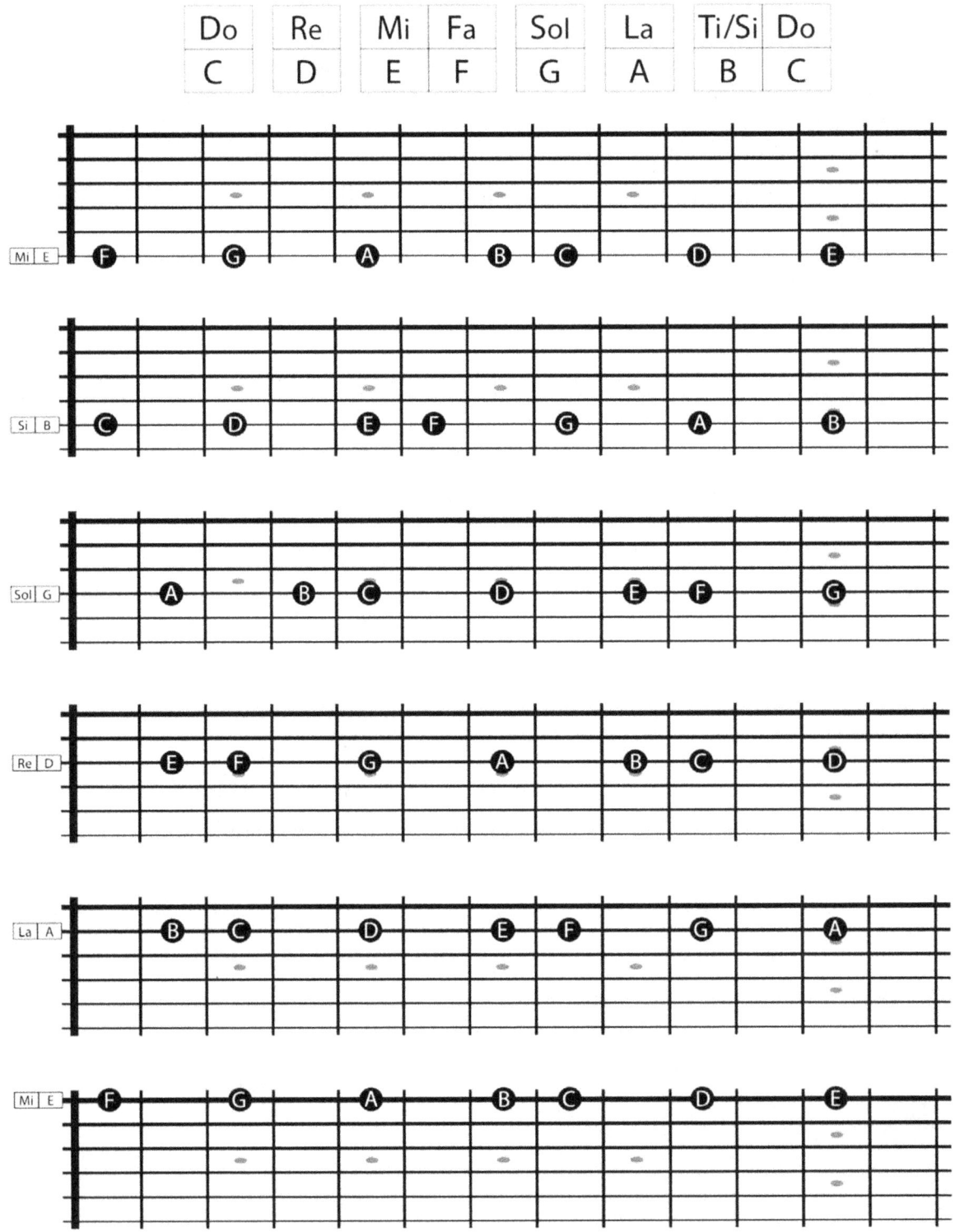

Linear vs. In Position

Your journey toward fret board mastery must include single-string soloing. Without it, you don't really get the complete guitar training you deserve.

That's why it is so odd that in music schools all over the world, the guitar is still primarily taught in position. "In position" playing means you stay in one location with your hand, each finger assigned to an adjacent fret, and you play scales and learn the fret board vertically.

For example:

When you play in second position, your index finger is taking all the notes on the second fret, your middle finger takes all the notes on the next (third fret), your ring finger takes all the notes on the fourth fret, and your pinky covers the fifth fret.

Now it's an understatement to say that this is not the best way to teach guitar. Yet, this is how music educators teach stringed instruments, including some of the best and most prestigious music schools worldwide.

There are three distinct disadvantages to this system of learning scales that slows down guitar students' progress.

1. Too many notes to deal with

There are only seven notes in a scale (Do re mi fa sol la si/ti).

However, with the "in position" system of learning scales, there are not seven but twenty-four notes thrown at you all at once (four fingers covering six strings). Logically this is way too much information to start with for any guitar student.

Whereas, when you play on one string at a time, you only deal with twelve notes at a time.

2. No visible organization or structure

Because the note organization over multiple strings is not easily nor visually apparent, it's challenging for a guitar student to understand the structure of a scale when viewed vertically. All the notes seem all over the place with the "in position" approach for learning scales. That is why it takes guitar students who learn scales with in position fingerings a considerable amount of time to memorize the note locations or scale fingerings. People tend to memorize information much more easily when there's a clearly visible logic behind things.

On the other hand, when you learn a scale on one string, you benefit from all the advantages that piano players have. There's a reason why beginning piano students always improve much more quickly on their instrument than beginning guitar students. People who learn piano can play songs in no time. They also tend to have a better understanding of music theory and harmony, and are better able to apply all the theory they learn on their instrument right away.

The reason for this seems obvious. Piano players clearly visibly see all the music theory linearly laid out under their fingertips. You don't have this advantage as a guitarist when you learn in position, but you do have that same advantage when you think like a piano player: **linearly**.

There is at least one country in the world, that I know of, where students of stringed instruments learn linearly. As a matter of fact, the musicians in this country spend their whole long-lasting careers, sometimes of many decades, playing one string. That country is... India.

It's always striking to see Indian musicians play their sitars. Their fretting hand is horizontally moving all over the place. They play all their melodies on one string only. The sitar does have multiple strings, but all the other strings are used to play drones, harmonically supporting the constantly evolving melodies.

While Indian musicians play their melodies on one string only, it is worth noting that:

- ▶ Indian music is the oldest on the planet. It's been around for thousands of years.
- ▶ Indian music is also the most complex and theoretically most involved music.
- ▶ And to top it all off, Indian music still keeps on flourishing and developing.

Isn't it rather interesting that in a culture where music possibly has some of the richest history and highest complexity of all music on the planet, the musicians conceptualize and play their instruments in what would seem to be the most basic, easiest way: on one string only?

Do you think that's a coincidence?

3. Conceptually too complex

There are too many directions and dimensions happening simultaneously when you learn a scale in position. This ties into previous points discussed.

In position, you play two or three notes on one string (horizontal) then go to the next string (vertical) where you play a couple of notes linearly again, then vertical again to the next string, linear again for two or three notes on that string, then vertical again to the next string, and so on. As if that is not quite difficult enough yet, sometimes your pointer finger needs to move diagonally from string to string.

You basically have to oversee too many dimensions simultaneously, which is obviously much more challenging than linear thinking. With one string at a time, your only options are: left to right, and right to left.

I'm Not Discarding "In-Position" Playing

In-position playing is an important part of guitar playing. It is just simply not the most efficient way to learn a new scale, and it leads to a less effective and less thorough fret board understanding among even advanced players. Position playing should not be where guitar education starts, but should be the next logical step after having spent a considerable amount of time on each string separately.

Before moving on, make sure to also read the freebie bonus PDF titled: *Some Bonus Benefits You Get from Single-String Soloing*. It lists more benefits, and shows why even advanced students improve quite a bit from this drill.

Let's check it out!

Single-String Soloing Explained in a Nutshell

1. You'll improvise on one string at a time in the key of C
2. Over songs or backing tracks (development of ensemble playing and ear training)
3. Playing short musical phrases of three notes (development of melodic awareness)
4. Using the right fingerings (guitar technique)
5. Singing the note names out loud of the notes you are playing (ear training, accelerated fret board awareness)
6. And this for only three minutes maximum per string. The short drills keep your concentration at peak performance. This helps you get the maximum out of your practice.

Let's get into the details of this approach now.

1. What is "Improvising"?

"Improvisation" means making up melodies on the spot. You'll create simple melody lines that you make up. It's like talking with your instrument, which is exactly what improvisers do.

2. You'll Be Doing This Over Songs.

You want to practice over music. It makes soloing and learning scales much more fun. A learning experience that is perceived as being more fun:

▶ Requires less concentration.

▶ Results in higher-quality learning. You learn with much less effort, and memorization takes substantially less time.

In addition, you get the best learning results when the material is presented in context. The music you play along with provides the context for the solo. When you practice a scale along with a backing track, you hear the scale being part of the music. Hearing how the scale sounds with music, you realize on a deeper level what you can do with that scale, and why you're practicing it or needing to learn it in the first place. The sense of purpose that you derive from practicing the scale within a musical context is also motivating because it makes you want to spend more time getting better at it.

Download your free C major backing track from the Bonus page.

3. Playing Three-Note Phrases

Music is a language. **Songwriting** is **storytelling**. You create melodies when you select a couple of notes from a scale and then play these notes one at a time. The resulting short melody is called a "phrase," and through repetition and development of melodic phrases, you build **musical sentences**. Repetition of sentences is how you form verses and choruses.

While five-or-more-note phrases are not that uncommon, most melodic phrases in well-written songs tend to have four notes or less.

Here are some examples.

The Beatles – "She Loves You"

▶ Phrase 1: "She loves you" (three notes)

▶ Phrase 2: "Yeah, yeah, yeah" (three notes)

The Beatles – "Help"

▶ Phrase 1: "Help" (one note)

▶ Phrase 2: "I need somebody" (three notes: F F E E D)

The Eagles – "Hotel California"

▶ Phrase 1: "On a dark desert highway" (two notes)

▶ Phrase 2: "Cool wind in my hair" (two notes)

▶ Phrase 3: "Warm smell of colitas" (two notes)

▶ Phrase 4: "Rising up through the air" (four notes)

You want to improvise in short phrases of three, maximum four different notes. This will develop your melodic awareness.

(This will also improve the quality of your melodies in your songwriting.)

4. Fingerings

There are only two fingering principles. These two rules cover every scale fingering that exists, whether you're playing on one string or vertically in position. When you know these two fingering principles, you have mastered the foundation needed to figure out any in-position fingering for any scale.

The two fingering rules are:

▶ **The One-Finger-Per-Fret Rule**

When a half step (two adjacent frets; e.g., E-F and B-C) is involved, then the three notes fall within a range of four adjacent frets. In that case, use the one-finger-per-fret rule: four fingers cover four consecutive frets. Each finger is assigned to a fret.

Having four fingers cover four adjacent frets, you play the notes with the fingers that are right on top of each fret. The following guitar neck shows how the notes D, E, and F cover four frets.

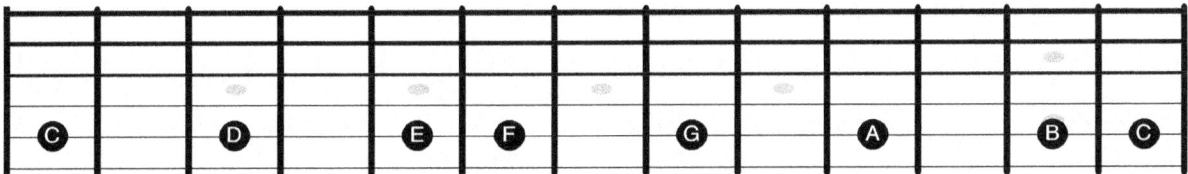

You see the same four-fret range for the notes:

▷ E, F and G
▷ A, B and C
▷ B, C and D

All these three-note groupings fall within a four-fret range, because they all have an E-F or B-C half step involved.

▶ **The Stretch Fingering Rule**

When there's no half step, or in other words, when the three consecutive notes span a five-fret range: Always use the first, second and fourth finger.

These fingers are the **index finger, middle finger** and **pinky.**

That stretch fingering, as you can see in the above guitar diagram, happens on I, IV, and V in a major scale. In the key of C, that is:

▷ The first note C ➡ the notes C D E cover a five-fret distance
▷ The fourth note F ➡ the notes F G A cover a five-fret distance
▷ The fifth note G ➡ the notes G A B cover a five-fret distance

The reason for using index finger, middle finger, and pinky is because this is the most effective fingering. This fingering utilizes the stronger fingers in the hand, which are better equipped to more accurately perform the stretch. You never want to stretch between the third and fourth fingers if you can avoid it, because these are the weakest fingers of the hand. Weaker fingers lack the control, speed, and performance accuracy of the stronger index and middle finger. It makes sense that the fingers with less muscle mass don't have the same strength to execute the commands coming from the brain as effortlessly as the stronger fingers can.

I'm only bringing this up because I've coached god knows how many self-study guitarists who play this five-fret stretch using the much less effective index finger, ring finger, and pinky finger combination. Though that is the fingering they had gotten used to, those students always end up finding out that they can't perform certain melody lines with a high degree of accuracy with that fingering. It doesn't matter how huge or strong a student's hands are, or how many decades they've been playing that way; there's a certain amount of sloppiness in their performance that magically disappears the moment they start using the stronger fingering.

5. Singing Note Names While You Play

You want to sing the names of the notes you play with the following names:

do - re - mi - fa - sol - la - ti.

This system of naming the notes is called "solfeggio."

Why should you sing "do-re-mi" instead of the alphabet names for each note? As it turns out, experiments with groups of students have shown that students who sing the solfeggio note names need much less time to memorize all the notes on the fret board than people who sing "C-D-E..."

Here's Why Singing Solfeggio Will Bring You Better Results

1. It's more musical sounding.

The note names in the solfeggio system are much more musical sounding than the harder-to-pronounce sounds produced by the alphabet names. As a result, the more musical sounding "do re mi" names attune to the ear more quickly, and their locations on the string somehow get stored into memory sooner than the alphabet note names.

2. They're easier to pronounce.

I already touched upon this a bit in the previous point. As a test, sing a C major scale as C D E F G A B C, then sing the same scale with the note names do re mi fa sol la ti do. Do you notice a difference? If you're like most people, you will notice that there's a certain musical flow to the solfeggio note names that is missing when singing alphabet note names. You might notice that the solfeggio singing requires less effort of the mouth and facial muscles, too.

3. The note names are more distinctive.

The most important reason, though, why you want to sing solfeggio note names is this:

Each of the first five solfeggio note names has a significantly different vowel: do re mi fa sol la ti. Up through sol, they are all very different sounding from one another. In contrast, all the alphabet note names are much more alike sounding: C D E (F) G (A) B. Five out of the seven alphabet note names sound like [E]. Since there is much less distinction between each individual note name when using letters, it is much harder and takes much longer to memorize the location of each note on each string. The solfeggio names facilitate learning in a way that alphabet names for notes do not.

It's probably not a coincidence that in the majority of music schools all over the world, the solfeggio system that has been around for about a thousand years is still the preferred note-naming system. Teachers in music schools use solfeggio as the preferred system to teach students sight-reading, sight-singing, ear training, and music theory.

Memorization Drill for Solfeggio Note Names

How does the brain memorize things? Answer: Constant repetition.

The more regularly you repeat something, the sooner it gets logged into your brain. You want to memorize the solfeggio note names in no time so you can use them. Here's how:

1. Recite the line "do re mi fa sol la ti do" over and over again. You can do this anywhere.
2. When you get the hang of this, go backward (do ti la sol fa mi re do).
3. Next, practice the line starting from "re" ascending and descending.
4. Then, do it from "mi".
5. Continue until you can recite the solfeggio line from any note, ascending and descending.

You want to know that line so well that you can recite it in any direction, starting from any of the seven note names, without having to give it any thought and without any hesitation. Practice this anywhere (i.e., stuck in a car in traffic, waiting in line at the bank, and so on.)

Alphabet and Solfeggio Links

You also want to memorize the connecting alphabet and solfeggio note names.

- ▶ **C = do** (spells out "doc" when you put "do" and "C" together)
- ▶ **D = re** (spells out "Dre," like in "Doctor Dre," or the color "ReD")
- ▶ E = mi
- ▶ **F = fa** (fa is the only note name that has an "F" in it)
- ▶ G = sol
- ▶ **A = la** (A as in L.A.)
- ▶ B = ti

Memorize this in both directions: from alphabet name to solfeggio name, and from solfeggio name to alphabet name. The same holds true for this drill—repetition is key. The more you recite this, the faster you will get it memorized. *(You can make flash cards.)*

It should take you relatively little time to get this all in shape, but it will save you a lot of time in faster progress in the long run. Lastly, if ever you suddenly feel the desire or inclination to want to go to music school, you will have to know all this anyway. You'll have an edge on your peer students because you won't have to spend time anymore with having to learn all this.

6. You Know All You Need to Know: Time to Solo on One String

The above material explained the single-string training approach in great detail.

I can understand, though, how the above might seem like a ton of information, and that just for one drill. A quick short recap might be helpful, to help you get started. So, here, in a few words, is what the drill is and how to practice it:

Play a backing track in the key of C, solo on one string at a time in the key of C, playing three-note melodies with the right fingerings, for three minutes per string, singing the note names out loud (or quietly in your head if you're shy about anybody hearing you sing).

Don't practice on the bass E string. It's the same as the high E string.

Drill time:
5 strings x 3 min. = **15-minute daily drill**.

That's it!

If you still feel a bit unsure or insecure or you happen to be the type of person who prefers very regimented instructions, read the PDF titled *Detailed Single-String Soloing Instructions,* which you can download from the Bonus page.

Do everything *exactly* as explained above. You won't see the same great results if you leave anything out of the drill. The only exception is if you dreadfully dislike having to sing solfeggio, don't worry about solfeggio. Sing with letters, or don't sing at all if you don't want to. Just make sure you know what the notes are before playing them.

Common Single-String Soloing Mistakes and Some Pointers

So as not to get overwhelmed by the following list, focus on items 5-9 first. These specific pointers will help you get the most out of the single-string soloing drill. The first four items in the list are technique and physical performance corrections.

After that, maybe only add in two or three of the remaining items in the list a day.

1. Keep your thumb behind the guitar neck. It's not only good guitar technique, it's also close to impossible to stretch the fingers to cover a five-fret range with the thumb up too high.

2. Don't bend your thumb behind the guitar neck—keep the thumb joint straight.

3. Don't bend your wrist too much. Preferably, you don't want any bend at all in your wrist. The straighter you keep your wrist, the less likely you will ever have to deal with wrist problems.

4. FINGERINGS! Use the fingerings as explained. Bad fingerings = bad technique = more room for error when playing in front of people.

5. There is nothing wrong with doing this under other circumstances, but strictly as part of the single-string soloing exercise: **no out-of-position finger-slides**! Select three notes, play them with the right fingering, and then move to another location on that string that is not right next to where you just played. Don't slide up or down one or two frets with the pointer finger or pinky from where you just played to a neighboring note. That is what I call an out-of-position slide. Instead, after you have played a melody with the three selected notes, take your hand away and place it on an entirely different location on that string, farther away from where your hand was in the previous phrase. This rule is only in place because it makes you have to think more and take more chances. You want that because there is no growth if you only stay in your comfort zone.

   To be clear: I didn't say you can't add slides. By all means, you should slide. Slides are a phrasing tool that adds feel and expressiveness to melodies.

   However, if you want to slide, then slide within the position of the notes you selected, into the notes you selected, using the fingers you would normally use to play these notes. For example, if you want to play A, B, and C on the first string on frets 5, 7, and 8, you can slide with index finger to A, or with third finger to B, or with pinky into C. That is okay. What you don't want to do is to slide with your index down from A down to G, or with your pinky from C out of position to D. Those are out-of-position slides.

6. Don't start all phrases from the same finger, and don't play all three notes in the same order over and again. Be creative with the notes you have under your fingers. You can start any phrase from any of the three notes under your fingers, in any direction or any configuration. You can start a melody from the note that falls under your pinky, which is the highest note, or from the note that falls in the middle. Solos quickly become very predictable if every melody line starts from the lowest note under the pointer finger.

7. Avoid stepwise motion from phrase to phrase—leap around a lot. This is a bit of a reiteration of some points I brought up in my discussion of the out-of-position finger slides. After you have played the notes do re mi, avoid playing re mi fa in your next phrase or ti do re. If you move to the next or preceding letter with your pointer finger from where you just played, it will sound more like a scale exercise than a solo. There's nothing wrong with occasionally doing that, you just don't want your whole solo to be **that** stepwise. Moving up and down consecutive notes makes the solo too predictable, less interesting, and less cool sounding. In addition, you're not challenging yourself enough when you move up or down a letter from what you just played. You learn way more when you leap around all over the string to random locations.

8. Don't avoid the note groupings where the three notes are two whole steps apart (the five-fret stretches). Oftentimes, students avoid the locations where there are stretchy fingerings in favor of the more comfortable one-finger-per-fret note groupings. You don't want

to do that, because it's skipping too many scale notes you could be using. Only playing in the four locations where the three notes fall in a four-fret range makes your solo less colorful. It also diminishes the added fret board memorization benefits you will get out of this drill. The stretches get easier the more you play them. You can't get stronger or more flexible if you avoid the opportunities to train that strength and flexibility.

9. Don't stay in the same range too long. Play one phrase, short and to the point, then move to another location on the string. The more you move around, the more you have to think, and the more progress you will see. You don't want to play the same three notes for x number of phrases in a row. Doing so not only makes the drill less fun, it also robs you of the opportunity to be more adventurous all over the string.

10. **Space** and **silence** are extremely important. Silence is as important as sound. It was Miles Davis who supposedly said something along the lines of: "The notes you don't play are as important as the notes you do play." Don't play too much. Play short phrases and leave silence in between them.

11. Let me say that again: "Leave **even more** silence in between phrases." It might seem redundant that I'm repeating this, but it's only meant to illustrate how often I need to keep telling it to students after I've already told them the above. It sometimes seems as if guitar students are "afraid" to allow silence and space.

12. Make phrases short and poignant. It's like talking with your instrument. Don't linger on.

13. **Rhythm.** Be more creative with the note placements and lengths. Avoid playing the notes at even lengths and even spacing. Go nuts: rush some notes, play super fast ones, mix the short notes up with slow, long, sustained notes, and so on. It's not good enough to merely hit all the right notes. You also want to play cool, interesting rhythms with them.

14. Don't be afraid to play a note numerous times in a row. When you hit every note only once in your melodic phrases, you sound like you're meandering about without ever really saying something on your guitar. A phrase where you hit a note x number of times in a row always sounds like a statement. That note repetition makes it come across as if you *really* meant to say what you said. Of course, play rhythmic games with that note you're repeating. Try to surprise your listeners with where you place that note in time when repeating it.

15. **Dynamics.** Don't play each note in a phrase equally loud. Give each note its own intensity and volume, as if it is the most important note you've ever played in your life. This is like adding voice-inflection in storytelling. Dynamics is one of the musical tools we use that allows us to add drama, emotion, and feel to a guitar solo.

16. **Alternate pick** as much as possible. Avoid playing all down strokes only.

17. You can play the occasional two-note phrase, but overall, have more three- than two-note phrases. A two-note phrase should only be played every once in a while.

18. Regularly switch pick-up settings to give parts of your solo different guitar timbres. When you see top guitarists, like for example Steve Morse, you'd be surprised to see how often they change pickups or change their volume knob settings to create different sounds.

19. Experiment attacking the string with your pick on different string locations. Sometimes pick a note closer to the bridge, sometimes closer to the middle of the string or closer to the neck. This is a great technique to create different timbres.

20. Add vibrato to make the notes come to life. An added touch of vibrato will instantly make your solos sound a lot better.

21. Use phrasing techniques that add feel to melodies. Hammer-ons, pull-offs, bends, and slides are tools that we use to express ourselves within our solos. If we don't use these tools, our solos sound less expressive, less rich in texture, less emotional, less deep, and possibly less interesting.

You will find many of these soloing pointers reiterated in chapter 34.

CHAPTER 5: THE MINOR PENTATONIC SCALE

These are the five fingerings of **the A minor pentatonic scale.**

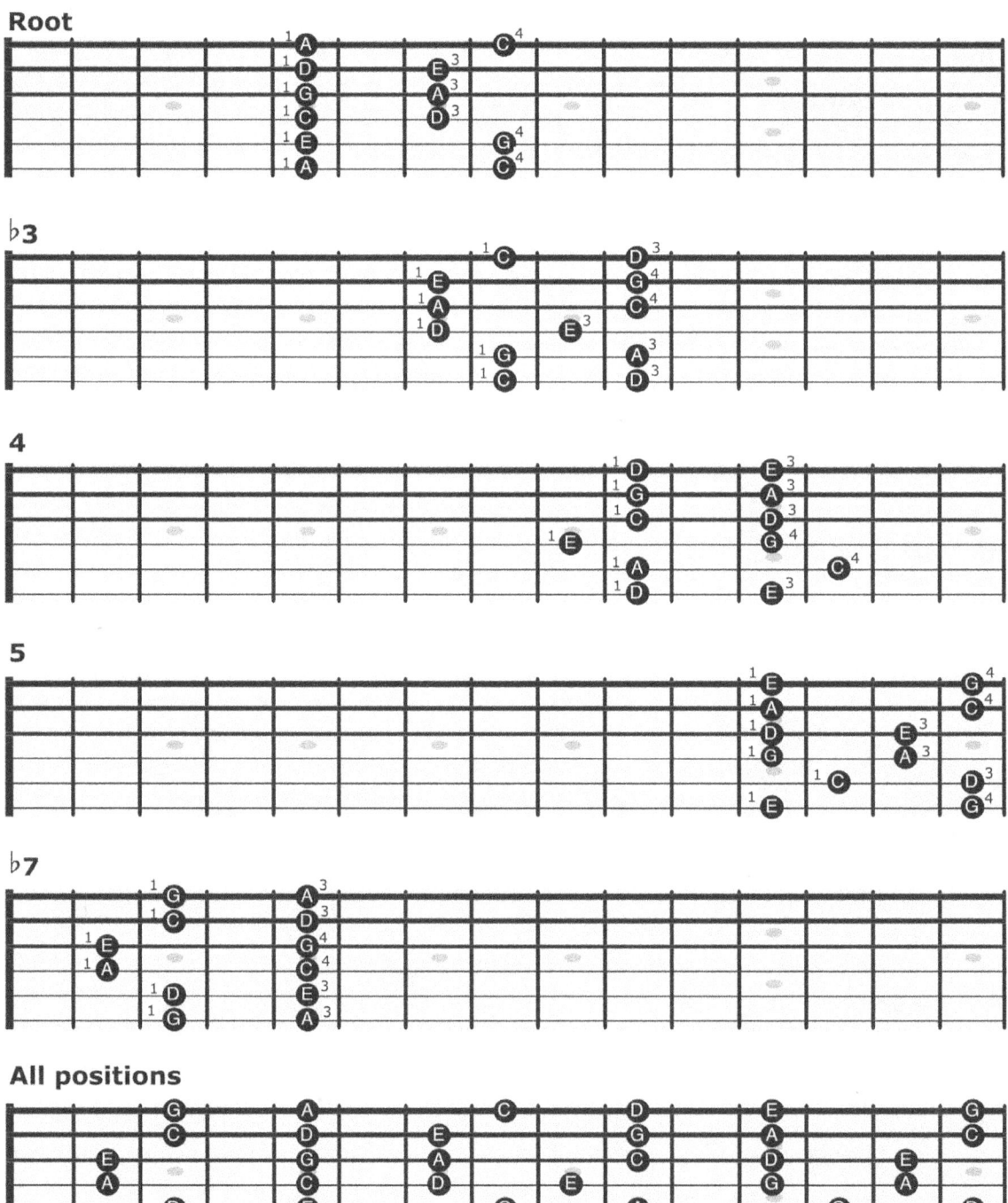

From Jimmy Page, to Robbie Krieger in The Doors, to Jimi Hendrix to Jeff Beck or Santana and so many more, the minor pentatonic scale is *the* must-know scale for improvisation in blues, rock n' roll, rockabilly, rock, hard rock, classic rock, country, and folk music. The minor pentatonic scale is even used in jazz and fusion.

If you practiced the fret board exercise, you will find that it's easier to memorize the A minor pentatonic scale fingerings. Notice that the notes are: **A C D E G** *(You want to memorize this.)*

The Greek word "penta" means "five." The minor pentatonic is the most commonly used five-note scale. Because you can start the scale from each of the five notes, there are only five in-position fingerings to learn.

(The lowest guitar neck on the above page shows all five pentatonic fingerings mapped out on one guitar neck.)

Fingerings

Notice how these in-position pentatonic scale fingerings consist of two notes per string.

These two notes on each string are either spaced:

▶ **A whole step apart.** (Play these notes with pointer finger and ring finger.)

▶ **A minor third apart.** (Play these notes with pointer finger and pinky.)

That sums up everything there is to know about fingerings for the minor pentatonic scale. It's either going to be fingers 1 and 3, or fingers 1 and 4.

Some guitar teachers teach their students how to play these scale fingerings using the strict one-finger-per-fret, in-position type of fingerings. This fingering approach requires you to also use your middle finger to play the notes that fall under that finger. As an example: the ♭7 fingering would be played with fingers 2 - 4, 2 - 4, 1 - 4, 1 - 4, 2 - 4, 2 - 4. Try this fingering and you'll immediately realize how very impractical that fingering system is.

That is why you'd be hard pressed to see a pro guitarist on stage using these "academic" in-position fingerings when improvising with the minor pentatonic scale. The fingerings I gave above are what every pro would normally play because these are the most practical fingerings.

Some Quick Pentatonic Scale Theory

The formula for this scale is **1 ♭3 4 5 ♭7**

▶ 1 is whatever note the scale starts on. It could be each one of the twelve notes we have in music. I've often seen this note being called the "root" in books that teach the minor pentatonic scale. This is a bit odd considering that the word "root" in music typically refers to the starting note of a **chord**, not the starting note of a scale. The first note in a scale is usually called the **tonic**.

▶ ♭3 is another name for minor 3rd. The minor 3rd is the note that makes a scale sound minor (As opposed to 3, a major 3rd, which is what major scales have.)

▶ 4 is the note that is four letters above 1.

▶ 5 is the note that is five letters above 1.

▶ ♭7 is the note that is always a whole step below 1.

As you can see on the graphic depicting the A minor pentatonic scale fingerings, each fingering is named after the lowest note where the fingering starts on the low E string. The fingering that starts on a C note is called the ♭3 fingering because C is the minor 3rd in the key of A minor. The fingering that starts on a D note is called the 4 fingering because D is the 4th in the key of A.

How to Learn and Practice These Five Scale Shapes

1. Learn and memorize the root fingering first. This is the easiest fingering to learn because it looks very much like a square block. Focus on the notes. To that end, feel free to say or sing the notes out loud while playing them. Solo with that fingering over a C major or A minor backing track.

Drill time:
Do 3 practice sessions of 2 min. a day = **6 minutes**

2. After two days or so, learn the ♭7 scale shape next. The reason why it's better to learn that fingering next is because it is visually the second-easiest shape to memorize. Solo over a C major or A minor backing track.

Drill time:
Do 3 practice sessions of 2 min. a day = **6 minutes**

Solo for another three minutes, combining the root and ♭7 fingerings. There are different ways you can approach this. You can play one phrase in one fingering, then play the next phrase in the other fingering, moving back and forth between the two positions. You can also start a phrase in one position and then continue the same phrase without stopping in the other position. This adds a horizontal approach to the vertical in-position approach.

3. After two days or so, learn the ♭3 scale shape. Practice it the same way as you did previous fingerings. Solo for another three minutes, combining the three fingerings.

4. After two days or so, learn the 4 fingering. Practice it the same way as you did previous fingerings.

5. Lastly, learn and memorize the 5 fingering, again practicing it the same way.

Drill time:
From that point on, solo two minutes per fingering,
= **10-minute daily drill.**

Once you start feeling pretty confident, you should start soloing in all twelve keys with the pentatonic scale. If you're a bit new to this, you might think to yourself: "What? Already?"

It's actually not as hard as it might seem.

As an example, let's say that you choose to solo in the key of Dm.

- ▶ You'd play the root fingering on the tenth fret, which is where the note D is on the low E string.
- ▶ The ♭7 shape is two frets below that, which in other words is on the note C.
- ▶ The ♭3 shape is three frets above the root. This is the thirteenth fret, three frets above D, which is where we find the note F on the low E string.
- ▶ The 4 shape starts on the letter that is four letters above D, which is the note G (as in D E F **G**).
- ▶ The 5 shape is played starting on the letter a 5th above D. Counting up five letters from the letter D on your fingers gives you the letter A, which is on the fifth fret, which is where you would position the 5 shape.

Of course, you can find backing tracks in all twelve keys on the Free Bonus materials page.

Soloing in Major Keys With Minor Pentatonic

There are good reasons why many guitar players, including top-level guitarists, always think of this scale as a **minor** pentatonic scale, even when used over major keys. One of the reasons has to do with the many ways you can use this scale (as we'll cover later on in the Pentatonic Substitution chapter). It simplifies the thought processes if you always think of this as a minor pentatonic scale in every situation in which you can use that scale.

As it turns out, when you know the minor pentatonic scale, then you also already know the major pentatonic scale. When you solo with the A minor pentatonic scale over an Am chord or a song that starts on an Am chord, the scale sounds like an A minor pentatonic scale. No surprise there, right? When, however, you solo with the same scale over a C chord or a song in the key of C, then that scale no longer sounds like an A minor scale but like a C major pentatonic scale. In other words, this scale is a C major **and** an A minor pentatonic scale. The scale sounds like either one or the other depending on what chord you solo over.

We call these **relative scales**, which are defined as **different scales** that consist of the same notes. Which major scale has the same notes as an A minor scale? Answer: C major. Both scales consist of all naturals. A is the **relative minor** to C major. C is the **relative major** to A minor. Notice how the relative minor (A minor) is down three frets from its relative major scale (C).

That right there is the trick to figure out which minor pentatonic scale to solo with over major keys. When the song is in the key of E, you'd solo with C♯ minor pentatonic (three frets down from E). In the key of A, use F♯ minor pentatonic. You simply **go down three frets from whatever the major key is, and then play the minor pentatonic scale from there. It will sound like a major pentatonic scale.** Another way to look at this: When you play the ♭3 shape on the tonic (instead of the root shape) you are playing the **pentatonic major** scale. The lowest note in the ♭3 shape is basically the tonic of the relative major key.

CHAPTER 6: THE HINDUSTAN SCALE

The Hindustan scale belongs to the group of the hexatonic scales. That is a fancy way of saying that it is a six-note scale.

It's actually a Mixolydian scale minus the sixth note. You can learn more about Mixolydian in the chapter on "Modes." Leaving a note out of a seven-note scale creates a new scale that has a more open feel.

Sometimes, less is more. Guitar players who want to be creative with scales often add notes to scales they already use or know, to add or create new colors or textures to that scale. Meanwhile, many overlook the equally resourceful tactic of leaving out notes in scales. Leaving notes out of an already familiar scale in order to get to a new scale with fewer notes can create equally drastic color changes.

A case in point really is the Hindustan scale. Not only does leaving the sixth note out of the Mixolydian scale create a sound quite different from the Mixolydian sound, it conjures up images of an "exotic" place on earth called... India!

Yes, it's called the Hindustan scale for a reason indeed. One can't help but feel that the scale has a strong Indian vibe and sound.

You see, leaving notes out of scales is fun. 😃

The formula for the Hindustan scale is: **1 2 3 4 5 ♭7**

As you already know, I'm a big proponent of learning scales one string at a time. It's much easier to see and understand a scale when it's shown on one line. This single-string approach is also the easiest, quickest way to be able to immediately improvise with any new scale. In-position fingerings take much longer to learn because they seem more all over the place and they cover two octaves.

As such, here's the Hindustan scale in the key of C, mapped out on each string.

The notes are **C D E F G B♭.**

Learning the scale on one string, you'll be able to play this in no time. I of course also teach the in-position fingerings to students who want to learn scales from all over the world or who want to become outstanding improvisers.

The Hindustan Scale

Do	Re	Mi	Fa	Sol	Te	Do
C	**D**	**E**	**F**	**G**	**B**♭	**C**
1	2	3	4	5	♭7	1

You can solo with that scale over a C7 groove (or C Mixolydian chord progressions).

Here are the in-position fingerings:

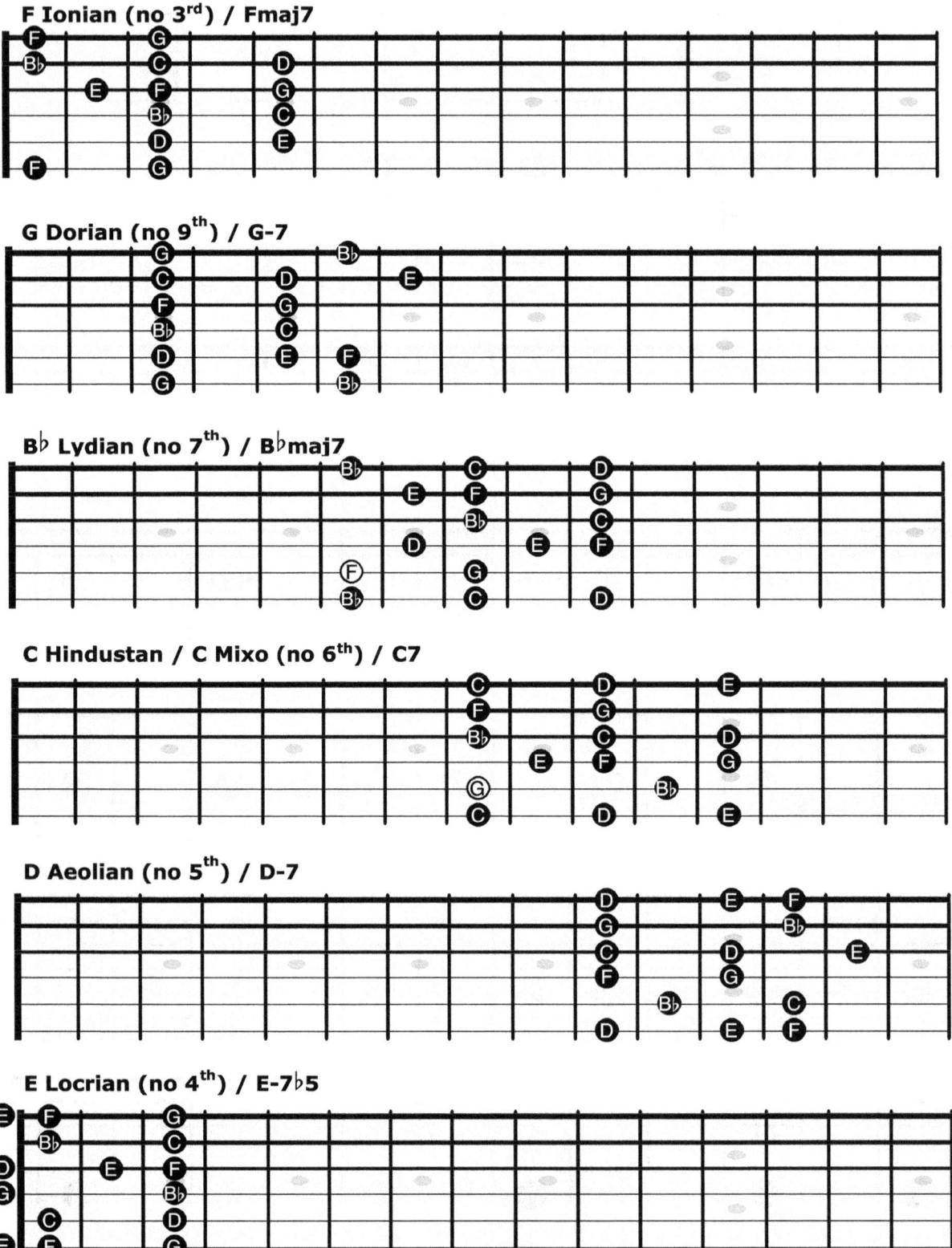

CHAPTER 7: PENTATONIC SUBSTITUTION

Almost every guitar player who uses pentatonic scales for soloing uses them in very limited ways. More specifically, most guitar players who see or hear a C chord immediately play an A minor pentatonic scale, not being aware that A minor pentatonic is not the only minor pentatonic scale one can use over a C chord.

That's why you want to know about **pentatonic substitution**. This improvisation concept teaches that you can play multiple possible pentatonic scales over any given chord. This is a really fun lesson, because this knowledge will make it possible for you to create and discover tons of new colors in your guitar solos, all without having to learn any new scales. You're merely using the minor pentatonic scale you already know, in entirely new ways.

Over a C Chord

You can play:

1. The minor pentatonic scale **up a sixth** from the chord:

    A minor pentatonic.

    This is the pentatonic scale almost all guitar players play all the time over a C chord, missing out on the many colors they can create if they'd also use following options:

2. The minor pent scale **up a major third** from the C chord root:

    E minor pentatonic.

3. The minor pent scale **up a seventh** from the root:

    B minor pentatonic.

    This creates a C Lydian sound. B minor pentatonic = **B D E F♯ A** (= 7th, 9th, 3rd, ♯11th and 13th over a C chord)

4. The minor pent scale **up a whole step** from the chord:

    D minor pentatonic.

    The notes in the D minor pentatonic are **D F G A C**.

    It's a bit more challenging to make this scale sound right over the C chord. The reason is because the most important note in a C chord is the note E, which is missing in the D minor pentatonic scale. In addition, the F in the scale creates a harsh clash with the E note in the C chord. The trick is to end all your melodic phrases as much as possible on the notes C or G. When you play the F note, resolve it up a whole step to G.

You want to memorize this with math, not with note names. Instead of memorizing "I can solo over a C chord with Am, Dm, Em, and Bm pentatonic scales," memorize that over every major chord, you can solo with the minor pentatonic scales:

1. Up a whole step from the chord root (two frets up)
2. Up a major 3rd from the chord root (four frets up)
3. Down a minor 2nd from the chord root (one fret down)
4. Down a minor 3rd from the chord root (three frets down)

The best and most fun way to enjoy these new sounds is by soloing with these four scales over a C or Cmaj7 one-chord groove type of backing-track. Be patient with the D minor pentatonic option. It does work. You just have to be diligent in resolving to the right notes, which might take some getting used to.

Enjoy the new sounds. You have made another great step forward in your musicianship now you know that you can solo over any given major chord with four different minor pentatonic scales.

One last note before moving on: These four scale options work really well over a C **one-chord groove**. However, in **chord progressions** in the key of C major (which has an F note) you would not be able to use the B minor pentatonic scale because the F♯ note in the scale would clash with the F notes in the chords. That doesn't mean that you can't use the B minor pentatonic at all, you just have to be careful that you only hit the F♯ note on chords that don't have an F note. All that said: while you could theoretically do that, it's unusual to solo with a scale that has an F♯ over a chord progression with chords that have F notes. It makes the solo sound disconnected from the harmony and makes the storytelling less fluent. But it **can** work. We'll cover a chord progression in the key of C where using B minor pentatonic actually sounds great.

Over a Dm Chord

You can play:

1. The minor pentatonic scale from the root:

   D minor pentatonic.

2. The minor pent scale up a major 2nd from the chord:

   E minor pentatonic.

   The E minor pentatonic scale over a Dm chord creates a D Dorian scale sound. You want to memorize this: When you solo over a minor chord with a minor pentatonic scale that is up a whole step from that minor chord, you are playing a Dorian sound. Feel free to first go have a look at the chapter on Modes if you want to learn what a Dorian scale is.

3. The minor pent scale up a 5th from the root:

   A minor pentatonic.

Have fun soloing with these three scale options over a one-chord groove in D minor. Enjoy the cool new improvisation sounds these scale options create over the chord.

If you would like to solo with them over **chord progressions** in D minor:

- ▶ The minor pentatonic scales **from the root** and **from the 5th** work over chord progressions in Aeolian, also called the natural minor scale. As an example, the notes in the D Aeolian scale are **D E F G A B♭ C**. You can solo with D minor pentatonic and A minor pentatonic over the chords of the D Aeolian scale, but not with the E minor pentatonic, which has a B note. That B note in the E minor pentatonic scale is going to clash with the B♭ notes in the chords of the D Aeolian scale.
- ▶ The minor pentatonic scale up a whole step from the root (E minor pent over a Dm chord) is the minor pentatonic scale of choice over chord progressions in Dorian (in this example: D Dorian).

If you are a little unsure about all this theory, your safest bet for now would be to just improvise over a one-chord groove. In later chapters, you'll learn more about modes and about chord progressions used in the different modes. The explanations above about chord progressions will make more sense once you get to those chapters.

Also, practice what you learn in this chapter in different keys. Solo with the four minor pentatonic options that work over major chords, not just over C chords, but also over the other eleven keys. For example, over an F chord, you would solo with the minor pentatonic scale:

- ▶ Up a whole step from the root = G minor pentatonic scale
- ▶ Up a major 3rd from F = A minor pentatonic scale
- ▶ Down a half step from F = E minor pentatonic scale
- ▶ Down a minor 3rd from F = D minor pentatonic scale

The same holds true for the minor chords: Solo over the other eleven minor keys besides the key of Dm.

Over Altered Chords

First off, what are **altered chords**?

An "altered chord" is the name we give to **dominant 7 chords** with "**altered tensions**": ♭9, ♯9, ♭5, and ♯5. The chords look like this: A7♭5, E7♯9, D7♭9, G7♭9♯5, and so on.

You might already know at least one altered chord. E7♯9 is an altered chord. Many guitar teachers call this "The Jimi Hendrix Chord" because Hendrix used it in so many of his songs.

"Dominant chords" are **V** chords. What this means is that the 5th (V) chord in a major scale is called a dominant chord. It is called that, because the V chord is the chord that has the most tension in a scale. It always wants to resolve back to I (the first chord in the scale). So, the altered chord is a V chord with altered 9ths and/or 5ths. In the key of C, the V chord is G7. Adding the altered tensions gives you G7♭9, or G7♯9 or G7♭5 or G7♯5 or any combinations of an altered 5th with an altered 9th. This chord name can also be written as Galt or G7alt.

Adding those altered tensions to the V chord adds even more tension to an already tense chord. This makes the resolution to the I chord all the sweeter. That's why jazz guys *love* altered chords.

They love the complex colors, the harsher tension, and the stark contrasts between that harsher tension and the sweeter resolution that follows it.

You would think that over a chord that sounds so complex, one would have to learn an entirely new, complex-sounding scale to solo. You would be right. The scale used to solo over altered chords is called **the altered scale**.

It is the seventh mode of the melodic minor scale.

Don't worry about that if that doesn't make sense because—lo and behold—there actually is a minor pentatonic scale that contains the five most important notes of the altered scale.

That minor pentatonic scale is the one up three frets from the root of the V chord.

In other words, over the **G alt** chord, you can solo with a B♭ minor pentatonic scale.

The notes in a B♭ minor pent scale are **B♭ D♭ E♭ F A♭**.

When we compare those notes against the G chord, we glean the following insights:

1. B♭, which can also be called A♯, is a ♯9th interval in relationship to G.

2. D♭ is a ♭5th interval in relationship to G.

3. E♭, which can also be called D♯, is a ♯5th interval in relationship to G.

4. F is the ♭7th in the G chord, one of the most important notes in the chord.

5. A♭ is the ♭9th interval in relationship to the G chord.

To sum up, playing the minor pentatonic scale up three frets from the root of a major chord gives you all the altered tensions: ♭5, ♯5, ♭9 and ♯9.

Let's put this all together now over *the* most heavily used chord progression in jazz. This is where it all comes together and where the minor pentatonic substitution fun really begins.

Minor Pent. Substitution Over a II - V - I Chord Progression

The most common chord progression in jazz music is **II V I**.

As you now know, jazz musicians love making the V chord an altered chord.

This gives the following chord progression in the key of C:

IIm7	V7alt	Imaj7	Imaj7
Dm7	G7♯9	Cmaj7	Cmaj7

Putting it all together, you know that over the:

1. **Dm** chord, one of the pentatonic minor scale options is **A minor pentatonic.**

2. **G7** altered chord, we only have one option: **B♭ minor pentatonic.**

3. **C** chord, we have a couple of options, from which we'll choose **B minor pentatonic.**

This yields:

Dm7	G7♯9	Cmaj7	Cmaj7
A min. pent.	B♭ min. pent.	B min. pent.	

I chose these particular scale options for a reason. Not sure if you noticed, but the scales move up one fret for each chord. It goes from A minor pentatonic scale, up a fret to B♭ minor pentatonic, up a fret to B minor pentatonic. Then when it starts over again with the Dm chord after four bars, move back down two frets to A minor pentatonic.

The chords move up in 4ths, while the scales move up in half steps. This creates a really cool sound. Notice how we're ending with two bars of Lydian sound, playing B minor pentatonic over the Cmaj7 chord. Though the first two chords have an F note (F is the minor 3rd in Dm and the ♭7th in G7), the F♯ note in the B minor pentatonic scale sounds great over the C chord mainly for two reasons:

1. The listener's ear "accepts" the F♯ note instead of rejecting its sound, because the consecutive half step motion of the three scales creates a sense of symmetry and expectation by the time the third scale gets hit.

2. The ear (or should we say "the brain") loves symmetry. There's a half-and-half symmetry: two bars with an F note (in the chords) and two bars with an F♯ note (in the scale).

This application of pentatonic substitution makes it fairly easy to solo over this more complex chord progression. Moreover, it's another step up in your jazz chops. Who would have thought that you could almost sound like an advanced jazz guy, using the fairly simple minor pentatonic scale in such creative ways?

Chapter 8: Creative Pentatonic Chord Progressions

Improvisers are trained to think in terms of, "Which scales go over these chords?" The study of improvisation always starts from the idea of, "Here's an intricate chord progression... and these are the scales you can use to solo over this progression."

But how interesting would it be to go completely backward on this: learn how to improvise odd, intricate, or unusual chord progressions underneath a set scale, instead of improvising with a scale over a set chord progression. This idea can lead to interesting songs or to really cool music being produced during jam sessions.

This harmonic technique can be used with pentatonic melodies or when playing with a lead guitarist whose style is very pentatonic based. One of the cool features of a scale with less notes is that you can use that scale to solo over complex chord progressions that combine chords from various larger (seven-note) scales, as long as these seven-note scales contain the notes of that smaller scale. To put this differently, any given seven-note scale only works over the chords that one can form with the notes of that scale. When the chord progression has a chord that is foreign to that scale, the improviser needs to switch to another scale over that chord.

Let me explain this with a real-life musical situation.

In a jam session, there's going to be someone laying down the harmony and rhythm, and someone else improvising lead melodies. The musicians agree upon a key before the playing starts, and everybody operates within that chosen framework. For example, if the chosen key is A, the musicians will play the notes of an A major scale and the chords that go with that scale: **Amaj7 Bm7 C#m7 Dmaj7 E7 F#m7 and G#m7♭5.**

In this situation, there's no wiggle room. Seven notes in the scale; seven chords can be formed with those seven notes. Everybody in the jam session is playing the same seven notes.

If you, the rhythm player, throw in anything other than these seven chords in the jam, that chord is more than likely going to clash with the notes of the person who's soloing.

When the soloist primarily uses the pentatonic scale, however, there's a lot more you can do harmonically, because the omission of two notes that turns a seven-note scale into a pentatonic scale, open up a lot of harmonic possibilities.

Pentatonic Substitution Chords

Consider the A minor pentatonic scale, which consists of the notes **A C D E G**. Building further on what was covered in previous pentatonic substitution chapter, we can conclude that there are three major scales that contain these five notes. *(The major scales that are down a whole step (G), down two whole steps (F) and down a major 6th (C) from A)*

1. C major scale **C D E F G A** B
2. F major scale F **G A** B♭ **C D E**
3. G major scale **G A** B **C D E** F#

The chords in a C major scale are: **C Dm Em F G Am Bdim C**.
The chords in an F major scale are: **F Gm Am B♭ C Dm Edim F**.
The chords in a G major scale are: **G Am Bm C D Em F♯dim G**.

Since, as shown above, these three major scales all have the notes of an A minor pentatonic scale in them, that means that you can play an A minor pentatonic scale over any combination of chords that are in these three scales.

You are now, as a rhythm player, no longer confined to just the seven chords of a C major scale. You can play any of the following chords under the A minor pentatonic melodies of the improviser:

C, Dm, D, Em, Edim, F, F♯dim, G, Gm, Am, B♭, Bdim, Bm.

You get even more options when you play the four-note versions, called **7th chords:**

The 7th chords in a C major scale are **Cmaj7 Dm7 Em7 Fmaj7 G7 Am7 Bm7♭5**.
The 7th chords in an F major scale are **Fmaj7 Gm7 Am7 B♭maj7 C7 Dm7 Em7♭5**.
The 7th chords in a G major scale are **Gmaj7 Am7 Bm7 Cmaj7 D7 Em7 F♯m7♭5**.

Putting these chords in alphabetical order starting from C, we get:

Cmaj7, C7, Dm7, D7, Em7, Em7♭5, Fmaj7, F♯m7♭5, Gmaj7, G7, Gm7, Am7, B♭maj7, Bm7♭5, Bm7.

Adding in the triads:

C, Cmaj7, C7, D, Dm, Dm7, D7, Em, Em7, Edim, Em7♭5, F, Fmaj7, F♯dim, F♯m7♭5, G, Gm, Gmaj7, G7, Gm7, Am, Am7, B♭, B♭maj7, Bdim, Bm7♭5, Bm, Bm7

Chords Taken from Blues

It doesn't end there—there are more chords.

In major blues, the preferred scale of choice for improvisation is the minor pentatonic scale. While you *can* solo over a major blues using the major pentatonic scale, it doesn't entirely nail the blues sound. Blues guys primarily use the minor pentatonic scale to solo over major blues.

The A minor pentatonic scale, is the preferred scale to solo over a blues in the key of A major. The chords in a blues in A are: A7, D7 and E7.

When we now update the list of chords, adding in A7 and E7, we get:

C, Cmaj7, C7, D, Dm, Dm7, D7, Em, Em7, Edim, Em7♭5, E, E7, F, Fmaj7, F♯dim, F♯m7♭5, G, Gm, Gmaj7, G7, Gm7, Am, Am7, A, A7, B♭, B♭maj7, Bdim, Bm7♭5, Bm, Bm7

Those are **thirty-two chords** that work with the A minor pentatonic scale... but it still doesn't end there yet.

The Dom7alt Chord Pentatonic Substitution

Remember the minor pentatonic substitution chapter? As you might remember, we can use the minor pentatonic scale to solo over V7 altered chords. The minor pentatonic scale that works over an altered chord is the one up three frets from the chord.

That means that to find the altered chord that works over a given minor pentatonic scale, we need to go down three frets from the tonic (first note) of that minor scale. Three frets down from A minor pentatonic = F♯.

In conclusion, we can add F♯alt to the chord list, adding up to thirty-three chords. This is harmonically a huge step up from the fourteen (seven triads and seven 7th) chords of the C major/A minor scale that most guitar players play when jamming with a pentatonic-based soloist.

Given that the V7alt chord can have any combination of altered 5^{ths} and 9^{ths}, this means that the alt dominant chord can take eight forms:

- ▶ F♯7♭5
- ▶ F♯7♯5
- ▶ F♯7♭9
- ▶ F♯7♯9
- ▶ F♯7♭5♯9
- ▶ F♯7♭5♭9
- ▶ F♯7♯5♯9
- ▶ F♯7♯5♭9

When we consider these eight forms of the altered chord as eight separate options, then the list adds up to forty chords we can use to create chord progressions for minor pentatonic melodies.

Cool Chord Progressions for the A Minor Pentatonic Scale

You can literally combine any of the above thirty-three chords any way you want. Imagine the compositional possibilities! The use of these harmonic improvisation ideas is not confined to jamming or performance. This harmonic concept works really well in composition, too. Next time you write a pentatonic melody, experiment coming up with very interesting chord progressions for that melody, applying what you learned here.

As for jamming, I apply this above knowledge absolutely *all* the time when I'm playing rhythm guitar for someone who mostly solos with pentatonic scales. The musicians I play with love it when I do this, because of the really interesting and sometimes surprising harmonic colors it creates for them to solo over.

These rich, intricate sounding chord progressions make the lead guitarist sound very advanced, even though they're playing guitar solos using a simple, easy scale. It's a great way to make your friends sound really good or much more advanced, even if they aren't that good yet at playing guitar solos.

Here are some cool chord progressions for you to have fun with. All of the following chord progressions work with the A minor pentatonic scale. Of course, ideally you will want to practice these in all twelve keys over time.

G | F | C | B♭ D |

A7 | G7 | C7 | D7 |

Blues in A: chords are A7, D7 and E7

Blues in G: chords are G7, C7 and D7

You could combine these two blues keys into one longer chord progression.

G7 | D7 | C7 | A7 | D7 | E7

Or

G7 | A7 | C7 | D7 | E7

Gm | B♭ | D7

Cmaj7 | B♭maj7 | Gmaj7 | Fmaj7

A7 | B♭maj7

B♭ one-chord groove (Lydian)

B♭ | A | C | Dm

F | G | A7 | B♭

F | G | A | B♭ | C | D

F | Gm | A

A7 | F♯m7♭5 | B♭maj7

A7 | F♯m7♭5 | Fmaj7 | B♭maj7

F | Gm | A7 | B♭ | C | D | Em

Em7 | F♯7alt | Bm7

Em7 | F♯7alt | Bm7 | B♭maj7

C7 | F♯7alt | Bm7

Be creative, and above all, have fun with this. Come up with your own chord progressions combining any of those thirty-three chords.

It's a lot of information, so you want to take your time and be patient with this.

Applying this takes time. You will find, though, that the time it takes to learn and memorize this is time well spent.

The excitement you'll feel when you see the flabbergasted look on the faces of your pentatonic guitar buddies who can't believe your chord progressions—priceless.

CHAPTER 9: KEY SIGNATURES

The Key Signature Theory

A quick side-note before going into key signatures: Know that the words **key** and **scale** are very often interchanged as if they mean the same thing. Such is the case here in the study of key signatures. Anytime you see the word "key" being used in this chapter, know that this also means "scale" (and vice versa). Knowing this ahead of time will avoid a lot of confusion.

All that being said...

When you start a major scale on the note C, you get the notes **C D E F G A B**.

There are eleven more starting notes we can start a major scale from. These starting notes are what we call keys. While the key of C only counts naturals, the other eleven keys have sharps or flats in them. Each specific major scale key has a very specific number of sharps or flats. Hence, key signatures.

Key Signatures

A key signature is **a number of sharps or flats**. That number of sharps or flats signifies a specific major scale. There is only one major scale that has three ♯'s. There's only one major scale that has two ♭'s. You get the idea.

You can always find the key signature at the beginning of the staff, positioned at the beginning of a piece of music, right after the clef and before the time signature.

Key signatures look like this:

With the key signature placed at the very beginning of a piece of music, it's always one of the first things a musician looks at before learning or performing the music. It tells that musician what scale the song is written with. This makes it easier to sight-read the piece of music because it shows the musicians ahead of time which notes they're going to encounter throughout the piece. They know what to expect and are better prepared to perform the piece more accurately.

Since a key signature shows you what the notes are in a scale, you have the notes in all twelve major scales memorized when you have their key signatures memorized. That is the goal of this chapter.

Before we go into that, I want to touch upon something a student once asked me.

"Why bother? Can't we just write and perform everything in the key of C?"

Each key has a certain unique tonal color. Music written with an A major scale for example has a more vibrant, lively color than music written with an E♭ major scale, which is generally agreed to have a more warm, fluffy, soft-spoken color. It requires a well-developed ear and sensitivity to hear these differences in sonic personalities. However, just because people can't hear it doesn't mean they can't feel it. It's safe to say that your listeners will experience a very different emotional impact for either version when you play them a song you recorded, and then the same song recorded in another key. That's why there seems to be a general agreement amongst musicologists or high-level composers that Bach, Beethoven, and Mozart (to name a few) didn't come upon the keys of their compositions by accident or coincidence. They deliberately chose the one key that best expressed and represented the feel they wanted to convey in each composition.

Each Key Signature Signifies a Specific Major Scale

Example 1

The major scale starting from F has the following notes: **F G A B♭ C D E F**

In the key of F, in order to maintain half steps between 3-4 and 7-8, the 4th note B is flatted to B♭. By flatting the B to B♭ we get the necessary half step between the 3rd and 4th note.

That one flat "signifies" the key of F. It is its "signature" so to speak. There's only one major scale that has one flat, and that's the F major scale.

Example 2

The G major scale has the following notes: **G A B C D E F♯ G**

In the key of G, in order to maintain half steps between 3-4 and 7-8, the 7th note F has to be raised to F♯ so we have a half step between F♯ and G.

That one sharp "signifies" the key of G. It is its "signature." There is only one major scale that has one sharp, and that is the G major scale.

From there on we can conclude that since a scale has seven notes:

- ▶ From one up to a maximum of seven notes can be raised:

    1-7 sharps (1♯, 2♯, 3♯, 4♯, 5♯, 6♯, 7♯)

- ▶ From one up to a maximum of seven notes can be lowered:

    1-7 flats (1♭, 2♭, 3♭, 4♭, 5♭, 6♭, 7♭)

There is one major scale that has no sharps or flats. You already learned that scale: C major. This adds up to fifteen possible key signatures.

Because a key signature tells you how many accidentals (black keys) there are in any given major scale, that means that it basically shows you how many notes of that scale are different from the

C major scale. Looking at it that way, we can then conclude that a key signature doesn't only tell you what the black keys are but also what the white keys are in that scale. When a scale, for example, has four sharps, that means that that scale has three white keys. The number of accidentals plus the number of naturals will always add up to seven, because that is the number of notes that make up a major scale.

The Order of Sharps and the Order of Flats

The sharps and flats appear in major scales following a set order. Memorize the following lines:

The order of sharps

The order of flats

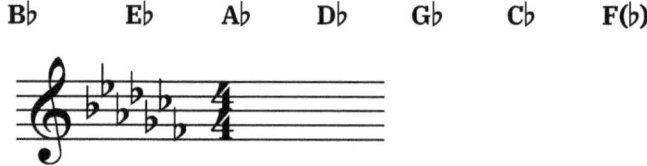

Notice how the order of ♯'s is the order of ♭'s backwards, and vice versa.

- The sharps go up in 5^{ths}
- The flats go down in 5^{ths} (which is up in 4^{ths})

This sequence in 5^{ths} is what led to the **circle of 5^{ths}** (covered in a later chapter).

What Does This Mean: "The Order of..."?

You want to memorize both these lines because you will be using them to figure out and to memorize what the notes are in all twelve major scales.

The "order of sharps" means that the sharps always happen in that order:

- In a scale that has one ♯, that note is F♯.
- In a scale that has two ♯'s, those notes are F♯ and C♯.
- In a scale that has three ♯'s, those notes are F♯, C♯ and G♯.
- And so on.

Same for the order of ♭'s:

- In a scale that has one ♭, that note is B♭.
- In a scale that has two ♭'s, those notes are B♭ and E♭.
- In a scale that has three ♭'s, those notes are B♭, E♭ and A♭.
- And so on.

Which Scales Have ♭'s and Which Have ♯'s?

1. Scales with ♯'s

You use the order of ♯'s for scales that start on **WHITE** keys (naturals):

1. G major
2. D major
3. A major
4. E major
5. B major

Two exceptions: The F♯ major and C♯ major scales.

Major scales that start on a natural always have sharps in them. There are two major scales that start on a black key that have sharps in them: F♯ and C♯

2. Scales with ♭'s

You use the order of ♭'s for scales that start on **BLACK** keys (accidentals):

1. B♭ major
2. E♭ major
3. A♭ major
4. D♭ major
5. G♭ major
6. C♭ major

One exception: The F major scale starts on a white key, but has one flat.

Major scales that start on accidentals (black keys) always have flats in them.

How to Apply This to Learn All Major Scales

This is where we're getting into the nitty-gritty.

The following explains a system that will enable you to memorize what the notes are in all twelve major scales using the order of sharps and the order of flats.

You will either know the key signature (and figure out the scale), or you will know the scale (and figure out the key signature), as explained here:

1. **Figure out the scale (based on a given key signature).**

   This is the situation where you want to learn a song from sheet music and the key signature is given at the beginning of the staff. That key signature tells you what the notes are with which that song is written. You want to be able to figure out, based on that given key signature, what scale it is that has those notes.

   Even if you aren't interested in learning how to read music, knowing how to figure out what the notes are in scales is a skill that will serve you well. This skill will, for example, make it easier for you to learn new songs. The more you know about music, the more connections you see. All pieces of the music theory puzzle are connected. Each connection you see is like an "anchor" that hooks into memory as a recognizable memory location. The more connections you see, the less you have to rely upon memory when trying to learn a new song. Thus, you end up learning new things much more quickly with less effort. It goes without saying that knowing the notes in scales also makes you a much better improviser. It's usually the guitarists who know what notes they're playing who have come up with some of the world's best guitar solos. Guitar players who base their solos on visual shapes and patterns are much less likely to produce the same quality of improvisations.

2. **Figure out the key signature (the notes in a given scale).**

   This is the situation where you jam with friends and they say: "Let's jam in the key of A." You need a system to figure out what the notes are in that scale so you can play solos and interact with your friends musically. Sure, you can just play scale shapes and patterns. There's nothing wrong with that. But if you want to get your playing to the next levels, there's nothing but major benefits to not being dependent upon shapes. It's not shapes that make music, it's sounds that make music. Focus on notes, not geometry.

Here's how to apply the order of sharps and flats to figure out the notes of the major scale in all twelve keys.

1. **For scales with sharps:**

   A. **Key Signature to Key**

   Apply the following trick **when you know the key signature** (learning a transcribed song) and are trying to figure out what the scale is:

   Whatever the number of sharps you see at the clef ➡ Go up a half step from the last ♯ in line, and that tells you what the scale is.

   Example

   When you see three ♯'s at the clef, they always are F♯, C♯, and G♯ ➡ last ♯ in line is G♯ ➡ up a half step from G♯ = A (major scale).

   Conclusion

   The key of A major has three sharps (F♯, C♯, and G♯).

B. Key to Key Signature

Apply the following trick **when the key is given.** (When in a jam session with musicians, somebody names a key, and you try to figure what the key signature is, meaning: what the notes are.)

Go over the line of ♯'s ➡ stop on the sharp that is a half step down from the key you are looking for. That one is the last sharp in line. Count the number of sharps up till there.

Example:
Key of A ➡ The order of ♯'s is F♯, C♯, G♯... bingo ➡ This is the sharp a half step lower than A.

Conclusion
There are three sharps in the key of A major: F♯, C♯, and G♯.

2. For scales with flats:

A. Key Signature to Key

Apply following trick **when the key signature is given** and you are trying to figure out the scale (learning a transcribed song):

Go back one flat.

In other words: the one before the last ♭ in line ➡ = The key

Example
Two ♭'s at the clef ➡ Those two flats are B♭ and E♭ ➡ The one before the last flat is B♭ ➡ = the key.

Conclusion
The scale that has two flats is B♭ major. A B♭ major scale has a B♭ and an E♭ note, and five naturals.

B. Key to Key Signature

Apply the following trick **when the scale is given** and you are trying to figure out the key signature. (Jam session with musicians.)

Add the next flat past the flat with the same name of the key that is given.

Basically, count up the order of flats until you hit the flat that has the same letter like the key name, and then add the next flat past that.

Example
How many flats in the key of A♭? ➡ The order of ♭'s is: B♭, E♭, A♭ *(A♭ is the name of the key. We need to make this the one before the last flat. We do this by adding the next flat (D♭) to the key signature.)*
Going one flat further past A♭ gives us four ♭'s.

Conclusion
The A♭ major scale has four flats. Those flats are: B♭, E♭, A♭, and D♭. The naturals are F, C, and G. When you play these seven notes, you play an A♭ major scale.

Caution!

1. The scale that has six sharps: the sixth sharp is E♯. A half step up from E♯ gives us the key of F♯ major, not F major. The F major scale has one ♭, not sharps.

2. The seventh sharp in the order of ♯'s is B♯. Up a half step from B♯ is the key of C♯ major, not the key of C. The C♯ major scale has seven ♯'s.

3. You want to think of the "order of sharps" and the "order of flats" as continuous lines. When you think of the order of flats as a continuous line, then the last flat (F♭) comes before the first flat (B♭). That means that if you only have one flat, the "one before the last flat" is the one that comes before B♭, which is F. Thinking of the order of flats as a continuous line, makes it make more sense that the key of F major has one flat in the scale (the note B♭).

4. There is one little discrepancy in the whole system. Notice how in the order of flats, when you have:

    a. Two flats, the key is B♭

    b. Three flats, the key is E♭

    c. Four flats, the key is A♭

    d. Five flats, the key is D♭

    e. Six flats, the key is G♭

    f. Seven flats, the key is C♭

    g. However, when you have ONE flat, the key is not F♭ but F.

Notice how in the order of flats, the ♭ symbol in F♭ is in between parenthesis? That's to show this little discrepancy.

F♭ is the seventh flat in the order of flats. It's one of the seven notes in the C♭ major scale. But the scale you get when you look at the flat preceding B♭ in the order of flats is the F major scale, not the F♭ major scale. There is no F♭ major scale.

Some Fun Trivia for Music Theory Nerds (such as myself)!

A) Enharmonic scales/notes.

"**Enharmonic**" means different note names for the same sound.

(i.e. E♭ and D♯, F♯ and G♭, B and C♭, and so on)

The key signatures of enharmonic scales always add up to twelve.

Examples:

1. C♯ = 7 ♯'s ------- D♭ = 5 ♭'s = 12 ♯'s and ♭'s
2. C♭ = 7 ♭'s ------- B = 5 ♯'s = 12 ♯'s and ♭'s
3. G♭ = 6 ♭'s ------- F♯ = 6 ♯'s = 12 ♯'s and ♭'s

4. Now you would never call a scale a G♯ major scale, because scales that start on black keys use ♭ names. You would call that scale A♭. The following example is shown here merely to illustrate that key signatures of enharmonic scales indeed always add up to twelve consistently, even when using scale names we wouldn't theoretically use.

A♭ = 4♭'s ------- G♯ = 6♯'s + 1 𝑋 (double sharp = ♯♯) = 12 ♯'s and ♭'s

B) Why do we give scales that start on black keys ♭ names instead of ♯ names?

Let's use the aforementioned G♯ major scale to explain this. How did I, in the above example, get to 6♯'s + 1 𝑋 (double sharp = ♯♯) for the G♯ major scale?

The best way to understand this is to start from the idea that a G♯ major scale is a G major scale up a half step.

The key of G has six naturals and one ♯: G A B C D E F♯. When you raise that whole scale up a half step to the G♯ major scale, you raise all seven notes of the G major scale up a half step. You could say that you are in essence sharpening all seven notes, which is like adding seven sharps to the one sharp the G scale already had. This raises the G scale up a half step to a G♯ major scale. Doing so, you get the notes G♯ A♯ B♯ C♯ D♯ E♯ F𝑋

You can probably see the extra, added complexity with the double sharp? There are more sharps than there are notes in the scale. It's much easier to just call it A♭ instead.

That is why, with the exception of the keys of F♯ and C♯, scales that start on black keys of the piano are always called ♭.

C) Half step apart, but same alphabet note name.

For scales that are a half step apart but that share the same note name (A & A♭, F & F♯, B & B♭, etc.)
➡ the key signatures of these scales always add up to seven.

Examples:

- ▶ C = 0 ♭'s ➡ C♭ = 7 ♭'s = 7
- ▶ A = 3 ♯'s ➡ A♭ = 4 ♭'s = 7
- ▶ F = 1 ♭ ➡ F♯ = 6 ♯'s = 7
- ▶ G = 1 ♯ ➡ G♭ = 6 ♭'s = 7
- ▶ D = 2 ♯'s ➡ D♭ = 5 ♭'s = 7
- ▶ Etc.

And that's it! You now know all there is to know about key signatures. There's nothing more to it. The only thing still left to do is to practice and memorize them.

The best way to achieve this is with flash cards.

How to Practice Key Signatures

Make two stacks of flash cards:

1. Stack 1 ➡ 0♯, 1♯, 2♯, 3♯, 4♯, 5♯, 6♯, 7♯, 0♭, 1♭, 2♭, 3♭, 4♭, 5♭, 6♭, 7♭

2. Stack 2 ➡ C, C♯, D♭, D, E♭, E, F, F♯, G♭, G, A♭, A, B♭, B, C♭

   ▶ With the first stack of flash cards, you practice how to figure out the scale, based on a given key signature.

   ▶ With the second stack of flash cards, you practice how to figure out the key signature to a given scale.

Within only days, you will already have many memorized.

Go through each stack of flash cards, and apply the above explained practice systems.

Drill time:
Practice this for three minutes per stack of flash cards, twice a day. This adds up to a **12-minute daily drill**.

One last thing…

How to Efficiently Figure Out The Naturals in Scales With Lots of ♯'s or ♭'s?

You possess a much deeper understanding of a scale when you also know what the naturals are in that scale in addition to knowing its accidentals. To figure out the naturals, you could count all the way up until the end of the order of sharps or the order of flats to find out which notes did not get sharped or flatted, but there's a much faster and easier way.

Instead of working so hard, you want to use to your advantage the knowledge that the first flats are the last sharps and the last flats are the first sharps.

▶ The order of sharps is the order of flats backward.

▶ The order of flats is the order of sharps backward.

Sharps: **F C G D A E B**
Flats: **B E A D G C F**

Rather than counting all the way to the end of the order of sharps or flats to figure out the naturals, look instead at the beginning of the other line.

This will make more sense with following examples.

The key of E has four ♯'s. That means that it has three naturals. Those three naturals, the notes that are not sharped in the scale, are the last three letters in the order of sharps.

These three letters, A, E, and B, are also the first three flats.

It is way faster (more efficient) and easier to figure this out counting the first three flats, rather than to have to count all the way until the end of the order of sharps to figure out what the three notes are that did not get sharped.

Conversely:

The key of D♭ has five flats. A scale with five flats has two naturals. Those naturals are the last two letters in the order of flats. The last two flats in the order of flats are C and F. These are also the first two sharps. It is faster (read: more efficient) and much easier to look at the beginning of the order of sharps, than to have to count all the way to the end of the order of flats in order to figure out what the notes are that did not get flatted.

Use this information to your advantage to figure out more quickly what the naturals are in scales with lots of sharps or flats.

Examples:

1. The key of A♭ has four flats. What are the three white keys in that scale? Hint: don't count till the end of the order of flats to find out, but instead look at the first three sharps.

   Conclusion:

   The white keys in the key of A♭ are F, C, and G.

2. The key of B has five sharps. What are the two white keys in that scale? Hint: don't count till the end of the order of sharps to find out, but instead look at the first two flats.

   Conclusion:

   The white keys in a B major scale are B and E.

How is the above helpful or useful information?

Well, one of the benefits you get from this little piece of trivia is awareness. You understand and learn scales on a deeper level in a shorter amount of time if you're not only aware of what the key signature of the scale is (what the black keys are) but also aware of what the notes are that are not part of the key signature (the white keys in the scale).

That awareness also takes a huge load off of brain processing.

Think about it—isn't it easier, while soloing in a scale with lots of sharps, to just focus on what the couple of naturals are and make all the rest sharp? This surely beats constantly having to process each individual sharp in that scale while improvising.

CHAPTER 10: THE CIRCLE OF 4ths AND 5ths

The circle of 5ths (clockwise) is the circle of 4ths counterclockwise. Many people think this is a huge concept in music theory. All it really is is a graph that shows that major and minor scales have six out of seven notes in common when they are spaced in 4th or 5th intervals apart. In other words, there is only one note different between scales that are a 4th or a 5th apart. That's why it's always recommended to practice scales in this order (in 4ths or in 5ths), because you then only have one new note at a time to worry about. It's a very efficient way to practice, gradually moving to scales with more and more accidentals.

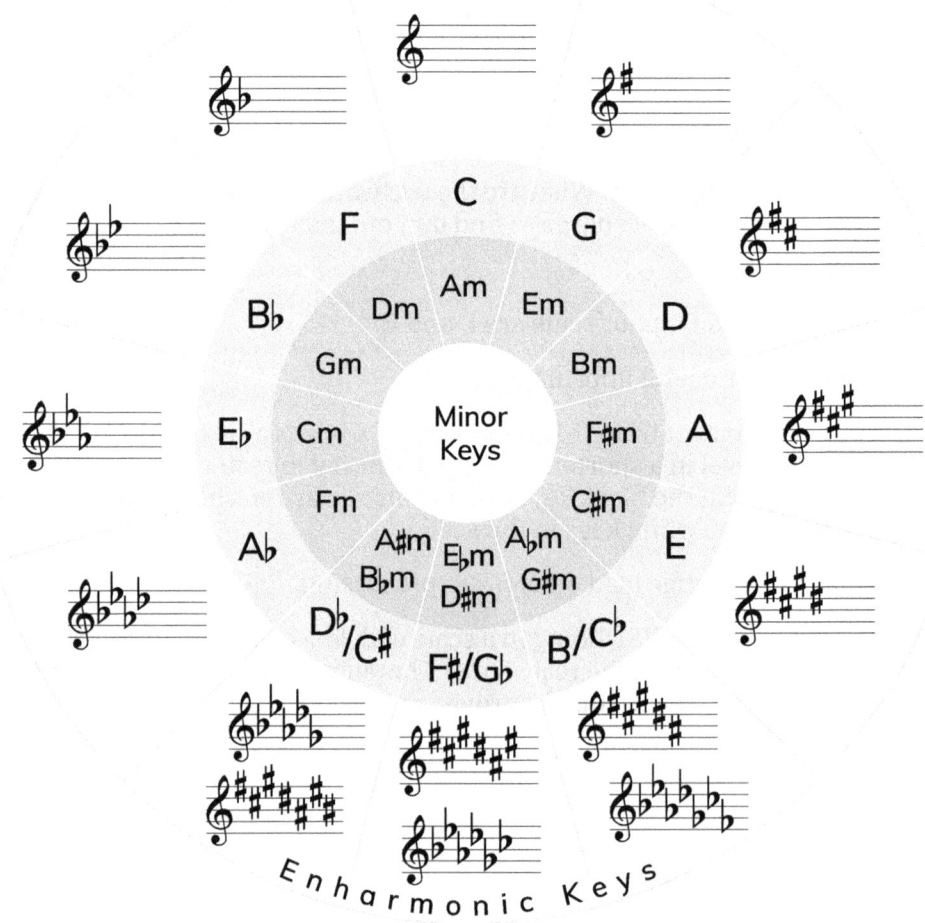

The keys on the inside of the circle are the relative minor keys. For each major scale there is a minor scale that contains the same seven notes. As a reminder, different scales that consist of the same notes are called "relative scales."

CHAPTER 11: THE MODES

Modes are rotations of a scale. You could also think of these rotations as (scale) inversions. "Inversion" is the name we use in the study of harmony to describe the rotation of notes in a chord. What all this means is that you could make the next note in a scale the first note of the scale, and then the next note, and so on, until all seven notes have served as the first note. This gives you seven unique, different scales, that all have their own structure and sound. Those scales are called modes (of one another).

Of course, all modes are relative scales because they all consist of the same seven notes.

You will notice below that there are three major modes and four minor modes. The major modes are explained and defined by comparing them to the major scale, which is also called the **Ionian** scale. The minor modes are explained and defined by comparing them to the regular minor scale, which is also called the **Aeolian** scale.

Here are all the modes of the major scale.

Ionian

Ionian is another name for the major scale. Pictured below is the C major scale.

This C major scale works over C, C6, and Cmaj7 chords.

Dorian

Dorian is the scale that is built on the second degree of the major scale. To say this differently: when you start a major scale from its second note up until you hit that same note again up an octave, you are playing a Dorian scale.

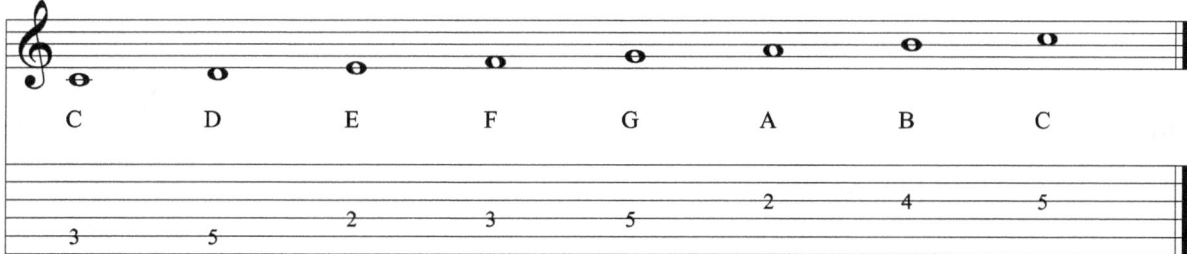

Dorian is a minor scale, and its characteristic tone, which distinguishes this scale from the natural minor (also called the Aeolian scale, covered on the next page), is the raised 6th. D Aeolian has a B♭ note, while D Dorian has a B note.

This D Dorian scale works over Dm and Dm7 chords.

Phrygian

This is the scale that is built on the third degree of the major scale. It is a minor scale and its characteristic tone is the flatted 2nd, which gives the scale its Spanish flavor.

This E Phrygian scale works over Em and Em7 chords.

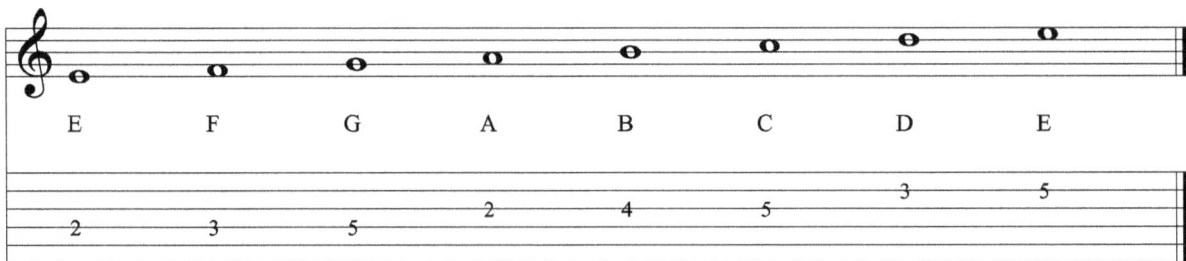

Lydian

This is the scale that is built on the fourth degree of the major scale. It is a major scale and its characteristic pitch is the raised 4th (B instead of B♭). Because of the three whole steps in a row, this scale is more open and brighter sounding than the regular major scale.

This F Lydian scale works over F, F6, and Fmaj7 chords.

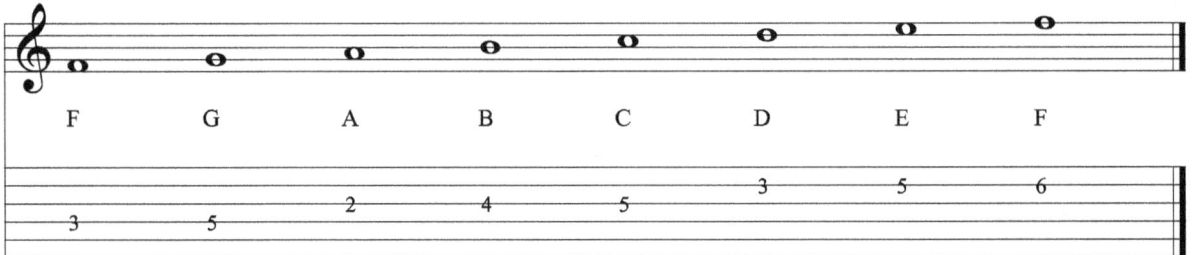

Mixolydian

You will oftentimes see this scale name in its abbreviated version "Mixo." This is the scale that is built on the fifth degree of the major scale. It is a major scale and its characteristic pitch is the flatted 7th.

The G Mixolydian scale works over G, G6, and G7 chords.

Aeolian

This is the scale that is built on the sixth degree of the major scale. This is the regular minor scale, also called the natural minor or relative minor, with half steps between 2-3 and 5-6.

This A Aeolian scale works over Am and Am7 chords.

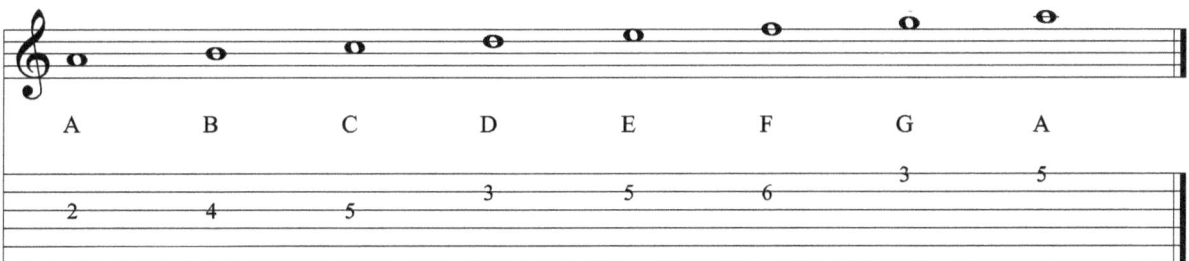

Locrian

This is the scale that is built on the seventh degree of the major scale. It is a minor scale and its characteristic pitches are the flatted 5th and the flatted 2nd.

The B Locrian scale works over Bdim and Bm7♭5 chords.

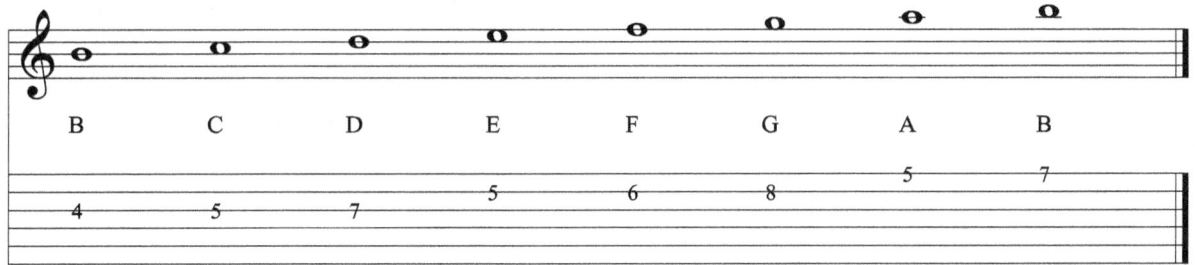

Modes: What's the Big Deal?

Now that we have gotten the theory about modes out of the way, this is typically where music teachers see blank expressions on students' faces. And the question that almost always arises right away:

"Isn't this all just a C major scale starting from different notes?"

NO! These really are seven different scales.

This chapter will resolve all possible confusion one might have about modes.

I remember how this was incredibly confusing to me back when I was first introduced to the concept of "modes" in music school. I could not understand how scales that all consist of the same seven notes could be seven different scales.

Unfortunately, I found that teachers generally tend to explain this material quite inadequately.

It always amuses me when my students showcase the same recognizable confusion and ask the same questions I once struggled with.

They typically always get it instantly when I share following information.

It all boils down to following simple concept:

The C major scale could **never** possibly sound like a C major scale **unless** it is played over a C major chord.

- ▶ When you play a C major scale over a Dm chord, then it sounds like a D Dorian scale.
- ▶ When you play a C major scale over an Em chord, then it sounds like an E Phrygian scale.
- ▶ When you play a C major scale over an F chord, then it sounds like an F Lydian scale.
- ▶ When you play a C major scale over a G chord, then it sounds like a G Mixolydian scale.
- ▶ When you play a C major scale over an Am chord, then it sounds like an A Aeolian scale.
- ▶ When you play a C major scale over a Bdim chord, then it sounds like a B Locrian scale.

Why does a C major scale become a different scale when played over another chord than C?

The reason has to do with your note choices in the scale you're soloing with.

You don't use the seven notes of the C major scale the same way over a Dm or over an F chord as you do over a C chord. When you solo over another chord than C, you change the sound of the scale from sounding like a C major scale to sounding like a different scale. This happens because the chord over which you improvise makes you outline and emphasize different notes in the scale than you would use over a C chord.

What does this mean: "outline" or "emphasize"?

Well, this is where things get interesting.

It simply means "the notes that you start and end your phrases on." The first and the last note in a melody are the notes that are the most "noticeable."

Even more so than the first note in your melodic phrase, it is the last note in your phrases that tends to stick out as the note that either creates tension or resolution when played over any given chord.

We all like resolution. Students tend to describe it as "the notes that sound pleasing." It is our inherent nature to dislike, to avoid, and to want to resolve tension. This human trait is immediately recognizable in how students approach their solos.

I say, "let's jam in the key of C major," and guess what?

1. The students tend to end most of their melody lines on either a C, or an E, or a G note over my C chord groove. That makes sense. C, E, and G are the notes of a C chord. These are the notes that sound pleasing to the improvising student's ear. We're in the key of C.

2. But when after saying "let's jam in the key of C major," I start off the jam playing a Dm chord groove instead of a C chord—pretty much all students tend to end their phrases on the notes D, F, and A now. These are the notes of a Dm chord. They usually aren't aware that they're doing this. They don't know it, but they are actually soloing in the D Dorian scale then. It doesn't matter that I said, "let's jam in the key of C major." They're playing all naturals, thinking we're jamming in the key of C. However, the scale they're playing doesn't sound like a C scale because they end all their melodies on the notes of a Dm chord. This makes their scale sound like a D scale that consists of all naturals. That scale is D Dorian.

3. Over an Em chord groove, students end most if not all their phrases on the notes E, G and B. You guessed it—the three notes of an Em chord. Playing all the naturals over an Em chord makes those seven notes sound like an E Phrygian scale. With its distinctive Spanish flamenco sound, this sounds nothing like a C major scale.

4. While playing guitar solos over an F chord groove, students end most of their phrases on the notes of an F chord: F, A, and C. In doing so, all the seven naturals sound like an F Lydian scale.

5. While playing guitar solos over a G chord groove, students end most of their phrases on the notes of a G chord: G, B, and D. In doing so, all the seven naturals sound like a G Mixolydian scale.

6. Over an Am chord groove, students naturally outline the notes A, C, and E more than any of the other four notes in the scale. This makes the seven white keys sound like an A Aeolian scale.

7. Lastly, you get the idea: Over a Bm7b5 groove, most of the student's phrases end on the notes B, D and F. Though nothing but naturals are played in the solo, the scale sounds very different from a C major scale. The sound we hear is the sound of B Locrian.

To sum it all up:

Students, usually without realizing they're doing this, let the chord they are soloing over influence their note choices in the scale they're improvising with.

When your melodic phrase ends on one of the chord notes that make up the chord you are improvising over, then your phrase sounds resolved. The colors match (same note in the solo as in the chord). Your melodic phrase resolves into the chord. The notes connect, and your phrase is in harmony with the chord. It sounds pleasing and lovely. When you play chord tones only in your solo, then there is no tension.

When, however, your ending note in a melodic phrase is not in the chord that is being played when you hit that note in your solo, then that note can create tension against that chord.

How do guitar students, who oftentimes don't have a good ear yet, know how to resolve their melodies to these "right" sounding notes?

It's a "feel" thing. Their "feel" has a way of leading their fingers to the notes that sound less "annoying" and more "pleasant." Even if the guitarist doesn't have a good ear yet, their fingers are led by what feels good and sounds pleasing. The fingers keep moving, only to pause when a note gets hit that is perceived as pleasant. That pause makes the phrase come to an end. The student might not be able to tell that that ending note is a chord note, but they will be able to tell that "that note sounded good" *(which basically means that it is probably a chord tone).*

So how do the notes you consistently end your melodies on turn what you thought was just a C major scale, into one of seven uniquely different-sounding scales?

The answer is that these ending notes in consecutive phrases create a sense of key. The part in the human brain that regulates auditory perception has a way of remembering the last note(s) in consecutive melodic phrases. Our inner ear (or should I say "brain") groups these notes together into chords. Even if nobody is strumming any chords, we end up perceiving the sound of a chord if x number of phrases in a row ended on a note of that chord. That chord we're hearing becomes the key center, the I chord.

As an example: When you play melodies using all the notes of a C scale, but start and end all your phrases with the notes of a Dm chord (D, F and A), your inner ear will hear a scale that is **centered** around a Dm chord now. All the white keys of the piano will no longer sound like a C scale, but like some sort of Dm scale now.

As a matter of fact: here's a fun experiment.

I urge you to improvise with all the white keys of the piano over a C chord, **not** resolving **one** single phrase to the notes C, E, or G. Don't end any of your melodies on C, E, or G. Instead, end all phrases on the notes D, F, and A. You can play the other four notes of the scale as well; just play them as passing notes between D and F and between F and A, and don't resolve to anything else than the notes D, F, and A.

You will be surprised at how incredibly bad and tedious this sounds over a C chord. After a while, the phrases will even end up sounding downright annoying to you.

Why?

It will sound tedious because every phrase-ending will clash with the C chord. You will get antsy because your inner peace of mind wants resolution. You will want the constant musical tension to end. You will crave to hear C, E, or G notes as ending notes. You will sound like a tone-deaf person trying to play melodies.

To say this differently:

YOU WILL SOUND LIKE YOU'RE PLAYING THE WRONG SCALE!

(Even though you're playing all the white keys of the piano over a C major chord.)

When you end all your melody lines with the notes of a certain chord, the scale you use to create those melodies ends up sounding like that chord. That is how you can make any seven-note scale sound like seven different scales.

This reiterates the point I've been hammering home: The seven modes really *are* seven different scales, even though they all share the same seven notes.

Each mode has its own particular:

    1. Structure of half and whole steps

    2. Distinctive sound created by that scale structure

The fun starts when you play music with those modes.

Download the C Ionian backing track from the FREE Bonus materials page and have fun improvising over the track.

Do the same over the D Dorian track. Solo with all the naturals. Notice how the scale has a totally different color and feel now—it is no longer a C major scale but a D Dorian scale.

Next, solo over the E Phrygian, F Lydian, G Mixolydian, A Aeolian, and B Locrian backing tracks.

Notice how the feel and atmosphere of these same seven notes (**C D E F G A B**) is entirely different over each track. You're playing the same notes, but they are, and sound like, a different scale over each track.

You just made an enormous leap forward in your musicianship if all the above makes sense. Enjoy the new sounds you're discovering.

CHAPTER 12: IN-POSITION SCALE FINGERINGS

These are the seven in-position fingerings of a C major scale. Learn and practice them. You also want to memorize the names of these seven fingerings. The best way to practice these fingerings: solo over a C Ionian backing track. (Two minutes per fingering.)

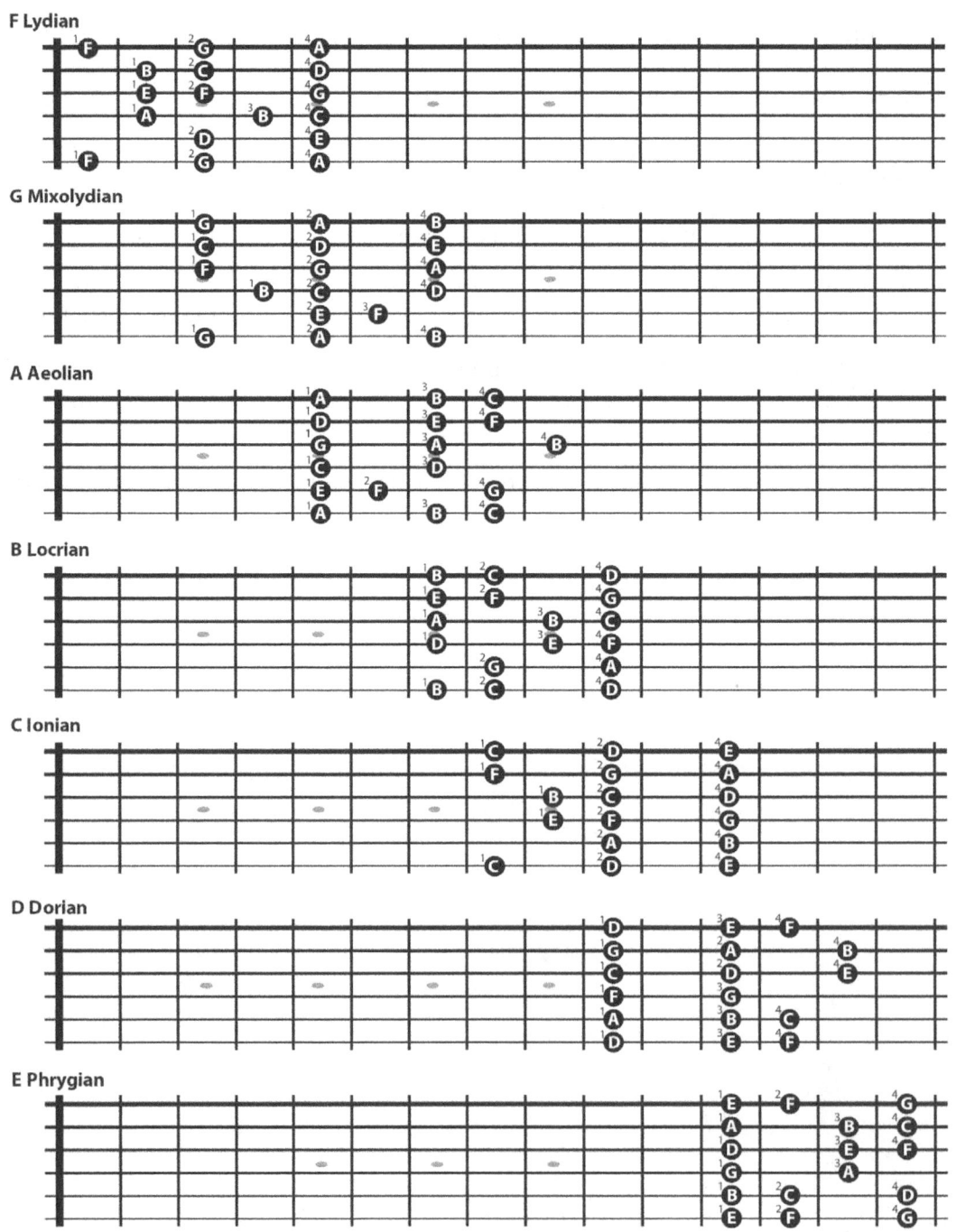

66

CHAPTER 13: IMPROVISATION OVER IVm MODAL INTERCHANGE

Cmaj7 | Cmaj7 | Fm7 | Fm7

Scales

This is the next level: Soloing with the in-position fingerings over more advanced chord progressions. Only tackle this when you feel confident about the in-position fingerings covered in previous chapter. Soloing gets really fun when you have to switch between different scales over a chord progression. Over the above chord progression, you would play:

C Ionian scale ➡ F Dorian scale

Whenever a chord progression has a minor chord that is foreign to the scale (for example an Fm chord in a C major song) you always play the Dorian scale over that minor chord. The reason: more notes in common between the two scales. To showcase this using the above chord progression as an example: F Dorian has three flats, which is closer to a C major scale than F Aeolian (four flats) or F Phrygian (five flats).

As you know from the previous page, every seven-note scale has seven different positions where you can play that scale. This results in seven fingerings. Below I have mapped out the closest connecting fingerings going from a C major scale to an F Dorian scale. This is something advanced level players and jazz guitarists practice on a lot. Being able to switch between different scales with the least amount of motion (meaning: staying on the same lowest note/position when possible) is a really good skill to have. The below mapped-out fingerings make it possible to play over the chord change and switch scales without having to move position.

Fingerings

- ▶ F Lydian fingering ➡ F Dorian fingering
- ▶ G Mixo fingering ➡ G Phrygian fingering
- ▶ A Aeolian fingering ➡ A♭ Lydian fingering
- ▶ B Locrian fingering ➡ B♭ Mixo fingering
- ▶ C Ionian fingering ➡ C Aeolian fingering
- ▶ D Dorian fingering ➡ D Locrian fingering
- ▶ E Phrygian fingering ➡ E♭ Ionian fingering

Drill time:
Solo 2 min. per location = **14-minute daily drill**.

Once this gets easier, transpose the chord progression to different keys. This is a fantastic drill to train the in-position scale fingerings. Here's another practice idea that will do a lot for your improvisation skills—solo over this chord progression on one string. Strongly recommended!

CHAPTER 14: IMPROVISATION OVER ♭VImaj7 MODAL INTERCHANGE

Cmaj7 | Cmaj7 | A♭maj7 | A♭maj7

This is basically the same idea as in the previous chapter, but with another chord progression.

Scales

C Ionian ➡ A♭ Lydian

Whenever a chord progression has a maj7 chord that is foreign to the scale (for example an A♭maj7 chord in a C major song) you always play the Lydian scale over that maj7 chord.

The reason: more notes in common between the two scales.

To showcase this using the above chord progression as an example: A♭ Lydian has three flats, which is closer to a C major scale than A♭ Ionian (four flats).

Fingerings

- ▶ F Lydian fingering ➡ F Dorian fingering
- ▶ G Mixo fingering ➡ G Phrygian fingering
- ▶ A Aeolian fingering ➡ A♭ Lydian fingering
- ▶ B Locrian fingering ➡ B♭ Mixo fingering
- ▶ C Ionian fingering ➡ C Aeolian fingering
- ▶ D Dorian fingering ➡ D Locrian fingering
- ▶ E Phrygian fingering ➡ E♭ Ionian fingering

Drill time:
Solo 2 min. per location = **14-minute daily drill.**

Here, too, you can use this chord progression as an opportunity to practice single-string soloing. You'll love what this will do for your improvisation skills and musicianship.

CHAPTER 15: KEY AND SCALE

As you learned in the key signatures chapter, the words "key" and "scale" are usually interchanged (and oftentimes confused). It's interesting to note how many musicians there are who have a hard time explaining the difference. Let's change that right here.

A **scale** is a series of notes organized from lowest to highest pitch. There are only 2,048 scales possible in our twelve-note system.

A **key** can be explained as a gravitational center that a song keeps coming back to. It is the one note you can sing throughout a whole song, without that note ever clashing anywhere with the chords in the song. You can play a scale, but you can't play a key. A key is a perception. It's to some extent a bit of an aural illusion. Some of the reasons why we hear that foundational pitch include:

1. The song is written with a scale that starts on that note.

2. The song (almost always) starts on the chord that is built on that note, basically the I chord.

3. That I chord keeps reappearing throughout the song, with all other chords either building up to it or resolving into it.

This entrenches the root of that chord in our ear.

The reason why you want to know the distinction between scale and key is because a song could at the same time be in a certain key throughout the whole song, while using different scales within that song. One of the easiest ways to showcase that distinction between key and scale is with the modal interchange chord progressions in the previous chapters.

Example:

||: Cmaj7 | Fmaj7 | G7 | A♭maj7 :||

This chord progression is in the key of C throughout all four chords. The A♭ chord is a modal interchange chord. Modal interchange chords are chords borrowed from parallel scales. Parallel scales are scales that are all in the same key. (All start on the same note). The A♭ chord is borrowed from the C minor scale, to be used in the C major scale chord progression.

Since the A♭maj7 chord is taken from another C scale, the above chord progression never leaves the key of C. However, you could not play a C major scale over the A♭maj7 chord.

Over A♭maj7, you play A♭ Lydian, which is relative to the C Aeolian scale.

Conclusion:

A key is not a scale, and a scale is not a key. They are two different things.

CHAPTER 16: THE WHOLE TONE SCALE

Songs that use mostly whole tone scale harmony are extremely rare, because of the sameness of sound. It's really only in jazz music that you would find tunes using this scale (e.g., "One Down, One Up," "Juju"). The intro to "You Are the Sunshine of My Life" (Stevie Wonder) has a whole tone scale line. Another great whole tone scale example is the main hook to "Coffy Is the Color" (Ron Ayers), from the soundtrack for the 1970s movie "Coffy" with Pam Grier in the lead.

The whole tone scale is a symmetrical scale. It consists of six notes spaced in whole steps. Symmetrical scales are scales that have all notes in the scale at equal distance from one another, dividing the octave into equal intervals. That is why all chords in symmetrical scales have exactly the same structure. Every note in a symmetrical scale feels like the tonic I.

There are only two whole tone scales: **C D E F♯ G♯ A♯**

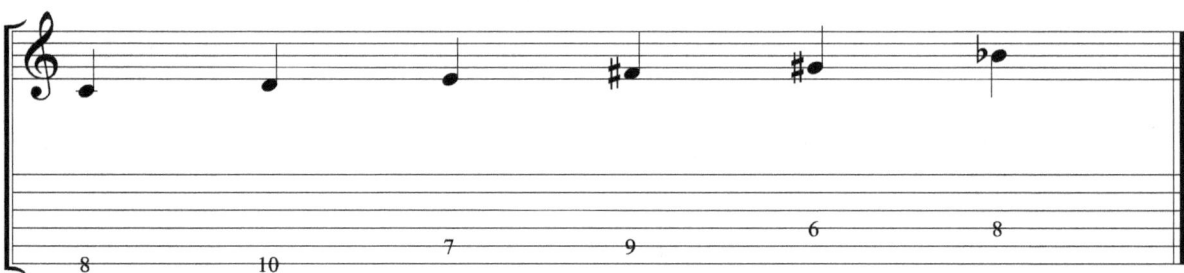

And **D♭ E♭ F G A B**

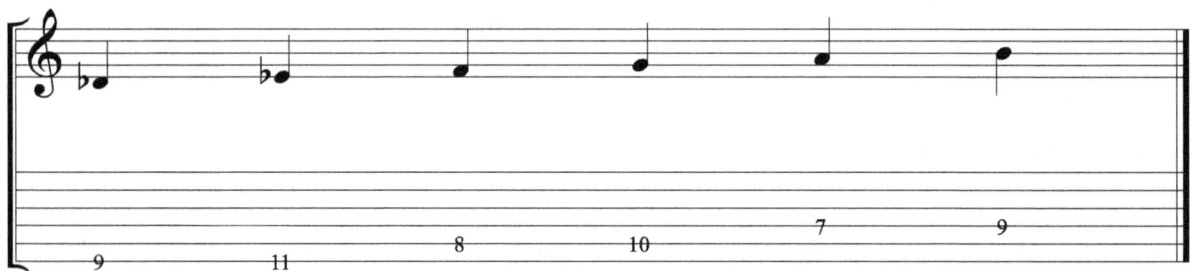

The scale formula is: **1 - 9 - 3 - ♯4 - ♯5 - ♭7**

Chords in the Whole Tone Scale

Triads: Augmented triads

▶ In the key of C, the chords are Caug, Daug, Eaug, F♯aug, G♯aug, B♭aug

7th Chords: 7♯5 and 7♭5

▶ C7♯5, D7♯5, E7♯5, F♯7♯5, G♯7♯5, B♭7♯5

▶ C7♭5, D7♭5, E7♭5, F♯7♭5, G♯7♭5, B♭7♭5

With tensions: dominant 9 chords

▶ C9♯5, D9♯5, E9♯5, F♯9♯5, G♯9♯5, B♭9♯5

▶ C9♭5, D9♭5, E9♭5, F♯9♭5, G♯9♭5, B♭9♭5

When and Where Do You Use the Whole Tone Scale?

You use the whole tone scale over augmented triads or dominant chords.
I've even heard the whole tone scale used over dominant chords that didn't have the ♭5 or ♯5. It sounded great.

Let's take the most common chord progression:

| C | C | F | G7 |

Over the G chord you can of course play G Mixolydian, but now you know that you can also play a G whole tone scale there. It creates a really cool, interesting, and surprising sound.

Of course, over this chord progression with the 5th altered in the G7 chord:

| C | C | F | G7♯5 |

The G whole tone scale sounds even better in this case because the ♯5 in the scale connects well to the ♯5 in the chord.

Check out the chord progressions with augmented chords in the chapter "The Augmented Line Cliché." You can use the whole tone scale to improvise over the augmented chord in those progressions.

This is the kind of knowledge and tools that instantly make one sound much more advanced. Yet interestingly enough, the whole tone scale fingerings are fairly easy to memorize and to apply. This is one of the fun features of symmetrical scales—there's only one finger pattern to learn. It repeats exactly the same on every note in the scale. Yes, pretty cool, right? You don't have six or seven different fingerings to learn.

While you should consider soloing with the scale on one string, you can learn the in-position fingerings on the following page. There are two ways you can finger this scale: starting with three notes or starting with two notes on the low E-string. Either of these fingerings can be repeated starting on each of the six scale notes.

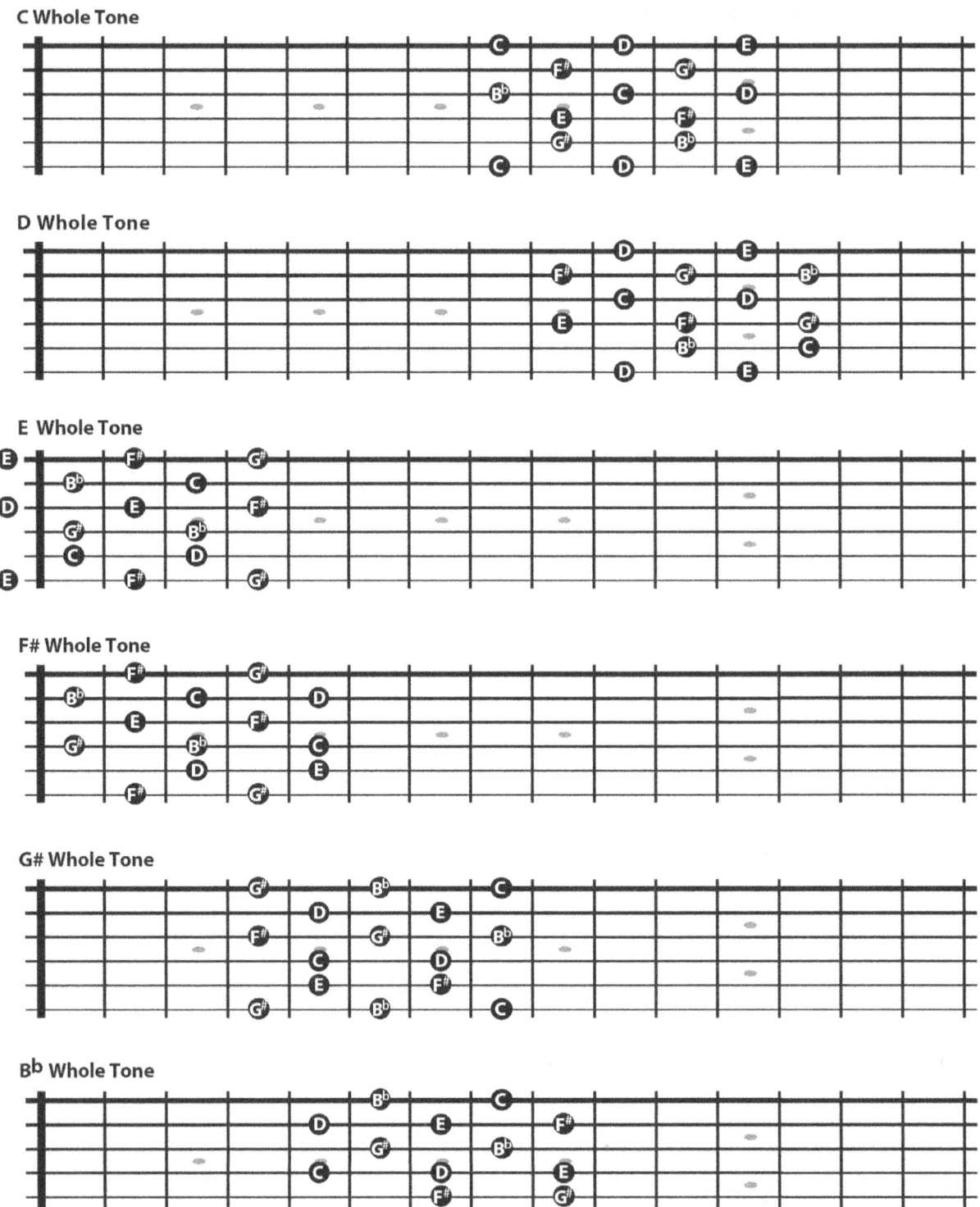

CHAPTER 17: THEORY OF INTERVALS

An interval is a distance between two sounds. This is where the study of harmony starts: the study of how notes interact when played simultaneously.

Before we get into intervals, here's harmony explained in broad strokes.

- ▶ **Two notes played simultaneously are called an interval.**

    - ▷ I've seen books where this is erroneously called a chord.

- ▶ **At least three different notes played simultaneously** is the definition of a chord.

    - ▷ Most of our music uses chords that are built by stacking 3rd intervals. When you stack 3^{rds}, you get a chord that consists of a root, a 3rd and a 5th.
    - ▷ Interesting tidbit: a power chord is theoretically speaking not a chord but an interval. It only consists of two different notes.
    - ▷ "At least" means that three notes are the minimum, but a chord can consist of more notes.
    - ▷ Three-note chords are called **triads.**

- ▶ **Four-note chords are generally called 7th chords.**

    - ▷ You get that 7th when you stack another 3rd on top of the 5th.
    - ▷ 6th chords are members of the four-note chord family, too.

- ▶ **Extended chords are chords with more than four notes.**

    - ▷ Those extensions, called tensions, are notes that fall above the octave: 9, 11, 13.
    - ▷ Notes below the octave (root, 3rd, 5th, and 7th) are called chord tones.

- ▶ **Clusters**

    When you play intervals smaller than a 3rd simultaneously, this is theoretically speaking not considered a chord but a **cluster.** If you want to hear how a cluster sounds, hit your full hand flat on a piano keyboard, hitting a number of adjacent keys. You can tell by the very dissonant sounds this creates that this is not really a musically useful sound. You would not write songs with that kind of harmony.

Now that we've got that covered, back to intervals.

Many students tend to get confused about what makes up an interval. Is it a number of frets? Is it a number of steps?

Let's clear up this confusion right away:

An interval is named after the number of letters that it takes to count from the lowest to the highest letter. From A to E for example is called a "5th" because it takes five fingers to count from the letter A to the letter E (**A B C D E**).

Students spend a lot of time in music schools on the study of intervals. The theory of musical intervals is an important part of music theory because intervals are the building blocks of music. After all:

▶ A **melody** consists of sounds at different intervals played one after another in time. (Horizontal writing.)

▶ A **chord** consists of sounds at different intervals stacked on top of one another and played simultaneously. (Vertical writing.)

Since we only have twelve sounds in our music, we also only have twelve intervals.

All Twelve Intervals and Their Names Starting From C

1	2	3	4	5	6	7	8
C	D	E	F	G	A	B	C

1. **C – D♭** ➡ minor 2nd = 1/2 step
2. **C – D** ➡ major 2nd = 1 step
3. **C – E♭** ➡ minor 3rd = 1 1/2 step
4. **C – E** ➡ major 3rd = 2 steps
5. **C – F** ➡ perfect 4th = 2 1/2 steps
6. **C – F♯** ➡ augmented 4th = tritone = 3 whole steps
   C – G♭ ➡ diminished 5th = tritone = 3 whole steps
7. **C – G** ➡ perfect 5th = 3 1/2 steps
8. **C – A♭** ➡ minor 6th = 4 steps
9. **C – A** ➡ major 6th = 4 1/2 steps
10. **C – B♭** ➡ minor 7th = 5 steps
11. **C – B** ➡ major 7th = 5 1/2 steps
12. **C – C** ➡ octave (8) = 6 whole steps.

Here's how all these intervals look on a staff and tablature.

The tablature also shows how the intervals are played on two strings.

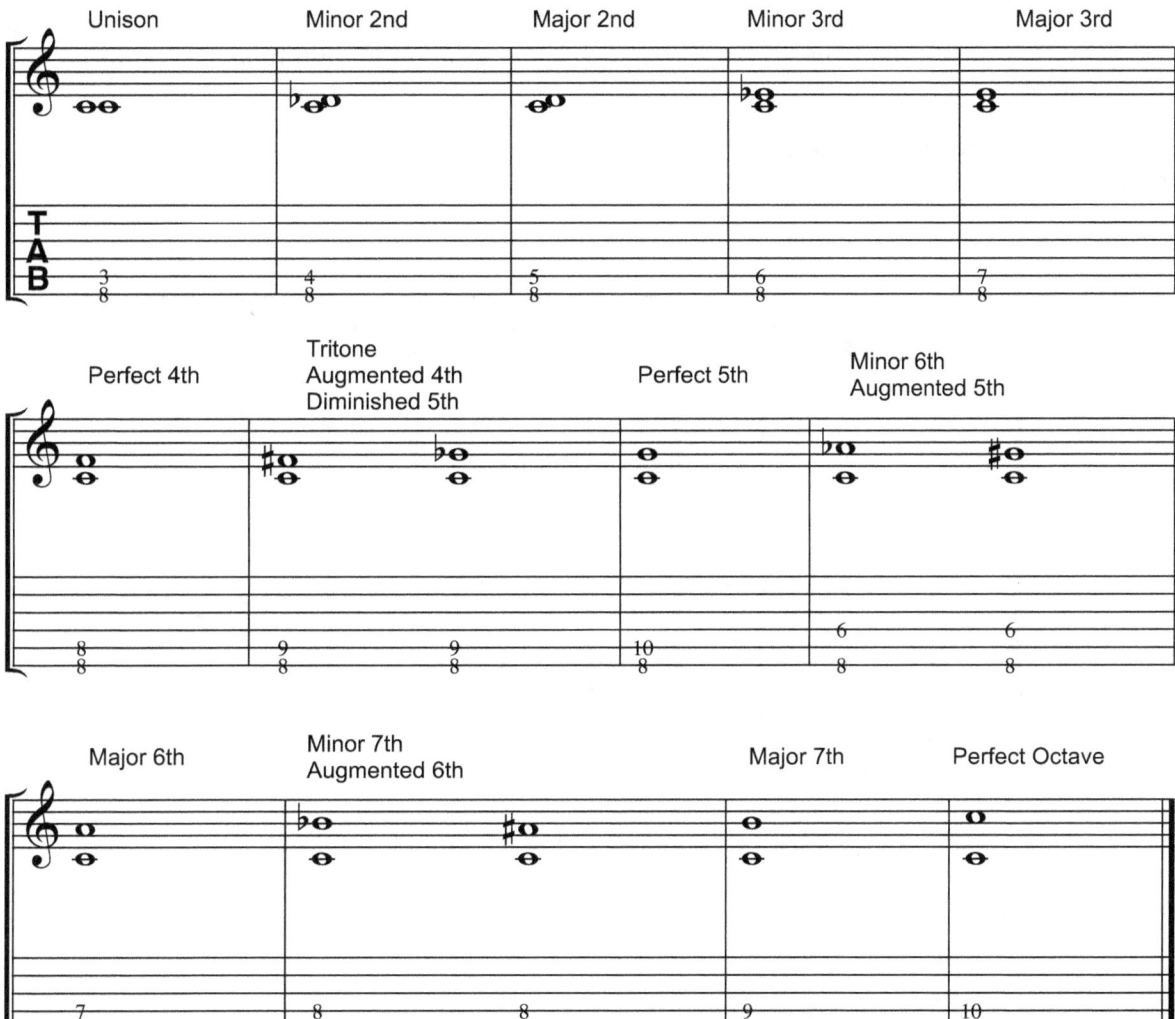

Intervals can be played one of two ways:

1. Melodically

The two notes are played one after another as a melody. You can play the notes on one string, or on multiple strings.

2. Harmonically

Both notes are played together as harmony. In this case, it is necessary to play both notes on two different strings so you can ring them together.

Did you notice the unison in the above graphic? Many music theory books neglect the unison a bit. Here's some quick info.

Guitar Essentials

The unison is technically speaking not an interval, as there's no distance between the two notes. It is really two versions of the same note played simultaneously.

In many theory books, the unison is not even mentioned. This probably can be explained by the fact that most music theory books use the piano as a foundation to explain music theory, and every note only appears once on a piano.

On a guitar, most notes appear numerous times on different strings, which makes it possible for us to play unisons.

Unisons look like this on every string set except the G and B string set.

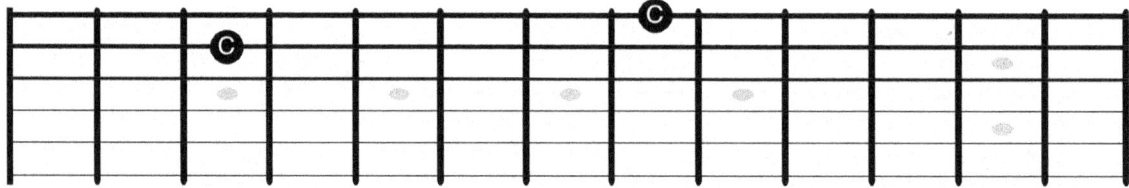

They are played like this on the G and B strings:

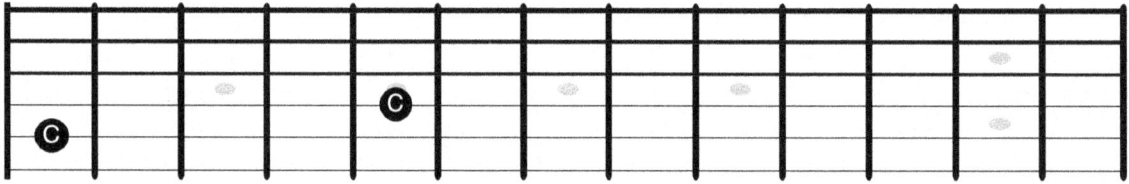

The shape and fingering for each interval looks exactly the same on each set of two adjacent strings, *except* on the G and the B string. The interval fingerings look different on these two strings only. (More about this later.)

Organization of Intervals

You can also organize all intervals into seven groups. In a major scale you have:

1. Unisons and octaves

▶ SEVEN unisons and octaves (one on every note in the scale)

2. Seconds

▶ TWO minor 2^{nds} (on III and VII in the scale)

▶ FIVE major 2^{nds} (on the other five notes in the scale)

3. Thirds

▶ THREE major 3^{rds} (On I, IV, and V)

▶ FOUR minor 3^{rds} (on II, III, VI, and VII)

4. **Fourths**
    - ▶ ONE augmented 4th (on IV)
    - ▶ SIX perfect 4^{ths} on the other six notes in the scale

5. **Fifths**
    - ▶ ONE diminished 5th (on VII)
    - ▶ SIX perfect 5^{ths} on the other six notes in the scale

6. **Sixths**
    - ▶ THREE minor 6^{ths} (on III, VI, and VII)
    - ▶ FOUR major 6^{ths} (on I, II, IV, and V)

7. **Sevenths**
    - ▶ TWO major 7^{ths} (on I and on IV)
    - ▶ FIVE minor 7^{ths} (on the other five notes)

Looking at it that way, you only have seven sets of intervals to learn and practice. When learning thirds, for example, you will play through a scale combining both major and minor thirds as they appear in the scale.

Following this lesson chapter, you will practice intervals soloing with harmonized lines on sets of two strings over songs.

You will start with 3rd intervals, because these are the most pleasant-sounding intervals. 3rd intervals are also the building blocks of all our harmony in the Western World.

The reason why all fingerings look different on the second and third string

The guitar is tuned in 4th intervals from low to high:

- ▶ E string to A string: E F G A
- ▶ A string to D string: A B C D
- ▶ D string to G string: D E F G
- ▶ B string to E string: B C D E

Because these four string sets are tuned the same, all interval fingerings look the same on these string sets. This means you only have to learn the fingering for each interval once, because it looks the same on each string set, except the G and B string.

The second and third strings are tuned in a different interval.

From G string to B string (**G A B**) is not a 4th but a major 3rd interval.

- ▶ A major 3rd interval = 2 whole steps distance between the two notes
- ▶ A perfect 4th = 2 ½ steps distance.

Conclusion:

The G and B string are tuned a half step narrower than all other sets of two adjacent strings. As a result, when playing intervals on the G & B strings, you have to make all your interval fingerings physically a half step (one fret) larger than on the other string sets.

What does that mean: "to make the fingering a half step larger"?

It means that you have to move the finger on the B string one fret closer toward the guitar body, which makes the distance between the notes on the G and B strings one half step larger than on the other string sets. If you, instead of doing this, play the same fingering on the G and B string as you do on the other string sets, then your interval will sound a half step smaller than on all other string sets.

Moving the note on the B string one fret farther away (up in pitch) from the lower note fingered on the G string, compensates for the half step smaller tuning distance between the two notes (G and B) that these strings are tuned to.

Meaning, a major 3rd fingering on the note C *(on any string set except the G and B strings)* gives you the notes C and E, which has exactly the same visual shape and fingering on each string set, but using that same fingering on the G and B string will give you the notes C and E♭ (an interval that is a half step smaller because the tuning between those two strings is a half step smaller).

CHAPTER 18: 3rd INTERVALS

As you know from the previous chapter, there are two kinds of 3rd intervals: minor 3rds and major 3rds. The 3rd intervals are important intervals. They are the building blocks of our harmony.

There is also quartal harmony: chords built stacking 4th intervals. Those are what we call the sus4 and sus2 chords. Apart from those sus chords, we build chords with 3rd intervals. Let's have a look at those very pleasant-sounding intervals.

The Minor 3rd

The minor 3rd interval is a half step larger than the major 2nd. A 3rd interval is called that because it spans a three-letter distance from the lower to the higher note **(C D E♭)**.

The interval distance between the notes a minor 3rd apart is one and a half steps. This is a three-fret interval.

As always, this intervallic distance corresponds to the same number of keys on a piano.

Just to avoid all confusion, I want to reiterate following: This is **not** a 3rd interval because there are three frets/keys from lowest to highest note. No: This is a 3rd interval because it's a three-letter distance.

There are four minor 3rd intervals in the major scale.

The minor 3rd occurs in all the locations where the 3-4 and 7-8 half steps are located.

   1. The 2nd note in the scale. In a C major scale, this is on the note D ➡ D – F

   2. The 3rd note in the scale. In a C major scale, this is on the note E ➡ E – G

   3. The 6th note in the scale. In a C major scale, this is on the note A ➡ A – C

   4. The 7th note in the scale. In a C major scale, this is on the note B ➡ B – D

Fingerings

The following example shows how you play a minor 3rd interval on two adjacent strings.

This fingering is the same on all string sets except the G and B strings.

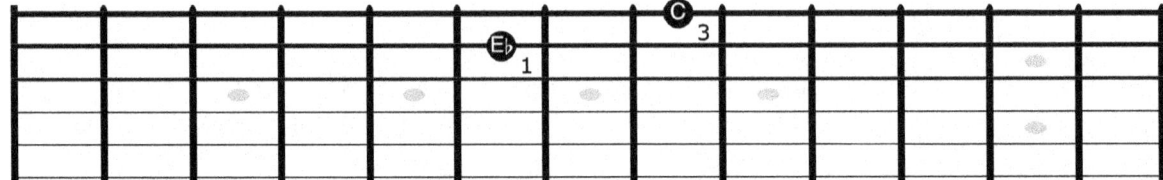

The following guitar neck shows the fingering for minor 3rds on the G and B strings.

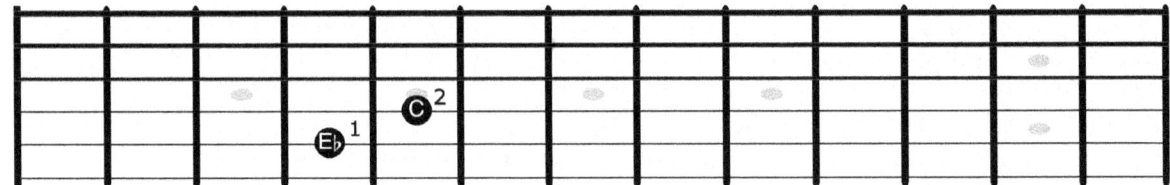

Important!

When soloing with intervals, it helps to only focus on the lowest of the two strings rather than trying to see what the notes are on both strings simultaneously. ("Lowest" means lowest in pitch.) Approaching it that way, soloing with intervals is very much like single-string soloing. You pay attention to the notes on one string only, on the lowest string, and harmonize every scale note with a note a 3rd above it.

The Major 3rd

The major 3rd interval is a half step larger than the minor 3rd.

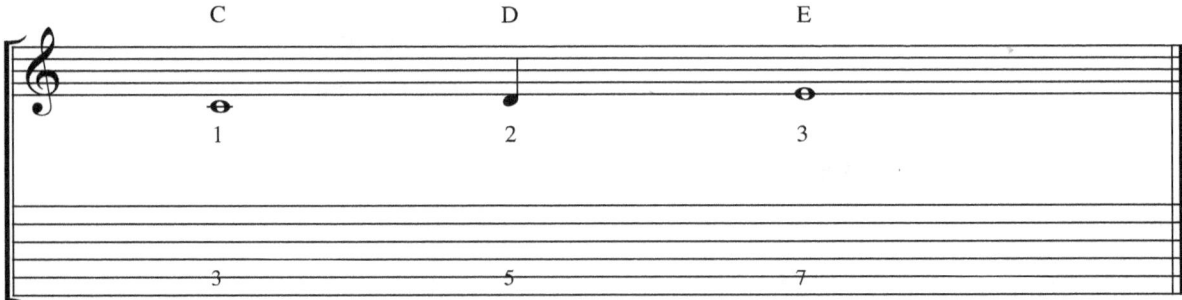

The interval distance between the notes is two whole steps, which adds up to four frets from note to note. As always, this intervallic distance corresponds to the same number of keys on a piano.

There are three major 3rd intervals in the major scale.

This interval occurs in the three locations where there is no half step involved over three notes.

You already know from single-string soloing that this is where you have the "three-note-over-five-fret" stretches. Within the structure of a major scale, the major 3rd fingerings are played on the following notes (which you want to see on the lower of the two strings):

1. The 1st scale degree. In the key of C, this is on the note C ➜ C – E
2. The 4th scale degree. In the key of C, this is on the note F ➜ F – A
3. The 5th scale degree. In the key of C, this is on the note G ➜ G – B

Fingerings

The following example shows how to play a major 3rd interval on two adjacent strings.

This fingering is the same on every string set except the G and B string set.

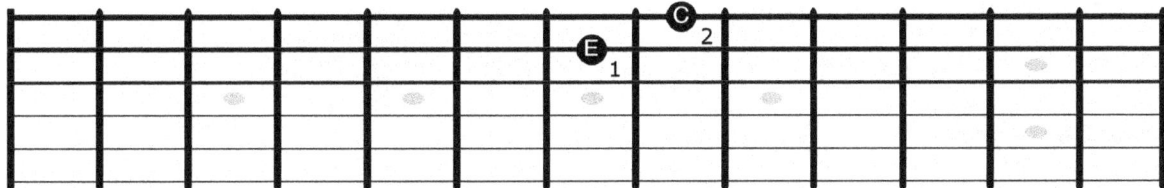

The following guitar neck shows the fingering for major 3rds on the G and B strings.

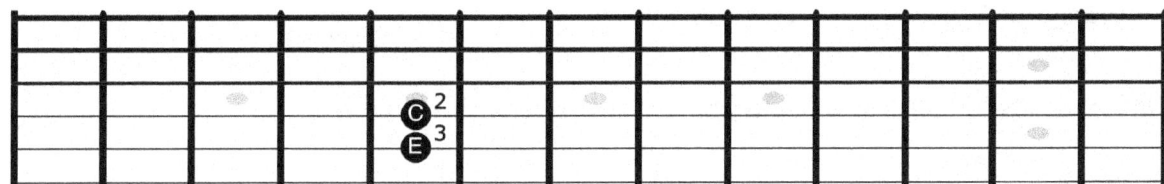

To simplify the thought processes for improvising with 3rd intervals, consider the following approach:

▶ Focus only on the major 3rd locations. The major 3rd intervals are on 1, 4, and 5. That's only three pieces of information for the brain to process. Focus on the location of the 1st, 4th, and 5th note on the lowest string only. Use these three locations as visual anchors to help you navigate around the neck.

▶ **Everywhere else:** Play the minor 3rd fingering.

This is basically on the 2nd, 3rd, 6th, and 7th note in the scale.

Drill time:
Solo with 3rd intervals over a backing track in C or Am for two minutes per string set.
Since there are five sets of two adjacent strings, this adds up to a **10-minute daily drill**.

CHAPTER 19: CHORDS AND INVERSIONS

Definition of a chord: **At least three different notes sounding simultaneously.**

How do you build a chord? You stack 3rd intervals. How do you get three different notes? You stack two 3rd intervals.

Example:

- ▶ Starting from the note C ➡ A 3rd above C is E
- ▶ Stacking another 3rd starting from E is G.

➡ Conclusion: The C chord consists of the notes **C ^{D} E ^{F} G**.

Another example:

- ▶ Starting from the note D ➡ A 3rd above D is F. This is a minor 3rd.
- ▶ A 3rd above F is A.

➡ Conclusion: The notes D F A form a Dm chord.

The Difference Between Major and Minor Chords

You already know that there are two kinds of 3rd intervals: major and minor 3^{rds}.

- ▶ **In major chords**, the first 3rd interval is a major 3rd.
- ▶ **In minor chords**, the first 3rd interval is a minor 3rd.

To demonstrate with some examples:

The notes in a Cm chord are: **C E♭ G** ➡ C to E♭ is a minor 3rd
The notes in a C chord are: **C E G** ➡ C to E is a major 3rd

The notes in a D chord are: **D F♯ A** ➡ D to F♯ is a major 3rd
The notes in a Dm chord are: **D F A** ➡ D to F is a minor 3rd

You can always use your guitar neck to figure out whether a 3rd interval is a major or minor 3rd. The best way to figure this out is by checking the notes on one string.

If the distance between the notes is two whole steps, it is a major 3rd. If the distance is a step and a half (three frets), it's a minor 3rd.

For example, when you look at the notes D and F♯ on the A string, you find these notes on the fifth fret and ninth fret on the A string. That distance is two whole steps. D to F♯ is a major 3rd.

Knowing that it is the first 3rd interval (of the ones you stack) that defines whether a chord is a major or a minor chord is a big step forward. Now you only have to know where the major 3rd and the minor 3rd intervals are in a scale, and you know where the major chords and the minor chords are.

Fortunately, you already know this from the previous chapter:

1. The major 3^{rds} are on I, IV and V

2. The minor 3^{rds} are on II, III, VI and VII

Which means that, since chords are built stacking 3^{rds}:

- The major chords are where the major 3^{rds} are.
- The minor chords are where the minor 3^{rds} are.

There is only one more thing to cover before we uncover all the chords in a major scale. Here's some little trivia: the 3^{rds} in major and minor chords alternate. If the first 3rd interval is major, the next one is always minor, and vice versa

Examples:

1. The notes in a C chord are **C E G**.

    a. C to E is a major 3rd (two whole steps distance).

    b. E to G is a minor 3rd (It has the E – F half step).

2. The notes in a Dm chord are **D F A**.

    a. D to F is a minor 3rd (It has the E – F half step).

    b. F to A is a major 3rd (two whole steps distance).

3. The notes in an F chord are **F A C**.

    a. F to A is a major 3rd (two whole steps).

    b. A to C is a minor 3rd (It has the B – C half step).

It always works out that way. Covering all the notes of all the chords in a C scale, we get:

- I =   C E G ➡ **C**
- IIm =   D F A ➡ **Dm**
- IIIm = E G B ➡ **Em**
- IV =   F A C ➡ **F**
- V =   G B D ➡ **G**
- VIm = A C E ➡ **Am**
- VIIdim = B D F ➡ **Bdim**

The first note in these chords is the note that gives the chord its name: We call that note the **root**. The next two notes are called the 3rd and the 5th of the chord.

1. Counting from C to E (C D E), you get 1 2 3. E is 3.

2. From C to G (C D E F G), you count 1 2 3 4 5. C to G is a 5th interval.

> ▶ C is called the root in the C chord.
> ▶ E is the 3rd.
> ▶ G is the 5th.

A major 3rd is written as 3. A minor 3rd is written as ♭3.

The chord formulas for major and minor chords, then, are:

> ▶ Major = 1 3 5
> ▶ Minor = 1 ♭3 5

There's one more chord to discuss: VII in a major scale. Did you notice in the list of C major scale chords that the B chord is neither major nor minor? The B chord has a different structure than the first six chords in the C major scale.

The notes are **B D F**.

Analyzing these 3rd intervals:

> ▶ **B to D** ➡ has the B – C half step over three notes, which is a minor 3rd.
> ▶ **D to F** ➡ has the E – F half step over three notes, which is a minor 3rd again.

This chord is more minor than minor. We call this a diminished chord.

The chord formula for diminished is:

> ▶ 1 ♭3 ♭5

You want to memorize this. The seventh chord in a major scale is always a diminished chord. Based on everything learned above, we can conclude that the chords in a C major scale are:

C Dm Em F G Am Bdim

Scale Degrees

Ideally, you want to memorize this with scale degrees. "Scale degrees" is the fancy music theory name for note locations in a scale. "First scale degree" is another way of saying "first note." Scale degrees are shown as Roman numerals:

I IIm IIIm IV V VIm VIIdim

Classical music theory books oftentimes show the minor chords as lowercase Roman numerals:

I ii iii IV V vi viidim

You will see both systems used interchangeably. I prefer the uppercase notation method, because I like how it is more consistent with how we would notate the chord names in a piece of music. **IIm** seems more consistent with normal chord notation than **ii**, because you wouldn't write a minor chord as **d** but as **Dm**.

The reason why you want to memorize chord locations in a music scale (or a song) as numbers is because math is universal, while chord names are not. Scale degree numbers apply to all keys, while specific chord names only appear in the major scale that happens to have these chords. This is why it's easier to transpose chords (in a song or a scale) from one key to all other keys when you memorize the order of the chords with numbers (**I IIm IIIm IV** etc.). Transposition is what we call it when music is moved up or down from one key to a higher or lower key. If you merely memorize chords using their letter names (**C Dm Em** and so on), then you're stuck in the key these chords belong to, which means that it becomes harder to transpose music written in that key to other keys.

You might wonder why.

The reason why it is easier to transpose music when you think of chords as scale degrees in relationship to I, instead of note/letter/chord names, is because it's easier to attach note names to numbers than it is to replace note names with other note names.

Examples showcasing this:

In a C major scale, as you know: I = C, II = Dm, III = Em, and so on.

Now if I want to transpose this up a whole step to the key of D, it becomes fairly easy to do so. You simply walk up the alphabet, assigning each consecutive letter a consecutive number, but now starting from the letter D instead of the letter C.

When the first chord in the scale is D, then:

- **II** is Em
- **III** is F♯m
- **IV** is G
- **V** is A
- **VI** is Bm
- **VII** is C♯dim

This makes sense, right? Think of chords not only as letters, but also as scale degree locations in relationship to I.

However, if you merely memorize that the chords in a C major scale are **C Dm Em F G Am and Bdim**, without awareness of their numerical location in relationship to the C chord, now when you want to transpose to the key of **D**, your thought process goes like:

- **C** becomes **D**
- **Dm** becomes **Em**
- **Em** becomes **F♯m**
- **F** becomes **G**
- **G** becomes **A**

- **Am** becomes **Bm**
- **Bdim** becomes **C#dim**

You see, rather than using a clean number system where you are attaching a note name alphabetically to a number, transposition now involves having to replace a chord name with another chord name. You end up juggling fourteen chord names, which requires too much unnecessary brain processing.

Top musicians are constantly aware of scale degrees while performing music. They think of chord progressions as number sequences. Some of the most common chord progressions are:

- I IV V I
- II V I
- VI II V I

In any case, there's reason for celebration at this point. In combination with your knowledge of key signature, you now know how to figure out all chords to any key. This enables you to write or perform chord progressions in any key. The only requirement of course is that you know the chord shapes. This is where bar chords come in really handy.

Bar Chords

Bar chords are E and A (and Em and Am) shapes that you move up and down the guitar neck barring your pointer finger as a capo over all six strings behind the E and A shapes.

The reason why we use E and A shapes to play bar chords is that their shapes are easy on the hand. The notes that make up the E and A shapes are on three adjacent strings. No tough stretches between the fingers. This makes E and A shapes physically much more practical than for example G or C chord shapes, which are a pain to move around the neck as bar chords.

Here are the E and A shapes:

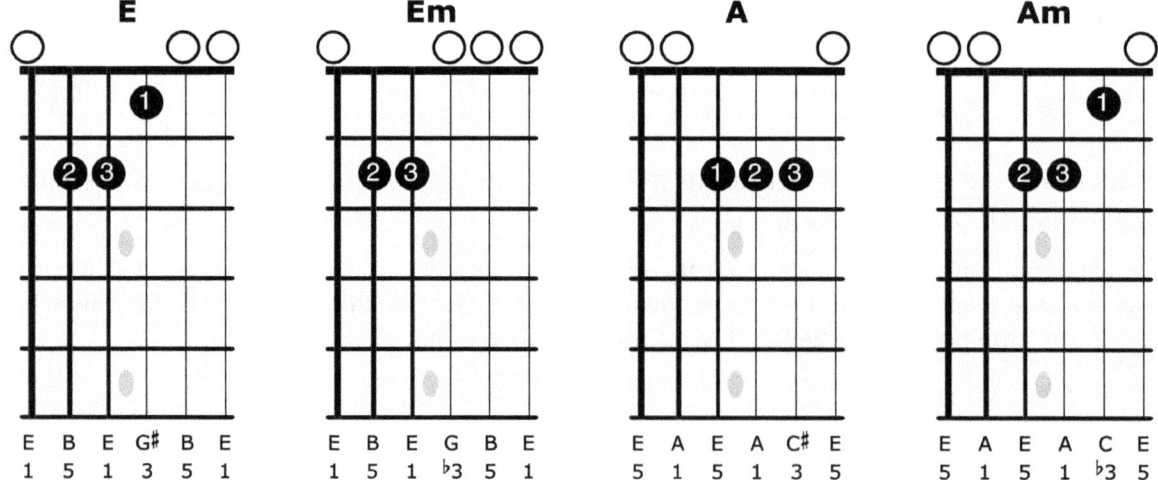

You could think of the guitar's nut as your capo or pointer finger.

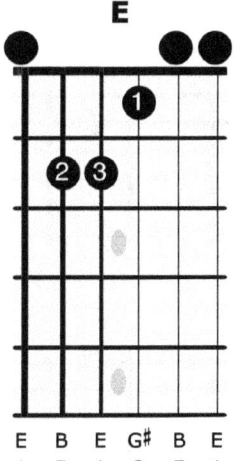 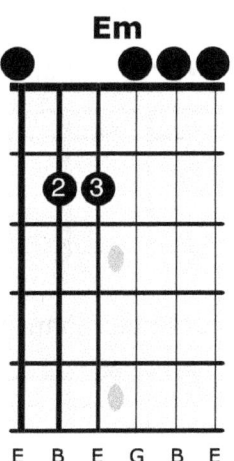 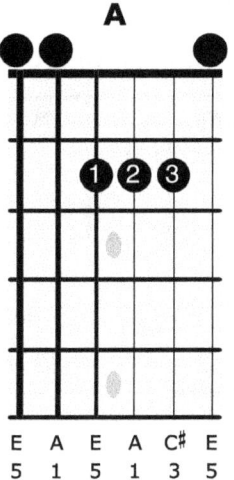 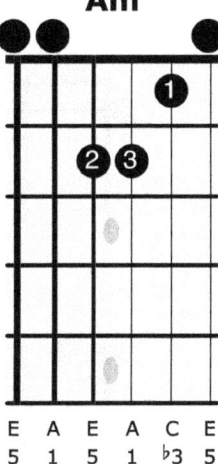

Moving this all up one fret, you get the following bar chords:

 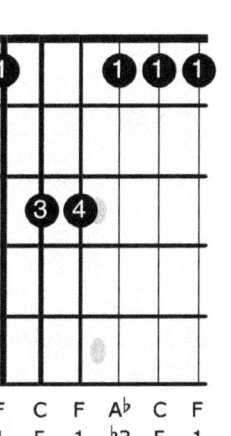 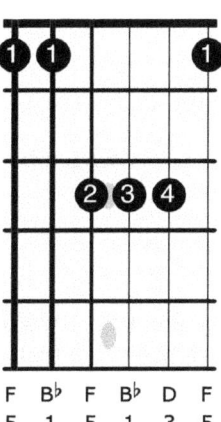 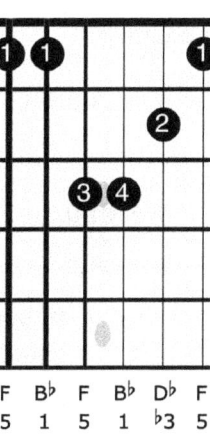

Here it is on the third fret:

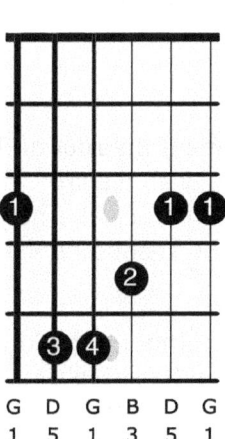 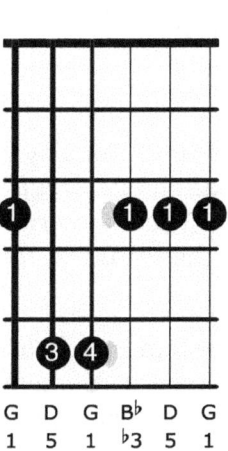 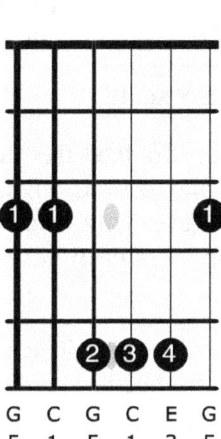 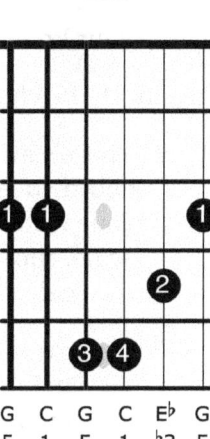

Since we form bar chords using E and A shapes, that means that the open E and A strings are where we can find the names of the bar chords.

> ▶ The notes on the A string give you the names of the A shape bar chord.

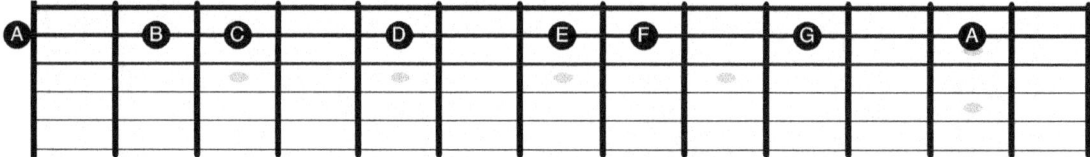

> ▶ The notes on the E string give you the names of the E shape bar chord.

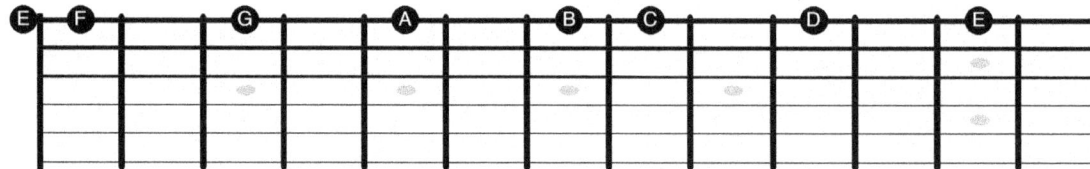

For example:

Place your pointer finger on the third fret, barring all six strings on the third fret.

There are four chords you can play with a bar in that location (third fret):

> ▶ C and Cm
> ▶ G and Gm
>
>> 1. When you play the A or Am shape while barring on the third fret, you play C or Cm chords because the third fret on the A string is where the note C is located at.
>> 2. When you play an E or Em shape while barring the third fret, you are playing G or Gm chords because the note under your bar on the third fret of the E string is the note G.

This now is where all fun starts. Bar chords provide a simple way to make up chord progressions, applying your knowledge of the major scale and scale degrees.

Let's play all the chords of an F scale.

> 1. There's an F note on the first fret of the E string. You play an E shape if the root of the chord you want to play is on the E string. Bar on that first fret and play an E shape with your remaining fingers. This is an F chord. Then conform to the structure of a major scale, move up two frets with your bar to the third fret to get to the second chord of the scale.
> 2. You are now on a G note. This is scale degree II in the key of F. II is a minor chord. You'd play an Em shape bar chord here. Since you know it's a whole step from II to III in a major scale, move up two frets again to chord III of the scale, which is on the fifth fret.

3. You are now on scale degree III. This is a minor chord again. In the key of F, this is Am. You don't have to change anything: Gm and Am are the same shape. They're both Em shape bar chords.

4. Move up one fret from here. Remember that 3-4 is a half step in a major scale. Your bar is now on the sixth fret. This is where B♭ is. We need a major chord here because B♭ is chord number IV in F, and IV is a major chord. You bar an E major shape here.

5. Move up two frets to the eighth fret. We need a C major chord here because this is V. V is always a major chord in the major scale. You can just move your B♭ chord up two frets as is.

6. Then move up two frets from C on the eighth fret to D. VI is a minor chord in the major scale. We need Dm. Play an Em shape while barring the tenth fret.

7. Then we'll skip chord VII for now because diminished is a much lesser used chord than the first six chords in the scale. There is also no bar chord version for diminished chords. We will cover that chord later.

Of course, you can also do all this with A shapes. In the key of F, the I chord as an A bar chord shape is located by barring on the eighth fret, which is where the note F is on the A string.

All this above is just to illustrate how useful bar chords are in coming up with chord progressions in any key. All you need is a visual understanding of the major scale mapped out on one string, and knowledge of scale degrees and the bar chord shapes. Having some fret board knowledge comes in handy too. But that's it—that's everything you need to write songs or perform chord progressions in any keys.

Bar chords are big, bulky-sounding chords that have some of the three chord tones appearing multiple times over six strings. This makes sense when you consider that bar chords are three-note chords, yet they cover all six strings. The shapes are big and good for strumming, but not really very well suited for composition or voice leading. There is little control over the individual notes in those chords. We can't easily change the order of the chord tones because the chord shapes take up all six strings and the chord tones are all over the place within the chords. This renders those chords useless for the finer art of composition, in which the ability to change the order of the notes in a chord is a necessity without which you can't smoothly connect chords in the organized and structured ways that the art of composition requires.

That is why you want to know about...

Inversions

You invert a chord when you change the order of the notes. The notes in a three-note chord can be configured x number of different ways.

Using the C chord as an example, the configurations are:

- ▶ C E G ➡ This is called **root position**.
- ▶ E G C ➡ This is called **1st inversion**. The 3rd of the chord is in the bass.
- ▶ G C E ➡ This is called **2nd inversion**. The 5th of the chord is in the bass.

A three-note chord has a root position and two inversions, while a four-note chord has a root position and three inversions, as shown in the following Cmaj7 chord:

- ▶ C E G B ➡ This is a root position Cmaj7 chord.
- ▶ E G B C ➡ This is a 1st inversion Cmaj7 chord.
- ▶ G B C E ➡ This is a 2nd inversion Cmaj7 chord.
- ▶ B C E G ➡ This is a 3rd inversion Cmaj7 chord.

Inversions are best understood in chord shapes where every note only appears once. This is shown in the following C triads.

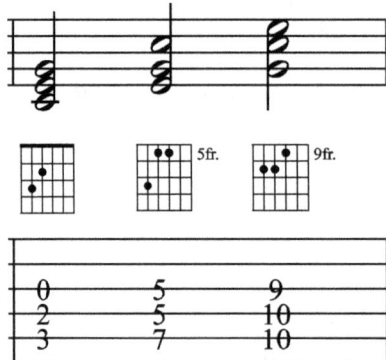

- ▶ The first C chord is in root position; the notes from low to high are C E G.
- ▶ The 2nd C chord has the 3rd in the bass (1st inversion).
- ▶ The 3rd C chord has the 5th in the bass (2nd inversion).

You can immediately hear how these three C chords all have their own sound. These three-note C chords sound more defined than the bar chords or the beginner C chord. Because every note only appears once in these C chords, you clearly hear how the first C chord has C as the lowest note, the next one has E as the lowest note, and the last one has G as the lowest note.

When you play these C chord inversions one after another, you immediately hear new harmonic possibilities that are not possible with the bulky beginner or bar chords.

Imagine the following two rhythm guitar scenarios.

1. A rhythm part where you strum the beginner C chord for two bars, or
2. A rhythm playing style where you strum moving around the three above C triad inversions for two bars.

The latter makes your rhythm playing sound more composed and more melodic. It sounds more like an actual, more memorable part, rather than just an accompaniment. I've heard some people describe the latter as a more pianistic style, sound, and approach to your rhythm playing. Those people probably made that association because piano players usually wouldn't hit chords with a ton of doubled and tripled notes. In addition, the nature of the guitar is more percussive than piano. Guitar also sounds less big and full than a piano. That's why guitar players tend to bang away on a same chord that consists of many repeated notes over and over again when accompanying a vocalist, while piano players tend to move around different chord inversions to create a bit of a composition underneath the singer's melodies.

Piano of course also lends itself better to understanding, seeing, and learning chord inversions, because of the linear organization of the notes on a keyboard. We guitar players have a ton of shapes to learn and are definitely dealing with a more complex note map on the fret board.

All that being said, it pays off to learn your chord inversions or at least understand the theory, because it allows you to delve into more compositional rhythm approaches and arranging techniques on guitar.

Here are the notes for all chords in a C major scale (**C, Dm, Em, F, G, Am, and Bdim**) written vertically from low to high note, lowest note at the bottom.

All root position:

G	A	B	C	D	E	F
E	F	G	A	B	C	D
C	D	E	F	G	A	B

All 1st inversion:

C	D	E	F	G	A	B
G	A	B	C	D	E	F
E	F	G	A	B	C	D

All 2nd inversion:

E	F	G	A	B	C	D
C	D	E	F	G	A	B
G	A	B	C	D	E	F

In the next chapters, you'll learn all the shapes for all triads in the key of C, with all inversions on every string set. Learning all these triads is going to keep you busy, but is ultimately going to be very rewarding.

CHAPTER 20: THE NOTES IN ALL TRIADS

I'm never going to forget my dad's answer when I asked him what the most important thing was that I should learn first and foremost.

I was sixteen and had barely been playing guitar for a couple of weeks when I asked him that question. My father is a really good musician. He started learning accordion with a reputable teacher when he was six years old. I was excited about the great advice I was sure dad was going to give me. At the very least, I was hoping or expecting to get some cool, fun pointers or tricks to propel me forward and keep me motivated at the start of my guitar journey.

Dad's response, "Kid, it's absolutely imperative that you memorize all the notes in all the chords!"

I was dumbfounded! Here I was at the beginning of my guitar journey, and the best, most exciting advice dad could come up with was to memorize the notes in all chords. At the time that advice seemed beyond silly. I felt pretty sure there had to be quite a number of things that were much more fun and more useful that I could learn first: chords, rhythms, songs, and so much more.

As I became a better musician, however, I understood why dad was adamant I should learn this first. He knew how many major benefits one gets as a result of knowing the notes in chords.

For one, you make better-informed note choices in your guitar solos. Knowing which notes to outline, greatly improves the quality of your guitar solos. Solos become more melodic and connect better to the harmony when you hit more chord tones.

You also spend much less time figuring out chords to songs or to songs you're writing. When a melody line that you are trying to figure out the chords for starts on a C and ends on an E, that greatly narrows down the number of chord choices that will work well with that melody line. You are more than likely going to want a C or Am chord there.

Other possible, but slightly less likely options, are Fmaj7, Dm9, or any chord that has a C and an E note.

Basically, knowing the notes in chords makes you a much better musician. Here they are:

Major Chords

C	=	C	E	G
C♯	=	C♯	E♯	G♯
D♭	=	D♭	F	A♭
D	=	D	F♯	A
D♯	=	D♯	F𝄪	A♯
E♭	=	E♭	G	B♭
E	=	E	G♯	B
F	=	F	A	C
F♯	=	F♯	A♯	C♯
G♭	=	G♭	B♭	D♭
G	=	G	B	D
G♯	=	G♯	B♯	D♯
A♭	=	A♭	C	E♭
A	=	A	C♯	E
B♭	=	B♭	D	F
B	=	B	D♯	F♯

Minor Chords

Cm	=	C	E♭	G
C♯m	=	C♯	E	G♯
D♭m	=	D♭	F♭	A♭
Dm	=	D	F	A
D♯m	=	D♯	F♯	A♯
E♭m	=	E♭	G♭	B♭
Em	=	E	G	B
Fm	=	F	A♭	C
F♯m	=	F♯	A	C♯
G♭m	=	G♭	B♭♭	D♭
Gm	=	G	B♭	D
G♯m	=	G♯	B	D♯
A♭m	=	A♭	C♭	E♭
Am	=	A	C	E
B♭m	=	B♭	D♭	F
Bm	=	B	D	F♯

How do you memorize these? Well first off, you always want to work smart, not hard. You can narrow that list down a lot.

Notice how there's only one note different between major and minor chords?

That note is the 3rd of the chord.

For example:

C = C E G

Cm = C E♭ G

That means that you don't have to spend time on the minor chords. Only memorize the major chord notes, and lower the 3rd down a half step for minor chords.

In addition, notice how half the major chords are ♯ and ♭.

♯ means white key up a half step, and ♭ means white key down a half step. When you know what the notes in a B chord are, then you also know the notes in a B♭ chord. You simply lower the three notes in a B chord and you get the notes in the B♭ chord—same three letters, with ♭'s added to them or ♯'s dropped.

That means that you only have seven chords to memorize: C, D, E, F, G, A, and B major. You can extrapolate all the other chords from those seven.

The flash card approach is a good system for memorizing these chords. Make a flash card for each chord.

Drill time:
Do three sessions of three minutes a day
= a **9-minute daily drill**

At that rate, you'll get all these chords memorized in no time.

CHAPTER 21: ALL TRIADS IN THE KEY OF C

This is fun material. These are all the chords of the C major scale with all inversions, mapped out on every string set. I would suggest you learn all seven chords one string set at a time.

C major triads (1 3 5)

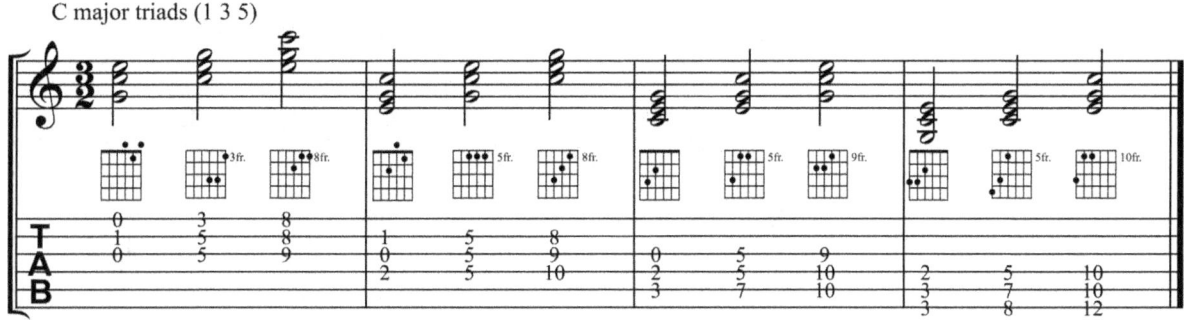

F major

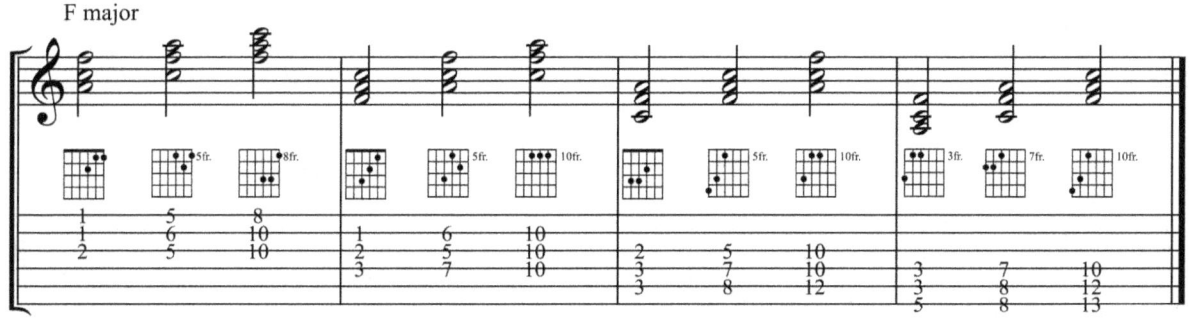

G major

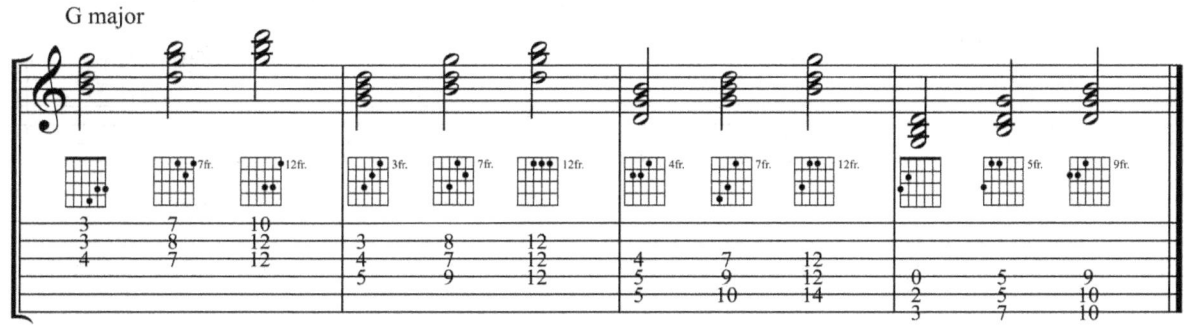

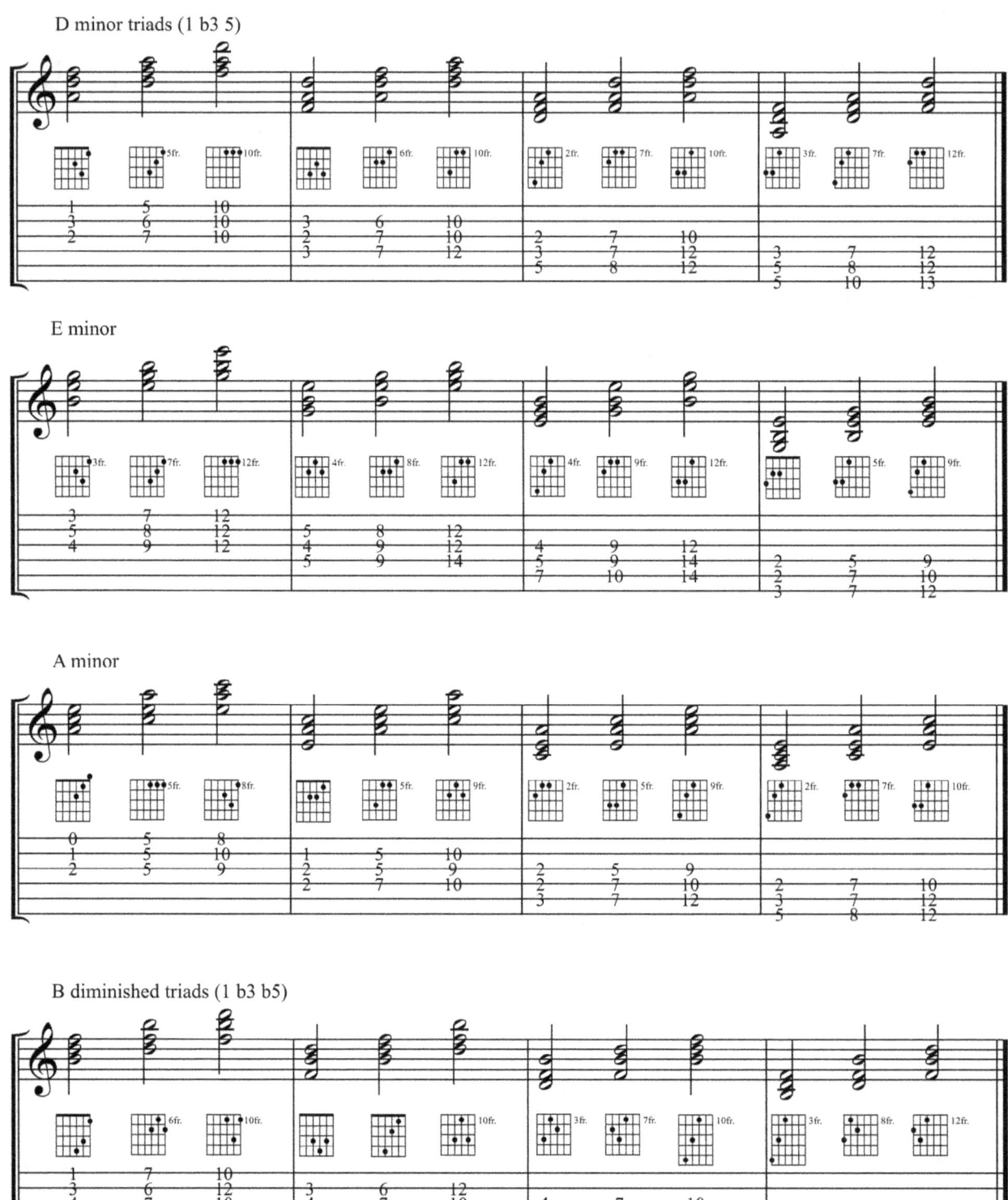

CHAPTER 22: CYCLES: THE STUDY OF VOICE-LEADING & COMPOSITION

When you know all seven C major scale triads of the previous chapter pretty well on (at least) one string set, only then are you ready for what we're going to cover now.

Voice-leading is the study of how to move from one chord to another with the least amount of motion between the notes from chord to chord. You will love how this sounds. It's a bit like weaving a dense tapestry of sound with the notes from chord to chord.

One of the best ways to practice voice-leading is by cycling through all the chord inversions in a scale, spaced at a certain reoccurring interval, until you hit your starting chord again.

You can tell by looking at the bold printed chord progressions for each cycle on the next page what the numbers refer to in the names Cycle **2**, Cycle **3**, Cycle **4**, and so on. Those numbers refer to the interval spacing between the chords.

Each cycle is twenty-one chords long (seven chords in a scale times three inversions for each chord). Cycles always start on the I chord. All cycles are shown in the key of C. I recommend that you start every cycle on the root position C chord, because you then start with the first note of the scale as the lowest starting note in the first chord.

I can't even begin to tell you how much you will get out of practicing this. Your chord knowledge will improve, along with your fret board knowledge, your music theory understanding, your interval knowledge, your song writing, your soloing, your ear, your arranging and production skills, your ability to write for other instrument groups, and so much more.

For some added bonus advice: You will improve even more and get more out of your practice time when you don't look at the notated chord sequences while practicing the cycles. Try to figure out what the next chord is by counting or using brain-power, rather than just reading it from the page. This will improve your interval memory: memorizing where every chord is in relationship to every other chord.

For cycles where the chords move in larger distances, you will run out of space on the guitar neck at some point. For cycles that move down, at some point you will run out of frets at the nut, before you get to the end of the cycle. You resolve this by simply moving up twelve frets with whatever your last shape was, then continuing the cycle from there. The same will happen with cycles that move up. For some cycles you will end up very high on the neck and run out of frets. In that case, at any given point past the twelfth fret, you can simply move your last chord shape down an octave (twelve frets) then continue the cycle from there.

In terms of how to practice this, you could do two cycles a day. You might be slow the first couple of days. As with anything, you will get faster and it will get easier. The benchmark you are aiming for is twenty seconds or less for each cycle. If you can play them that fast, you really master your triads in that key on that string set.

Cycle 2

C   D-   E-   F   G   A-   Bdim   C

- Chords move **down** the neck. This is in the opposite direction of what you are thinking. You're thinking ascending alphabet. The chords are moving up the scale, but your hand is physically moving down the neck for each chord.
- The chords move from Root position ➡ 2nd inversion ➡ 1st inversion

Cycle 3

C   E-   G   Bdim   D-   F   A-   C

- **Two common tones** stay and connect the two consecutive chords.
- One note moves **down**. That note is the root of the chord you are on. It moves down and becomes the 5th of the following chord.

Cycle 4

C   F   Bdim   E-   A-   D-   G   C

- **One common tone** stays and two notes move **up**. It is the root that stays and becomes the 5th of the next chord.
- Two notes move **up**: the 3rd and the 5th of the chord you're on. They become the root and 3rd of the next chord.

Cycle 5

C   G   D-   A-   E-   Bdim   F   C

- **One common tone** stays and connects the two consecutive chords. It is the 5th that stays. That 5th becomes the root in the next chord.
- Two notes move **down**. The root and 3rd move down, and in doing so become the 3rd and 5th of the next chord.
- This is exactly the opposite motion of cycle 4. Because 4ths and 5ths are inversions of each other, the end of cycle 4 is the beginning of cycle 5, and vice versa.

Cycle 6

    C   A-   F   D-   Bdim   G   E-   C

- ▶ **Two common tones** stay and connect the two consecutive chords.
- ▶ One note moves **up** the neck. It's the 5th of the chord that moves up to become the root of the following chord.
- ▶ This is exactly the opposite motion of cycle 3, as 3^{rds} and 6^{ths} are inversions of each other. The last chords in cycle 3 are the first chords in cycle 6, and vice versa.

Cycle 7

    C   Bdim   A-   G   F   E-   D-   C

- ▶ Chords **move up** the neck. This is in the opposite direction of what you are thinking. You're thinking descending alphabet. The chords are thought of as moving down the scale, but your hand is moving up the neck.
- ▶ The motion from chord to chord is: Root position ➡ 1st inversion ➡ 2nd inversion.
- ▶ This is exactly the opposite motion of cycle 2, as 2^{nds} and 7^{ths} are inversions of each other. The end of cycle 2 is the beginning of cycle 7, and vice versa.

For mastery, ideally you aim to:

1. Be able to play these cycles on each string set
2. In any key

It doesn't end there either.

You can also practice cycles with 7th chords arranged as drop 2 voicings, drop 3 voicings, or other drop voicings. You can even practice voice-leading cycles with quartal harmony chords and even hybrid chords.

This might seem overwhelming or intimidating, but always keep in mind that you *can* travel the whole world one footstep at a time. All it requires is to keep going. That is all it takes.

Another motivating thought is that the beginning is always the hardest. The time it will take you to be able to pull this off with triads is absolutely no indication of how long it will take you to do this with 7th chords or other harmonies. Each new piece of knowledge you acquire is connected to other pieces. It will take you less time to master cycles with 7th chords once you ace them with triads. You're building further on what you already know at that point.

CHAPTER 23: Dm & Em OVER G7 TRIAD SUBSTITUTION

Triad substitution is a really fun, cool improvisation technique more guitar players should know about. The idea is this: The band or rhythm section is jamming over a given one-chord groove, and you improvise over the groove, using the notes of different chords than what the band is playing.

For example:

The band is grooving on a G7 chord. You solo using Dm or Em triads instead of the notes of a G chord. When you solo with both Dm and Em triads over a G7 groove, you're soloing with what is called a **triad substitution pair**.

- ▶ The notes in a G7 chord: G B D F.
- ▶ The notes in a Dm chord: **D F** A.
- ▶ The notes in an Em chord: E **G B**.

When you analyze the relationship of these notes against the G chord that the rhythm section is grooving on:

- ▶ **The Dm triad creates a G9 sound**: D is the 5th, F is the $\flat 7^{th}$, and A is the 9th
- ▶ **The Em chord creates a G13 sound**: E is the 13th, G is the root, and B is the 3rd

When you put the notes of a Dm chord and an Em chord in alphabetical order, you get: **D E F G A B**

This spells out an almost complete C major scale. The only note missing is C. Yet, when you think of the notes as Dm and Em chord shapes, rather than thinking of them as a partial C major scale, you create a very different sound and texture with the notes. The musical phrases you come up with are going to be very different than if you thought of these notes in alphabetical ascending order as a scale.

The reason for this is that you use these six notes differently when you think of them as two groupings of three notes, organized within known chord shapes, instead of a six-note scale. The result is a unique sound, which you could never get if you just thought of the notes as one grouping of six ascending notes, or in other words, "as a scale."

Using Triad Shapes

Here are all the Dm and Em chord shapes on the top three strings.

Em chords are easy to memorize once you have the three Dm chords down. You get Em chords when you move Dm chords up two frets.

Dm & Em Over G7 Triad Substitution

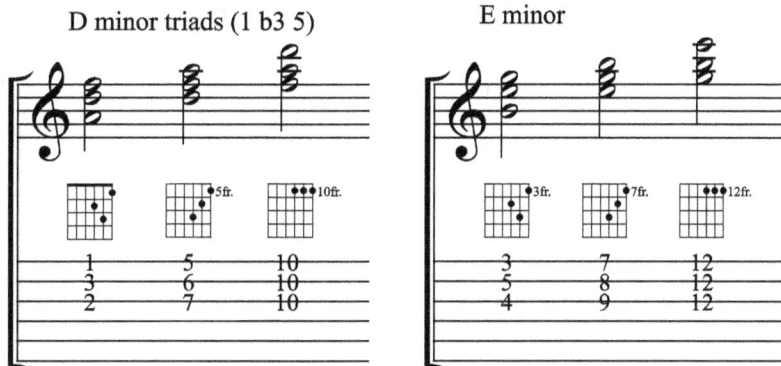

Here are a couple of ways you can improvise with those two chords over a G7 groove.

1. Chord Soloing With Block Chords

"Block chord" is a term from piano playing. It refers to a piano style where the chords are played with "locked-hands"—both hands simultaneously hitting all notes together as a vertical block of sound. "Vertical block of notes" is a good way to describe this because that is what block chords look like on staff paper. You can hear great examples of this in Supertramp's "Breakfast in America" or in Queen's "Killer Queen." The opposite of block chords are **broken chords**, which are what you play when you arpeggiate the notes in chords.

Applying this to soloing, over a G7 groove you can hit Dm and Em triads, moving around between their different inversions, or alternating between Dm and Em chords, as you see fit. You're basically soloing hitting full chords, moving around a lot to create melodies with the top notes of these chords.

All this is easiest when you stick to one string set of three strings and move horizontally through the inversions, rather than vertical over the six strings.

It's important to emphasize that this is about creating melodies. You don't want to hit any of these chords x number of times in a row as in a rhythm part. The same way you solo on one string is how you should solo with the Dm and Em shapes: lots of horizontal motion, but with full chord shapes. Every melody line you play with the top notes of the chords is harmonized with two notes underneath. It looks something like this:

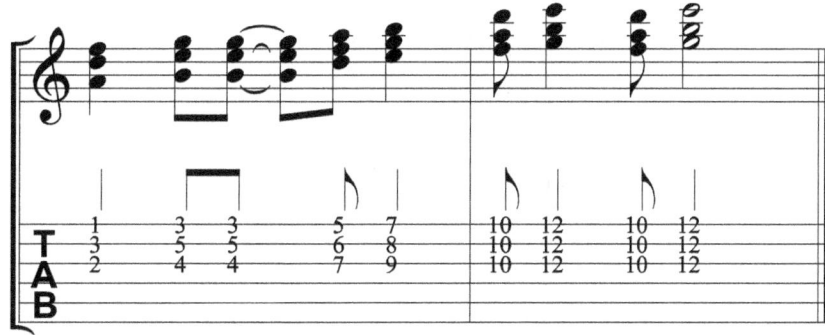

2. Arpeggiating the Notes in the Dm and Em Chords

With this approach, you don't hit the chords as vertical blocks, but rather separate the notes in the chord shapes to create single-note melody lines. Be creative: Avoid picking the three notes in each chord in order from low to high or from high to low all the time, so as not to make it predictable.

You don't even necessarily always want to play all three notes in every shape before you move on to another inversion. You could play one note in the Dm root shape, followed by, for example, two notes in the 1st inversion Em shape, followed by three notes in a Dm 2nd inversion shape, etc. The more random you get, the cooler it all sounds.

Important point:

You want this to sound like a solo, not like "House of the Rising Sun." Though you're working from chord shapes, lift up your fretting hand fingers after every note you play right before you play the next note. You don't want the notes to ring out into one another. Make it sound like a guitar solo, not like arpeggiated chord shapes.

Here's an example:

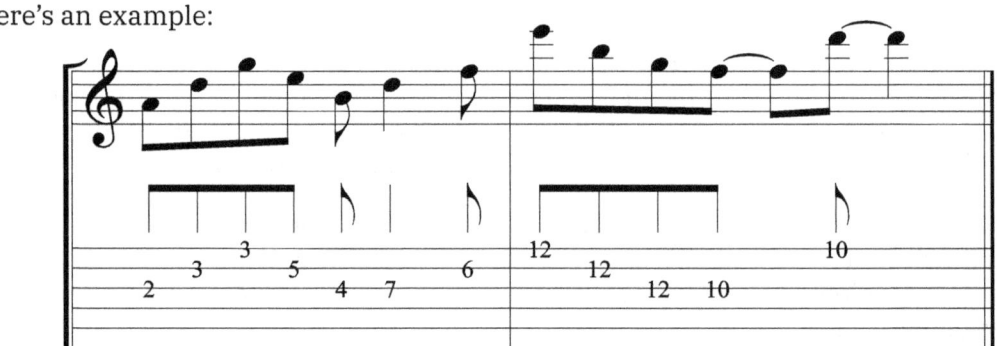

3. Abridging the Notes of the Two Triads Horizontally

With this approach, you play linear and vertical at the same time.

Here's how this works: Let's use the Dm and Em 2nd inversion (5th in the bass) shapes on the top three strings as an example.

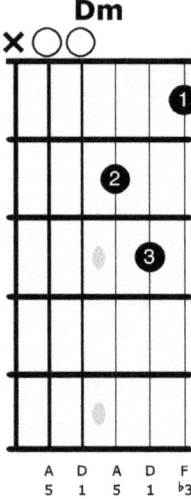

When you move that shape up two frets, you get an Em chord.

The lowest fingered note in that Dm chord, on the G string, is A, the 5th of the Dm chord.

So, the way this works is that you would play from the 5th of the Dm chord to the 5th of the Em chord, and then on the next string from the root of the Dm chord to the root of the Em chord, and on the high E string from the ♭3rd of the Dm chord to the ♭3rd of the Em chord. You're basically playing nothing but whole steps on every string (from the root of one chord to the root of the other chord a whole step up or down, from minor 3rd of one chord to the minor 3rd of the other chord, from 5th to 5th, from Dm chord to Em chord, or from Em chord to Dm chord).

In the above description I went from Dm note to Em note, ascending in other words, and from G string up to high E string. Needless to say, there are of course way more possibilities. You could go ascending or descending from an Em chord note to a Dm chord note, you could change the order of the strings, from E string to B string to G string, or skip strings, move horizontally all across the neck through all inversions of the two chords, and so on. The constant major 2nd intervals on each string, in combination with the vertical motion when you change strings, create a very unique type of phrasing. It makes you sound very advanced without necessarily having to learn or apply tough, advanced concepts.

Here's what it looks like when you move in whole step motion from a Dm note to an Em note, shown below in all three inversions.

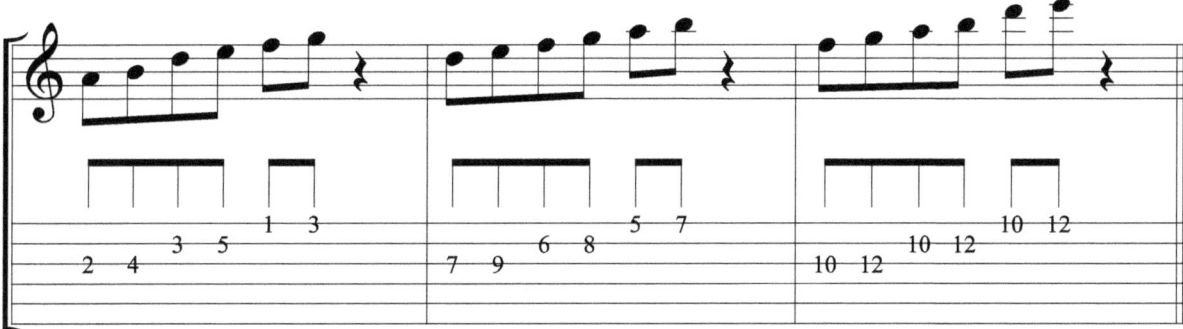

4. All the Above With Added Chromaticism

You can play the D♯m/E♭m chord in between Dm and Em. This added chromatic motion creates yet another unique sound in your solos, which is different from the sound of the aforementioned approaches.

Chromatic means moving by half steps. When you play all twelve notes in a row that is called the chromatic scale. There are two ways you can add chromaticism.

    1. **Chromatic approach chords**

        Hit the chord a half step above or below the chord you meant to hit, then resolve into that target chord.

        For example:

           ▶ C♯m to Dm. The Dm chord is approached from a half step below.

- E♭m to Dm. The Dm chord is approached from a half step above.
- D♯m to Em
- Fm to Em

2. Chromatic passing chords

Chromatic passing chords are played in between two chords a whole step apart.

For example:

- Dm D♯m Em
- Em E♭m Dm

I'm fully aware that such above descriptions are much easier to grasp when accompanied with a video. To hear how to pull off these four techniques, you can check it all out in a video I posted on the Free Bonus materials page.

CHAPTER 24: THE dim7 PASSING CHORD

Whenever you have two consecutive diatonic chords that are a whole step apart, you can place a diminished 7th chord in between those two chords as a chromatic passing chord.

The chromatic bass motion between two consecutive chords creates a strong sense of forward motion and direction in a chord progression. First off, you want to learn the three most-used dim7 chord shapes:

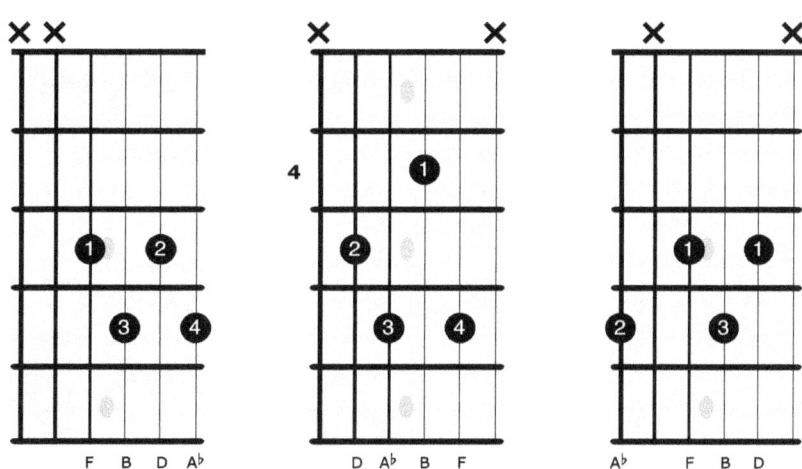

Let's have a look at a couple of examples of how to use the dim7 chord as a passing chord.

1. **C F F#dim G**

    The most common chord progression in all music is I IV V. In the key of C, those chords are C, F, and G. The following chord progression creates forward momentum from the F to the G chord by placing an F#dim7 chord in between F and G.

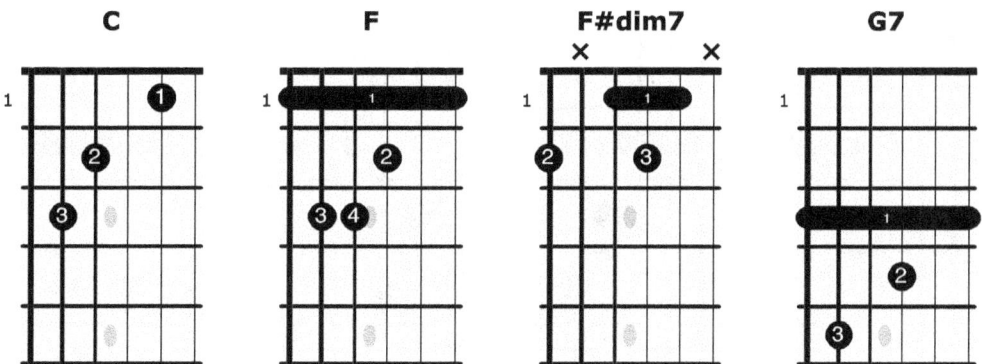

2. C G7 G#dim7 Am

This example has a passing chord between V and VI, in the key of C:

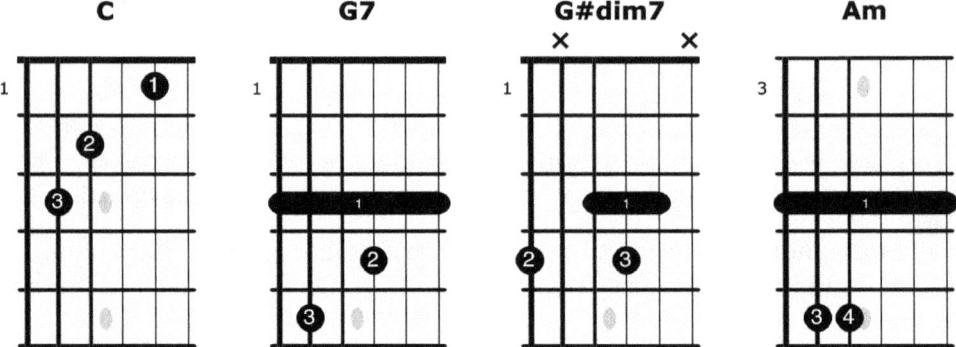

3. Cmaj7 C#dim7 | Dm7 D#dim7 | Em7 | Fmaj7 F#dim7 | G7 G#dim7 | Am7 A#dim7 | Bm7b5 ||

This example walks up *all* the chords of a C major scale, walking from chord to chord via an in between dim7 passing chord.

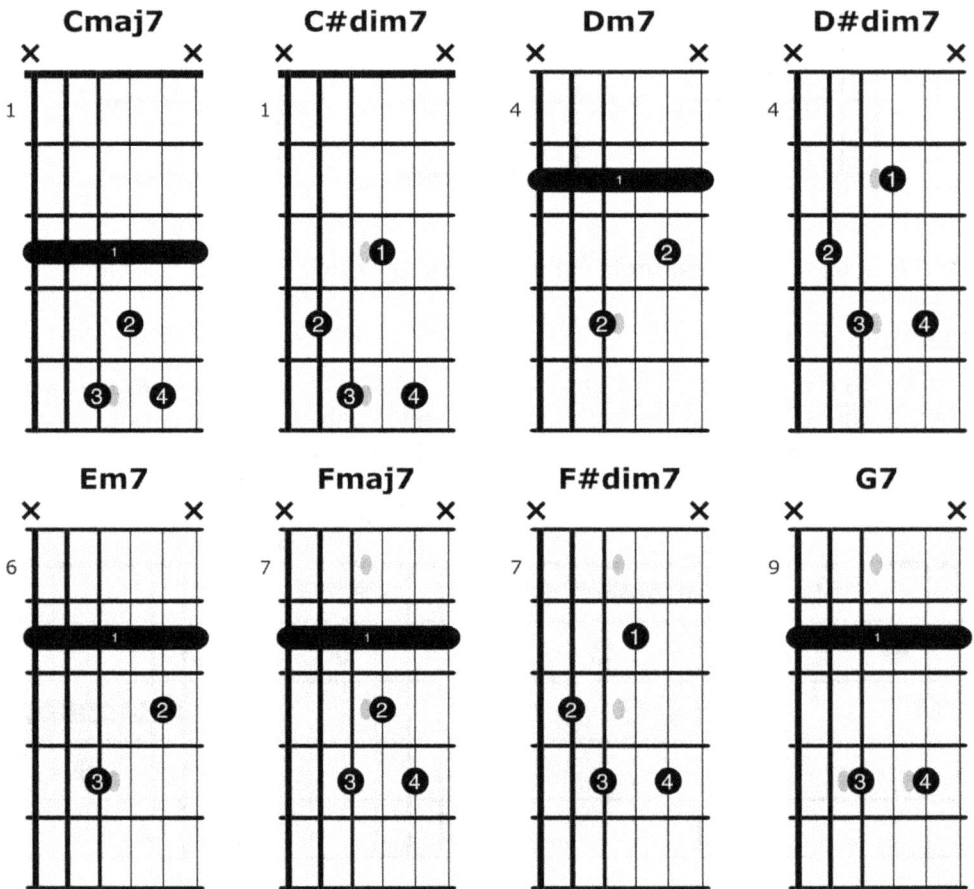

The dim7 Passing Chord

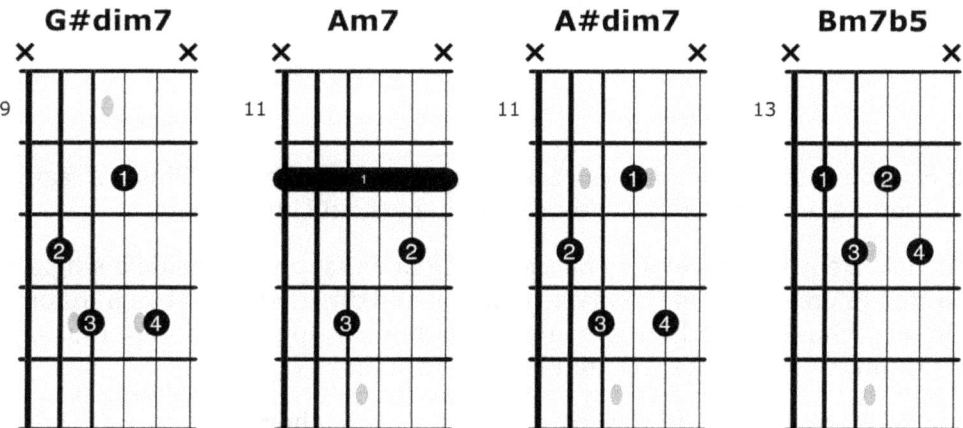

There are more really cool things you can do with dim7 chords. Our students at ZOT Zin Music have a blast discovering how to implement these cool sounds in their playing and their writing.

CHAPTER 25: THE AUGMENTED LINE CLICHÉ

This line cliché shows one of the ways you can use an augmented chord. This is a really cool composition and song-writing technique more songwriters should know about.

A line cliché is a stepwise descending or ascending line that moves inside a single, stationary chord. Line clichés create a sense of forward motion and direction in static chord progressions. They're a great technique to add interesting-sounding harmonic motion in musical passages where there is only one chord for an extended period of time.

The augmented line cliché can be played on the I or on the V chord.

On the I Chord

The following line cliché in the key of C creates a sense of direction from the I chord into the IV chord. In this case, the 5th in the C chord (the note G), moves up a fret to the ♯5 (G♯), then up another fret to the 6th (A), then up another fret to the ♭7 (B♭).

This gives the following chord progression:

| C | Caug | C6 | C7 | F ||

Analysis: **I Iaug I6 V7/IV IV**

V7/IV is called a secondary dominant chord. **V7/IV** is the dominant chord that wants to resolve down a 5th to the IV chord (F) of the key (C7 resolves to F).

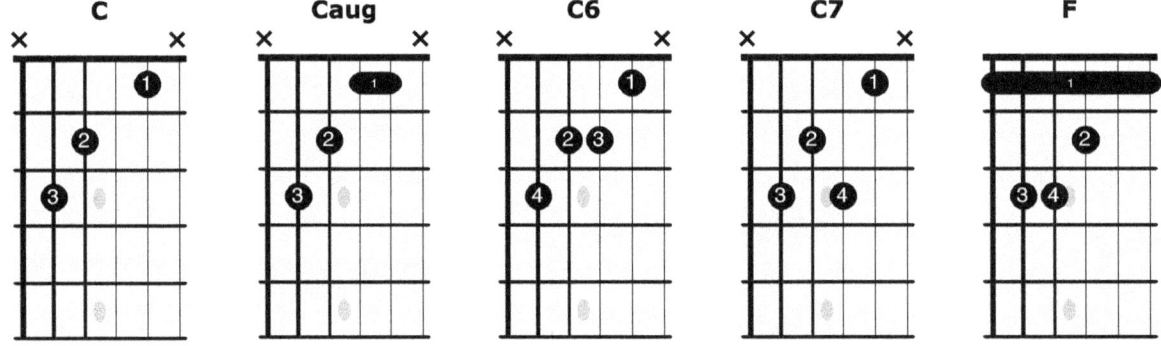

On the V Chord

This exact same line cliché can also be played in the key of F. In that case, the C chord is the V chord. The line cliché prolongs the V chord, creating a forward build-up from the V chord into the I chord. When you start the preceding chord progression on an F chord instead of a C chord, you are in the key of F, as in the following chord progression:

F | Bb | C | Caug | C6 | C7 | F ||

Analysis: **I IV V Vaug V6 V7 I**

When you finger the C chord with your pinky on the A string, ring finger on the D string, and middle finger on the B string, then you can move the shape up, using your pointer finger on the G string. In that case, you can move the above chord progression through all twelve keys. (You then just have to make sure you mute the two E strings.)

The following shows a G chord formed by a C chord shape moved up to the 7th fret:

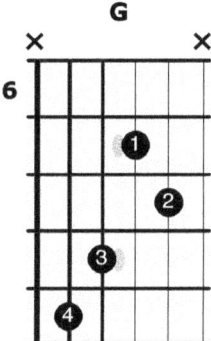

Here's what it looks like when you combine both the Iaug line cliché and the Vaug line cliché in the key of C:

| C | Caug | C6 | C7 | F | G | Gaug | G6 | G7 | C ||

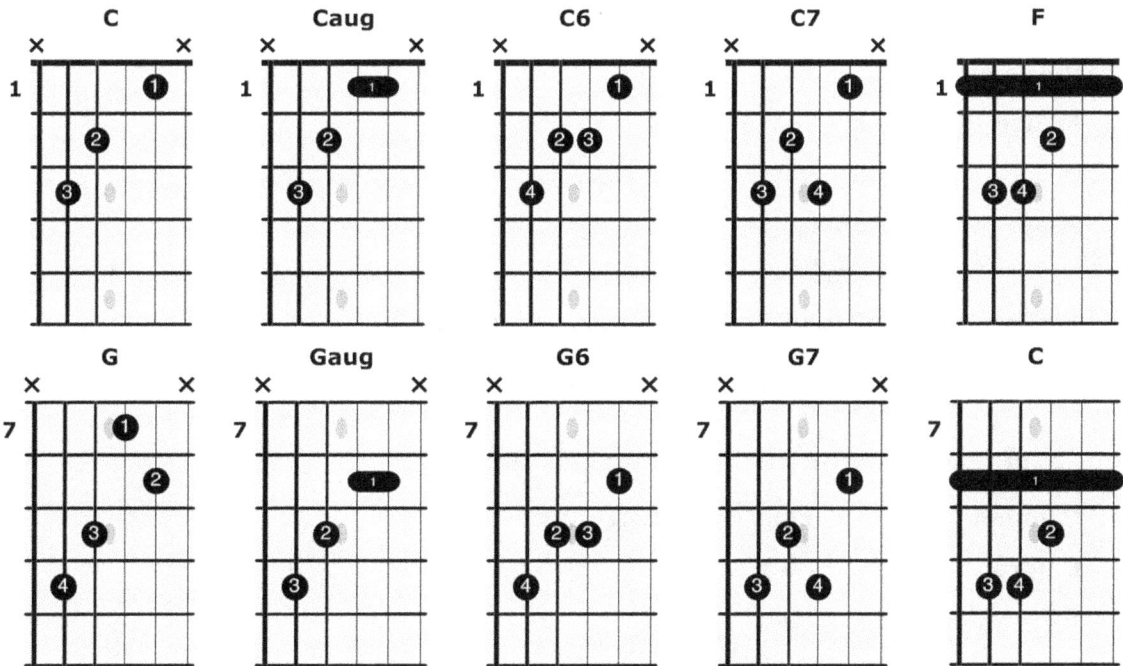

Have fun practicing this in all twelve keys.

CHAPTER 26: WRITING IN DIFFERENT MODES

Through the years, many students and musician friends have asked me how to write in modes.

While it's good to know the scale structure of each mode, a good start is to memorize some of the most common chord progressions for each mode:

With triads (three-note chords)

Ionian	I IV V I
Dorian	Im IV Vm Im
Phrygian	Im ♭II ♭III Im
Lydian	I II V I (or I ♯IVdim V I)
Mixolydian	I IV Vm I (or I IIm Vm I)
Aeolian	Im IVm Vm Im
Locrian	(Idim IVm ♭V Idim)

With 7th chords

Ionian	Imaj7 IVmaj7 V7 Imaj7
Dorian	Im7 IV7 Vm7 Im7
Phrygian	Im7 ♭IImaj7 ♭III7 Im7
Lydian	Imaj7 II7 Vmaj7 Imaj7
	Imaj7 ♯IVm7♭5 Vmaj7 Imaj7
Mixo	I7 IVmaj7 Vm7 I7
	I7 IIm7 Vm7 I7
Aeolian	Im7 IVm7 Vm7 Im7
Locrian	(Im7♭5 IVm7 ♭Vmaj7 Im7♭5)

In the key of C, all the above chord progressions are:

C Ionian	Cmaj7 Fmaj7 G7 Cmaj7
C Dorian	Cm7 F7 Gm7 Cm7
C Phrygian	Cm7 D♭maj7 E♭7 Cm7
C Lydian	Cmaj7 D7 Gmaj7 Cmaj7
	Cmaj7 F♯m7♭5 Gmaj7 Cmaj7

C Mixo	C7 Fmaj7 Gm7 C7
	C7 Dm7 Gm7 C7
C Aeolian	Cm7 Fm7 Gm7 Cm7
C Locrian	Cm7♭5 Fm7 G♭maj7 Cm7♭5

Locrian isn't a useful scale to write songs with. You probably can tell when you play the above chord progressions. Locrian doesn't feel like it's going anywhere.

The VII diminished chord has too much tension and is too unstable to feel like a I chord. It wants to resolve somewhere, not be resolved to.

Ionian is another name for the major scale. This is the most commonly used scale in the Western world. The notes in a C Ionian scale are **C D E F G A B C**.

Aeolian is another name for the minor scale. This is the second-most commonly used scale in the Western world. The notes in a C Aeolian scale are **C D E♭ F G A♭ B♭ C**.

Have fun playing around with the above chord progressions. When you sing a melody strumming the C Dorian chord progression, you're writing a song in C Dorian. When you sing a melody strumming the C Aeolian progression, you're writing a song in C Aeolian.

While the above examples list some of the most common chord progressions for each mode, it's fun to experiment, coming up with your own progressions. To that end, here are all the chords for each mode in the key of C.

- ▶ **C Ionian**   Cmaj7 Dm7 Em7 Fmaj7 G7 Am7 Bm7♭5 Cmaj7
- ▶ **C Dorian**   Cm7 Dm7 E♭maj7 F7 Gm7 Am7♭5 B♭maj7 Cm7
- ▶ **C Phrygian** Cm7 D♭maj7 E♭7 Fm7 Gm7♭5 A♭maj7 B♭m7 Cm7
- ▶ **C Lydian**   Cmaj7 D7 Em7 F♯m7♭5 Gmaj7 Am7 Bm7 Cmaj7
- ▶ **C Mixo**   C7 Dm7 Em7♭5 Fmaj7 Gm7 Am7 B♭maj7 C7
- ▶ **C Aeolian**   Cm7 Dm7♭5 E♭maj7 Fm7 Gm7 A♭maj7 B♭7 Cm7
- ▶ **C Locrian**   Cm7♭5 D♭maj7 E♭m7 Fm7 G♭maj7 A♭7 B♭m7 Cm7♭5

To write songs using modes in different keys, you'd just have to move all chords up or down a number of equal steps or frets. As an example: if you want to write a song in D Mixo, you will need to move up the C Mixo chords or chord progression up a whole step to the key of D. For A Aeolian, you'd move the C Aeolian chords or chord progression down three frets. The key of A is three frets down from the key of C.

Another technique that really helps with transposition is thinking in scale degrees, which you can learn about in the "Chords and Inversions" chapter.

CHAPTER 27: CHORD FORMULAS

Chord structures are represented by what we call **chord formulas**. A chord formula is a combination of numbers, with each number representing an intervallic relationship to the **root** of the chord, which is represented by the number 1. The root of a chord is the note that gives the chord its name. It is the note the chord is "built" on. The root of a C chord is the note C, the root of an A♭m chord is the note A♭, the root of an F♯m chord is the note F♯, and so on.

The root is always numbered as 1. If the next note in the chord is up a 3rd from 1, then that will get the number 3. If the next note is up a 5th from 1, then that note gets the number 5.

As an example, the notes that make up a C chord are **C E G**.

C = 1
E = 3 (C D E... 1 2 3 letters ➡ E is up a 3rd from C)
G = 5 (C D E F G ... 1 2 3 4 5 letters ➡ G is up a 5th from C)

Where it gets confusing for many people is understanding how to depict chord inversions with formulas. For example, when you see the following:

E G C

As the interval from E to G is a ♭3 and from E to C is a ♭6, the formula for E G C is **1 ♭3 ♭6**. Since the letter E is assigned to 1, the 1 ♭3 ♭6 formula implies that E is the root (1) and that this hence is some kind of E chord.

The problem with that reasoning is that this is not an E chord. If it were, you would have to call it Em♭6, which theoretically doesn't make sense. Em♭6 is not a chord you will ever see.

Why will you never see a chord called Em♭6?

Because it sounds like a C chord. You can try with all your might, there is no way to make this sound like any kind of E chord. We have mother nature's harmonic series to thank for this. When you hit one single C note on any instrument, that single note consists of a whole series of sine wave vibrations, the first six of which produce the notes C, E, and G.

That is why the notes **C E G,** or any inversion of these three notes, always sounds like a C chord.

The 1 ♭3 ♭6 formula is correct though—counting E as the root, G is up a minor 3rd and C is up a minor 6th. However, for the above reasons, the 1 ♭3 ♭6 formula isn't considered as a unique chord where 1 is the root, but as a first inversion (3rd in the bass) of a major chord, or in other words: 3 5 1.

The notes E G and C that you get when you start the formula 1 ♭3 ♭6 on an E note, feel more like a 3 5 1 (E = the 3rd, G = the 5th, and C = 1) in the key of C. The formula numbers 3 5 1 are out of order because the three notes E G C are out of order. This is a 1st inversion C chord, not an E chord.

If you didn't know that the notes E G C are a C chord, how can you figure out whether these notes form an E, a G, or a C chord?

It comes down to remembering (and then applying) a very important part in the study of harmony:

Chords are built by stacking 3rd intervals.

Here's how you apply this theory knowledge to figure out which chord the notes E G C add up to.

- ▶ Let's start with E. When you count up a 3rd up from E, you get G (E F G). So far so good.
- ▶ When you then stack another 3rd on top of G, you get B—not the note C. This is a dead giveaway that E is not the root.
- ▶ **Conclusion:** An Em chord consists of the notes E G B. Here we have E G C (a 3rd from E to G, and a 4th from G to C). This is not an E chord.

Maybe it could be a G chord? Let's follow the same logic.

- ▶ Stacking a 3rd on top of G (because again, that is how you built chords) gives us the note B. There is no B in the above chord.
- ▶ **Conclusion:** This is not a G chord. Stacking 3rd intervals on a G note gives us the notes G B D, which is what the notes are in a G chord.

There is only one possibility left: **C**

- ▶ Stacking a 3rd on top of C gives us the note E (C D E... 1 2 3). So far so good. Stacking a 3rd on top of E, gives us G (E F G ... 1 2 3).
- ▶ **C E G**. A 3rd and a 3rd. Bingo!
- ▶ **Conclusion:** After exhausting every option, C is the only note that could serve as the root. The notes E G and C can only be a C chord.

The notes E G C are out of order, which is again what we call an inversion. When reorganized in ascending order starting from the root, we get **C E G**—and indeed, these notes are all 3rd intervals apart. That is how you figure out what the root, and hence the name of the chord is, in any given combination of notes that are out of order.

Some Helpful Chord Formula Logic

As shown with the 1 ♭3 ♭6 example (that was really an out of order 1 3 5 formula): accounting for inversions in listings of chord formulas will lead to a disorganized mess that can cause a lot of confusion. Think about the disorganization: formulas starting on 3, others on 5, others on 6 or 7, and so on.

It organizationally makes much more sense to simply start all of them on 1. After all, formulas show the interval distances of all notes in a chord or scale, in relationship to the root 1. Not only that, it's actually unnecessary to list formulas of inversions in a study of chords or scales.

To understand this, consider that there are two ways we can think of formulas of inversions. Either way will show why it's unnecessary to start a formula on any other number than 1.

1. We can think of formulas 3 5 1 (EGC), 5 1 3 (GCE), 5 3 1 (GEC), and 3 1 5 (ECG) as an out-of-order 1 3 5 (CEG). They are different configurations, in other words inversions, of the formula 1 3 5. As such, all these different configurations are already covered by a formula that starts on 1: the 1 3 5 formula.

2. For every inversion of every scale or chord type, there is already a formula available that starts on 1. As an example: 3 5 1, thought of as an inversion of 1 3 5, is already covered in another formula that starts on 1, as we covered earlier—the 1 ♭3 ♭6 formula. C E G (1 3 5) inversion E G C = 1 ♭3 ♭6

Conclusion: Every possible chord, chord inversion, scale, and scale inversion (also called a mode) is covered by a formula that starts on 1. That is why it doesn't make sense to start a formula on any other number than the root or tonic.

We've got a lot of chord formulas coming up. Ideally, you want to learn and memorize them all. Here are some tips that will speed up the learning process:

1. Chords that consist of just a letter or a letter with an accidental are always major chords. You only specify it when it is not major, as in minor (m), diminished (dim), augmented (aug), or suspended (sus).

2. The words major and minor always refer to the 3rd of the chord.

    a. The first 3rd interval in major chords is major.

    b. The first 3rd interval in minor chords is minor.

3. The words augmented and diminished always refer to the 5th of the chord.

    a. A chord that has the word augmented in its name has a ♯5 (augmented 5th).

    b. A chord that has the word diminished in its name has a ♭5 (diminished 5th).

4. When you see the number 7 in a chord name, that chord has a ♭7 (minor 7th) interval.

5. When the chord name has maj in it, then that chord has a 7 (**major** 7th) interval. The appendix maj hence refers to the type of 7th in the chord, a major 7th. It does not refer to the chord being a major chord. We know it's a major chord because it always is when it doesn't have the minor chord appendix "m" or "-."

6. Sus means **suspended**. The word suspended refers to the 3rd. This means that the 3rd is replaced with another note, in this case always the 2nd or 4th.

    a. **Sus2**

    b. **Sus4**

7. **1 3 5 7** are considered chord tones. Chord tones are the meat and potatoes.

8. **9 11 13** are tensions. These are the spices added to the meat and potatoes.

9. There are three rules for tensions:

    a. In order for a tension to be available on a chord, it needs to be a note that belongs to the scale. For example:

i. Tension ♭9 on a Cmaj7 chord in the key of C is not possible because that note is D♭, which is not an available note in the C major scale.

ii. Chord III in the key of C, Em, cannot have tension 13 (= a major 6th above the root E) because that note is C♯, which is not an available note in the C major scale.

b. The tension needs to be a whole step above a chord tone. If a tension is only a half step above a chord tone, it's not available for that chord, because the harsh half step dissonance this creates muddies up the harmony, making it harder to clearly hear the notes in the chord.

i. Tension 11 is not an available tension on a I chord in a major scale. Cmaj11 is not a chord you will likely see. The F note, tension 11 on the Cmaj7 chord, clashes harshly with the E note in the C chord.

ii. Many theory books mention that tension 11 on the V chord, is not recommended either for the same reason. In the key of C, V7 is G7. Tension 11, a C note, will clash too harshly with the B note in the G chord.

However: I would consider this one of the blind spots in music theory. If the V chord, as we'll discuss next, can have any tension, why wouldn't the 11th work? I believe it does sound really good. Case in point: here's one of my favorite G7 chords.

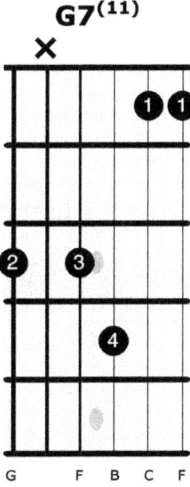

c. The V chord can take any and every tension: ♭9, 9, ♯9, ♭5/♯11, ♯5/♭13, 13.

The reason for this is that the V chord naturally is the chord with the most tension in the major scale, which is why it wants to resolve to I. Our ear expects that V will go to I. That expectation for the tense V chord to resolve to I is also why nothing you add to the V chord can sound "wrong" to our ear.

Our ear accepts any note you add to the V chord. You can't add any "wrong" notes to the V chord. On the contrary, any tense notes you add to the V chord make its resolution to the I chord sound all the sweeter. Our ear expects to hear tense notes on the V chord, and thus accepts any note you add to that chord.

To sum it all up, here are all the available tensions for every chord in a major scale:

Imaj7	9, 13
II-7	9, 11
III-7	11
IVmaj7	9, #11, 13
V7	b9, 9, #9, 11 *(see above remarks)*, b5 (#11), #5, b13, 13
VI-7	9, 11
VII-7b5	11, b13

Without any further ado, here are the chord types and their formulas.

Power Chord

Theoretically speaking, power chords are not chords because they only consist of two different notes. To be theoretically correct, they should be called power intervals.

Chord Type	Symbol	Formula	Notes	Example
Power Chord	5	1 5	C G	C5
Power Chord	5	1 5 8	C G C	C5

The Triads

Triads are three-note chords. Following are all the triad types.

Chord Type	Symbol	Formula	Notes	Example
Major	(none)	1 3 5	C E G	C
Minor	m, min, mi, -	1 b3 5	C Eb G	Cm, C-
Augmented	aug, +	1 3 #5	C E G#	Caug, C+
Diminished	dim, °	1 b3 b5	C Eb Gb	Cdim, C°
Suspended Fourth	sus4	1 4 5	C F G	Csus4
Suspended Second	sus2	1 2 5	C D G	Csus2

You might think: Isn't every three-note chord technically speaking a triad?

The answer to that question would be "no."

1. For example, the formulas 1 2 3, 1 b2 3, 1 2 b3, 1 2 7, 1 b2 7, 1 2 b7, 1 b2 b7, and so on are considered clusters. When you attach note names to these numbers, you notice you get three consecutive letters. The sound this produces is a dissonant cluster, not a chord.

2. Any formula that has the number 7 in it, like for example 1 3 7, 1 ♭3 ♭7, 1 3 ♭7 and so on are actually four-note chords with the 5th omitted. They appear to be three-note chords when you see the formula, but they sound like 7th chords minus a 5th.

7th Chords (in the Major Scale)

As you know, 7th chords are four-note chords. Knowing that you build chords by stacking 3rd intervals, you get a 7th when you stack another 3rd on top of the 5th.

The following are all the 7th chords that you can form with the notes in a major scale.

Chord Type	Symbol	Formula	Notes	Example
Major Seventh	maj7, △, 7	1 3 5 7	C E G B	Cmaj7, C△7, C7
(Dominant) Seventh	7	1 3 5 ♭7	C E G B♭	C7
Minor Seventh	m7, -7	1 ♭3 5 ♭7	C E♭ G B♭	Cm7, C-7
Half Diminished Seventh	m7♭5, -7♭5	1 ♭3 ♭5 ♭7	C E♭ G♭ B♭	Cm7♭5, C-7♭5
Dominant Seventh Suspended Fourth	7sus4	1 4 5 ♭7	C F G B♭	C7sus4

More 7th Chords

While there are five types of 7th chords in a major scale, as listed above, there are other types of 7th chords that you don't find in a major scale.

Chord Type	Symbol	Formula	Notes	Example
Major Seventh ♯5	maj7♯5	1 3 ♯5 7	C E G♯ B	Cmaj7♯5, C△7♯5
Major Seventh ♭5	maj7♭5	1 3 ♭5 7	C E G♭ B	Cmaj7♭5, C△7♭5. (Sounds like Cmaj7♯11)
Minor Major Seventh	mmaj7, -maj7	1 ♭3 5 7	C E♭ G B	Cmmaj7, C-maj7, C-△7
Diminished Seventh	dim7	1 ♭3 ♭5 ♭♭7	C E♭ G♭ B♭♭	Cdim7

6th Chords

Chord Type	Symbol	Formula	Notes	Example
Sixth	6	1 3 5 6	C E G A	C6
Minor Sixth	m6, -6	1 ♭3 5 6	C E♭ G A	Cm6, C-6

The 6th chords are chords with a major 6th interval, never a minor 6th interval. When you add a ♭6 to a 1 3 5 or 1 ♭3 5 triad, that ♭6 takes over and feels like the root. This becomes clear when you add note names to the numbers of the formula, as shown in following examples:

- **1 3 5 ♭6** = C E G A♭ = rearranging these notes in 3rds gives: A♭ C E G

    C E G A♭ sounds more like a 1st inversion A♭maj7♯5 chord, than a C chord.

- **1 ♭3 5 ♭6** = C E♭ G A♭ = 1st inversion of A♭ C E♭ G

    This sounds more like a 1st inversion A♭maj7 chord than it sounds like a C chord.

The "Add" Chords

Chord Type	Symbol	Formula	Notes	Example
Added Ninth	add9	1 3 5 9	C E G D	Cadd9
Added Fourth	add11	1 3 5 11	C E G F	Cadd11, Cadd4

Add 11 is quite a clash-y, nasty-sounding chord, with the E and the F note creating a lot of tension. I added it here for thoroughness, but I don't think I've ever encountered this chord in any song.

Chords With Tensions

Tensions is the name we give to the notes that you get when you keep stacking 3rd intervals on top of the 7th.

You get a:

- 9th when you stack a 3rd on top of the 7th ➜ **7 8 9**
- 11th when you stack a 3rd on top of the 9th ➜ **9 10 11**
- 13th when you stack a 3rd on top of the 11th ➜ **11 12 13**

maj7

Chord Type	Symbol	Formula	Notes	Example
Major Ninth	maj9, maj7$^{(9)}$, $\triangle 7^9$	1 3 5 7 9	C E G B D	Cmaj9, Cmaj7$^{(9)}$, C$\triangle 7^{(9)}$
Major Thirteenth	maj13, maj7$^{(13)}$, $\triangle 7^{13}$	1 3 5 7 13	C E G B A	Cmaj13, Cmaj7$^{(13)}$, C$\triangle 7^{13}$
Major Seven Sharp Eleventh	maj7#11, maj7$^{(\#11)}$, $\triangle 7^{(\#11)}$	1 3 5 7 #11	C E G B F#	Cmaj7#11, Cmaj7$^{(\#11)}$, C$\triangle 7^{\#11}$

The IV chord in a major scale can have tension #11. In the key of C, that is a B note added to an F chord. F to B is an augmented 4th interval, also labeled as #11. The chord this produces, **Fmaj7#11,** has what we call a "Lydian sound" because of the #4 added to the chord. Check the Lydian scale definition in the chapter "Modes" if that doesn't make sense.

maj7 With Tension Combinations

In chords with lots of tensions, you usually leave the less important notes out, like the 5th or even the root. Here are all the maj7 chords with tension combinations.

Chord Type	Symbol	Formula	Notes	Example
Major 9/13	maj9$^{(13)}$, maj7$^{(9,13)}$, $\triangle 9^{13}$	1 3 5 7 9 13	C E G B D A	Cmaj9$^{(13)}$, C$\triangle 9^{13}$
Major 9/#11	maj9$^{(\#11)}$, maj7$^{(9,\#11)}$, $\triangle 9^{\#11}$	1 3 5 7 9 #11	C E G B D F#	Cmaj9$^{(\#11)}$, C$\triangle 9^{\#11}$
Major #11/13	maj7$^{(\#11,13)}$, $\triangle 7^{(\#11,13)}$	1 3 5 7 #11 13	C E G B F# A	Cmaj7$^{(\#11,13)}$, C$\triangle 7^{(\#11,13)}$
Major 9/#11/13	maj7$^{(9,\#11,13)}$, $\triangle 7^{(9,\#11,13)}$	1 3 5 7 9 #11 13	C E G B D F# A	Cmaj7$^{(9,\#11,13)}$, C$\triangle 7^{(9,\#11,13)}$

m7

And here are the m7 chords with tensions 9, 11 and 13.

Chord Type	Symbol	Formula	Notes	Example
Minor Ninth	m9, -9, m7$^{(9)}$, -7^9	1 b3 5 b7 9	C Eb G Bb D	Cm9, C-9, Cm7$^{(9)}$, C-7$^{(9)}$
Minor Eleventh	m11, -11, m7$^{(11)}$, -7$^{(11)}$	1 b3 5 b7 11	C Eb G Bb F	Cm11, C-11, Cm7$^{(11)}$, C-7$^{(11)}$
Minor Thirteenth	m13, -13, m7$^{(13)}$, -7^{13}	1 b3 5 b7 13	C Eb G Bb A	Cm13, C-13, Cm7$^{(13)}$, C-7^{13}

m7 Tension Combinations

Chord Type	Symbol	Formula	Notes	Example
Minor 9/11	$m9^{(11)}$, $m7^{(9,11)}$, -9^{11}	1 b3 5 b7 9 11	C Eb G Bb D F	$Cm9^{(11)}$, $C-9^{11}$
Minor 9/13	$m9^{(13)}$, $m7^{(9,13)}$, -9^{13}	1 b3 5 b7 9 13	C Eb G Bb D A	$Cm9^{(13)}$, $C-9^{13}$
Minor 11/13	$m7^{(11,13)}$, $-7^{(11,13)}$, $m11^{(13)}$, $-11^{(13)}$	1 b3 5 b7 11 13	C Eb G Bb F A	$Cm7^{(11,13)}$, $C-7^{(11,13)}$
Minor 9/11/13	$m7^{(9,11,13)}$, $m9^{(11,13)}$, $-7^{(9,11,13)}$, $-9^{(11,13)}$	1 b3 5 b7 9 11 13	C Eb G Bb D F A	$Cm7^{(9,11,13)}$, $C-7^{(9,11,13)}$

Dominant 7

Jazz guys *love* dominant chords: *especially* even more so when they have altered tensions.

Dominant chords (1 3 5 b7) with altered tensions b5 #5 b9 #9 are called altered chords.

The altered chord is the I chord in the altered scale, which is the 7th mode of melodic minor. What this means is that when you play a melodic minor scale starting on the 7th note of that scale, you are then playing what's called the altered scale.

For example, the C melodic minor scale is: C D Eb F G A B
The seventh mode of C melodic minor is: B C D Eb F G A

This scale contains all the altered tensions, making this the preferred scale for improvisation over the altered chord. *(In this case: B7alt).*

    B to C = b9
    B to D = #9 (you can think of that D as C^x)
    B to Eb = 3 ➡ (Eb = D#)
    B to F = b5
    B to G = #5 ➡ (G = F^x)
    B to A = b7

Chord Type	Symbol	Formula	Notes	Example
Dominant Seventh b5	7b5	1 3 b5 b7	C E Gb Bb	C7b5
Dominant Seventh #5	7#5	1 3 #5 b7	C E G# Bb	C7#5
Dominant Ninth	9	1 3 5 b7 9	C E G Bb D	C9
Dominant Seventh b9	7b9	1 3 5 b7 b9	C E G Bb Db	C7b9
Dominant Seventh #9	7#9	1 3 5 b7 #9	C E G Bb D#	C7#9
Dominant Seventh b5 b9	7b5b9	1 3 b5 b7 b9	C E Gb Bb Db	C7b5b9

Chord Formulas

Chord Type	Symbol	Formula	Notes	Example
Dominant Seventh ♭5 ♯9	7♭5♯9	1 3 ♭5 ♭7 ♯9	C E G♭ B♭ D♯	C7♭5♯9
Dominant Seventh ♯5 ♭9	7♯5♭9	1 3 ♯5 ♭7 ♭9	C E G♯ B♭ D♭	C7♯5♭9
Dominant Seventh ♯5 ♯9	7♯5♯9	1 3 ♯5 ♭7 ♯9	C E G♯ B♭ D♯	C7♯5♯9
Dominant Seventh 11	11, 7^{11}, 7/11	1 3 5 ♭7 11	C E G B♭ F	C11, C7^{11}, C7/11
Dominant Seventh 9 13	9^{13}, 9/13, 7$^{(9,13)}$	1 3 5 ♭7 9 13	C E G B♭ D A	C9^{13}, C9/13
Dominant Seventh ♭13	7$^{♭13}$, 7/♭13, 7♭13	1 3 5 ♭7 ♭13	C E G B♭ A♭	C7$^{♭13}$, C7♭13
Dominant Seventh 13	7^{13}, 13	1 3 5 ♭7 13	C E G B♭ A	C7^{13}, C13
Dominant Ninth sus4	9sus4, sus9	1 4 5 ♭7 9	C F G B♭ D	C9sus4, Csus9

m7♭5

Chord Type	Symbol	Formula	Notes	Example
Minor Seven Flat Five 11	m7♭5^{11}, -7♭5^{11}	1 ♭3 ♭5 ♭7 11	C E♭ G♭ B♭ F	Cm7♭5^{11}, C-7♭5^{11}
Minor Seven Flat Five ♭13	m7♭5$^{♭13}$, -7♭5$^{♭13}$	1 ♭3 ♭5 ♭7 ♭13	C E♭ G♭ B♭ A♭	Cm7♭5$^{♭13}$, C-7♭5$^{♭13}$
Minor Seven Flat Five 11 ♭13	m7♭5$^{(11♭13)}$, -7♭5$^{(11♭13)}$	1 ♭3 ♭5 ♭7 11 ♭13	C E♭ G♭ B♭ F A♭	Cm7♭5$^{(11♭13)}$, C-7♭5$^{(11♭13)}$

The 6/9 Chords

The 6/9 chords are basically 6th chords with tension 9 added to the chord. It's very common for jazz musicians to end a song on a I6/9 chord instead of a Imaj7 chord.

The 6/9 chords are most commonly played on I and IV. On a fun side note, you can also hear the chord in some of Stevie Ray Vaughan's playing. You can find a great passage with 6/9 chords in Stevie's "Love Struck Baby" solo at 1:18. Stevie plays a series of 6/9 chords chromatically moving up from the I chord to the IV chord.

Chord Type	Symbol	Formula	Notes	Example
Six Ninth	6/9	1 3 5 6 9	C E G D A	C6/9
Minor Six Ninth	m6/9, -6/9	1 ♭3 5 6 9	C E♭ G D A	Cm6/9, C-6/9

It's beyond the scope of this book to also list all the chord shapes for each one of these chords. However, memorizing their formulas will give you a huge head start.

CHAPTER 28: IMPROVE YOUR TIMING

You will see amazing improvement in your timing if you do these drills every day. These four drills are short and focused, but challenging.

Exercise 1
E7#9

Exercise 2
E7#9

Exercise 3
E7#9

Exercise 4
E7#9

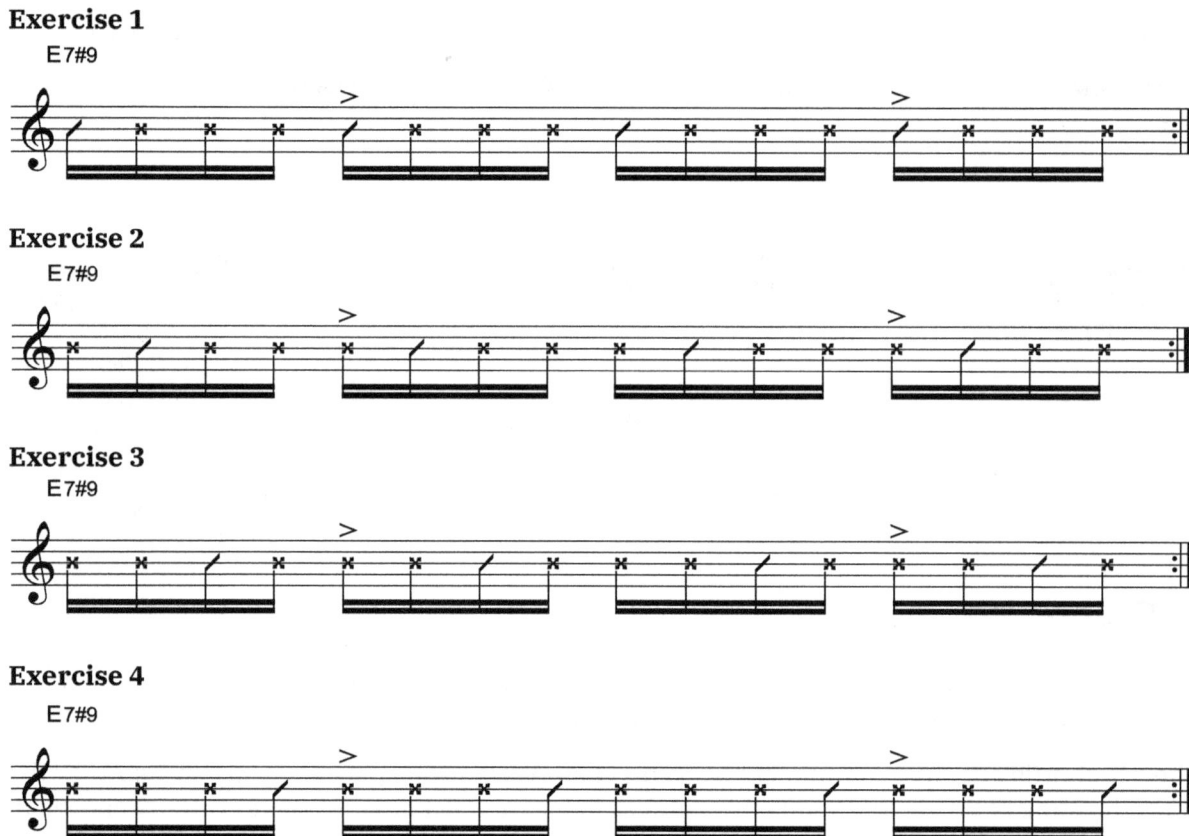

Slashes represent chord sounds.

You get a chord sound when you gently squeeze the strings against the frets.

X's represent mutes.

Mutes occur when you rest your hand on the strings without pressing them down against the frets. They sound percussive because you prevent the strings from vibrating.

Improve Your Timing

How to do these exercises?

1. Put your metronome at minimum 52 bpm up to maximum 58 bpm.

2. Strum constant **down up down up**.

3. Use the E7♯9 chord for this. Many teachers call E7♯9 "the Jimi Hendrix Chord." While fingering this chord, grab over the guitar neck with your thumb to mute the low E string. You want to mute both E strings so no notes are ringing during the percussive mutes.

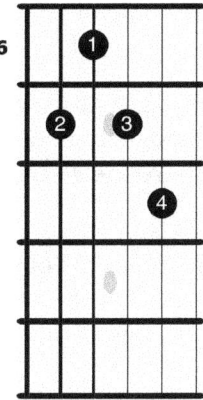

4. Notice the accent marks on the second and fourth beat. **Hit harder on beats 2 and 4.** Accent those beats—it will help you keep time and lock in better with the metronome.

5. You want to keep working on that first drill until you've reached the point where playing it with a metronome at that slow a tempo gets easier. Move on to the next exercise once you reach that level.

Practice the **third exercise** next. That's the next-easiest drill.

This drill, as you can tell, is significantly more challenging. The reason for this is that, unlike in the first exercise, now the **accented hits and chord squeeze no longer fall in the same location**. In addition to a time-feel exercise, the second, third, and fourth drills are also **coordination exercises.** Keep working on that third drill until it gets easier.

The next drill is number 4. Follow the same instructions as above.

Once you can play the fourth drill pretty well, you're ready to tackle the second exercise. We kept that one for last because the second drill seems to be the one most people struggle with the most. With all the previous training you got leading up to this, that second drill now won't be that difficult anymore.

Once you can play all four drills, you're ready for the new game plan. Practice each exercise back to back for three minutes each.

Drill time:
Practice each exercise back to back for three minutes each.
= **a 12-minute daily drill**.

CHAPTER 29: EAR-TRAINING

Of all the things to practice, ear training is the most important skill to develop. If all you did was ear training every day for a whole year without ever picking up your guitar, a year from now you would be a better guitarist.

Ear training is actually aural memory training. Every interval has its own unique flavor, feel and sound. You are training your memory to recognize and recall the sound of every interval. Since there are only twelve notes in our music, there are also only twelve intervals (distances between two sounds) to remember.

You'll train your ear with a website. You can access the ear-training practice pages for all intervals, from my site here: **https://www.zotzinguitarlessons.com/ear-training-links/** For your convenience, I posted this URL on the Free Bonus page so you can just click on it.

The links on that ear-training webpage lead to online ear-training practice pages. The first URL trains unison, minor 2nd and major 2nd intervals. The moment you click on the URL, you will hear a piano play two notes. Those two notes are either going to be a unison (same note twice in a row), a minor second (two adjacent frets) or a major 2nd. If you think that what you heard is, for example, a major 2nd, click on the button that says major 2nd. When you get it right, the piano will immediately play two new notes. If not, the button will turn red and you'll have to click on another answer.

Starting with the second URL, the unison is omitted, and a new interval keeps getting added. The next larger interval gets added with each consecutive URL.

The webpages have a clock running, and they show your score. Only move on to the next URL when you have a minimum 85% accuracy rate for three minutes non-stop.

Drill time:
I would suggest that you practice three sessions of three minutes a day, **= a 9-minute daily drill.**

You can do more than three sessions a day if you want to boost progress, but don't do more than three minutes at a time. Work your way through all of the URLs, moving on to the next level only after you have managed to maintain a minimum 85% accuracy rate in your current level.

Ear training is challenging. Don't get discouraged. Just keep getting at it every day, and I promise you will keep improving. Things will suddenly click. Treat it as a game. See if you can beat your score with every session. Also, hold on to the very motivating thought that you are developing your senses. This is brain development. You will be able to hear things most people can't hear or don't notice. You'll also enjoy music on an even deeper level, a much deeper level, when you hear all the colors much more vividly and lively, and with more detail.

The listed URLs on that webpage lead to drills that train the ear for ascending intervals played at a slow tempo.

Once you've worked through the whole list, you'll eventually also want to train your ear for faster tempos and descending and harmonic (the two notes played simultaneously) intervals.

Once you've worked through all URLs, move on to the following webpage:

https://www.musictheory.net/exercises/ear-interval.

In the upper right corner on that webpage, you can see a settings icon. When you click on that, a drop-down menu page opens up where you can change settings. Once you've worked through all URLs with a constant minimum 85% accuracy rate, start working through the different speed settings. Work up all the way to fastest.

After you've trained your ear to successfully hear all intervals ascending at the fastest setting, maintaining 85% accuracy, start practicing descending intervals at the slowest speed. You want to build things up again, starting with only three descending intervals until you reach 85% accuracy, to four intervals up to 85%, then five intervals to 85%, and so on, all the way up to all twelve intervals, all descending.

When you get that in shape, it's time to move on to harmonic ear training.

It might seem like a lot of work, but you want to look at this as a journey. Keep in mind that the descending and harmonic intervals are probably going to take less time to master. After all, by the time you get to them, you will already have acquired a cultivated ear.

Using Known Songs for Leverage

The following page lists songs for every interval.

First off, when you look at the first column, you can learn a lot about all the intervals and their names. Notice how the intervals get larger one fret at a time as you move down the column (unison, minor 2nd, major 2nd, minor 3rd, major 3rd, etc.). Ideally, you would want to memorize the names of all twelve intervals in music.

These songs are meant to help you identify which interval you hear the piano player play. For example: if you're not sure whether what you're hearing is a minor 2nd or a major 2nd, you can use the songs to guess whether what you're hearing sounds more like the first two notes in "It's Been A Hard Day's Night" or the first two notes in "Frère Jacques."

It's usually a bit easier to identify what interval you're hearing if you can compare the sound of the interval to the beginning of a song that starts with that interval.

If you don't know all the songs, you can always go on YouTube to listen to them. You can of course also do research on Google to find other songs for each interval.

Have fun with this. I can't overstate how important it is to train your ear. It might be really challenging now, but you will thank me later.

Interval	Ascending	Descending
Unison	▶ Happy Birthday To You ▶ La Marseillaise ▶ One Note Samba	
Minor 2nd **Half step**	▶ Jaws Theme ▶ Spanish/Flamenco chord progression (I-bII-bIII) ▶ It's Been A Hard Day's Night	▶ Für Elise ▶ Joy To The World ▶ Stella By Starlight ▶ Hernando's Hideaway
Major 2nd **Whole step.**	▶ Frère Jacques ▶ Silent Night ▶ Do-Re-Mi (Sound of Music)	▶ Satin Doll ▶ Yesterday ▶ Mary Had A Little Lamb
Minor 3rd **1 ½ steps**	▶ Brahms's Lullaby ▶ The Impossible Dream ▶ So Long, Farewell ▶ Greensleeves	▶ Hey Jude ▶ The Star Spangled Banner ▶ Frosty The Snowman
Major 3rd **2 whole steps.**	▶ When The Saints (Go Marchin' In) ▶ Kumbaya ▶ Morning Has Broken (Cat Stevens)	▶ Summertime ▶ Swing Low, Sweet Chariot ▶ Beethoven's 5th Symphony ▶ Giant Steps (Coltrane)
Perfect 4th **2 ½ steps.**	▶ Here Comes The Bride ▶ Amazing Grace ▶ Harry Potter Theme ▶ O Tannenbaum	▶ Adeste Fideles ▶ Star Trek ▶ Downtown (on the word "Downtown")
Tritone **(Aug 4th, Dim 5th)** **3 steps**	▶ The Simpsons Theme ▶ Maria (West Side Story)	▶ YYZ
Perfect 5th **3 ½ steps**	▶ Twinkle Little Star ▶ My Favorite Things (The Sound of Music) ▶ Also Sprach Zarathustra ▶ Star Wars Theme	▶ The Flintstones Theme Song ▶ Feelings
Minor 6th **4 steps**	▶ Black Orpheus ▶ Love Story (Francis Lai, 3rd and 4th note)	▶ Love Story (Francis Lai)
Major 6th **4 ½ steps**	▶ My Bonny ▶ NBC Theme ▶ Take The A-Train ▶ My Way	▶ The Music of The Night (The Phantom of the Opera) ▶ Sweet Caroline (Neil Diamond, 1st notes chorus)

Interval	Ascending	Descending
Minor 7th **5 steps**	▶ Stone Free (Jimi Hendrix, intro) ▶ Star Trek theme	▶ Watermelon Man (Herbie Hancock) ▶ An American in Paris
Major 7th **5 ½ steps**	▶ Take On Me (A-Ha, the chorus) ▶ Immigrant Song (1st and 3rd note of vocals in the intro) ▶ Theme from Fantasy Island	▶ I Love You (Cole Porter)
Octave **6 whole steps**	▶ Over The Rainbow ▶ Immigrant Song (Led Zeppelin) ▶ Blue Bossa	▶ Doogie Howser M.D. Theme ▶ Willow Weep For Me ▶ There's No Business Like Show business (2nd & 3rd note)

CHAPTER 30: THE FOUR SCHOOLS OF GUITAR TECHNIQUE TRAINING

If you ever wanted to gain amazing speed, accuracy, dexterity and control, this is how you will get there in a reasonably short amount of time. Most guitar players only practice technical skills one or two ways. This is one of the reasons why many of these players never reach the technical skill level they are trying to achieve.

When you combine these following four practice techniques, not only will you with an absolute guarantee reach your speed and dexterity goals, but you will do so in a much shorter time than you imagined possible.

1. With a Metronome

Start the metronome at a very slow speed (beats per minute).

Play any short three- or four-note phrase along with the metronome. Alternate pick every note. Focus on playing every note clean, even, and relaxed. When playing that phrase feels completely comfortable and relaxed, speed the metronome up (only by three to five bpm at a time).

Practice the same line at this new tempo, until again it feels and sounds totally relaxed, clean, and easy. Keep raising the tempo on the metronome a couple of bpm at a time, whenever the phrase you're practicing starts feeling easy and comfortable.

At some point, you will have a hard time keeping up. When this happens, either focus on relaxing your hand more while trying to keep up, or if the playing gets too sloppy, drop the metronome by twenty to thirty bpm. Slowly build the tempo up again from there with small increments of a couple bpm at a time.

This is slow but efficient practice. Gradually, over weeks, you will see your coordination between both hands and your picking-speeds improve.

2. The John Petrucci Way

The metronome approach is great, but it has its drawbacks. It shouldn't be the only way you practice technique. The whole idea of speeding up the tempo in small increments ensures that you gain control at any tempo. That's a really good thing. Some guitar players can play certain lines at a really fast tempo, but get sloppy when they need to play it a bit slower. That problem gets solved when you increase the bpm in small increments. So that is a good thing. But because the incremental speed increases are so minimal, the brain gets lulled into complacency and switches off or into automatic pilot mode after a while. That is **not** a good thing.

The increments are too small for them to be noticeable. As a result, the brain becomes less alert and less sharp after a while.

That is why, to really see progress and results, you should surprise your brain with novelty and shake it up about every fifteen to twenty minutes. Throw off your brain and shake it out of automatic pilot.

This leads us to the "John Petrucci" method. After fifteen to twenty minutes of metronome, you should do the John Petrucci exercise I'm going to outline here, for four to five minutes, to shake things up and keep your brain alert.

John Petrucci is one of the founding members of the amazing progressive rock band Dream Theater. John has a book out with guitar technique exercises.

He advocates the following technique exercise:

- No metronome.
- Play a short musical phrase, as slowly as you possibly can.
- Keep continuously repeating the melodic phrase back to back without pauses between the repetitions.
- Very, very slowly and gradually speed up...
- ... till you're playing that musical phrase so unbelievably fast that everything gets sloppy.
- Keep moving that super fast for a couple of seconds,
- Then very slowly and gradually, slow down again
- Until you're back at your starting speed.
- Then, without stopping, do this whole cycle over again.

Do this a couple of times in a row.

This is a great method to develop strong, advanced coordination between both hands in a relatively short time. It's an amazing exercise that will do a lot for your control, accuracy, strength, endurance, and so much more.

3. The Shawn Lane Way

Shawn Lane passed away way too soon. He's always been and will always be one of my all-time favorite guitarists. His coordination, speed, agility, and dexterity have been unmatched since.

Shawn explained in an interview that he never really practiced technique with a metronome all that much. Oddly enough, he also never really practiced things slowly all that much. He just right off the bat tried to play as fast as he possible could move is fingers, and then aimed to clean it up as he was going. It's an unusual approach to building technical facility, but hey—time has proven that it obviously worked really well for him. :)

So, put on your favorite song, and then go mad: Play as fast as you can move your picking hand and fingers. Force your fingers to move ridiculously fast. Don't worry about it being sloppy. Just fix it and clean it up as you're going.

Do this for about three or four minutes. That *really* will shake up your brain.

4. The Victor Wooten Way: Meditation – Visualization

Of all the things you could be doing to improve your technique, this is the most important. This drill will have the single greatest impact on your dexterity, picking technique, progress, and results. I used this approach myself many years ago to great success. I later found out that world-renowned bassist Victor Wooten wrote about this specific practice technique. In his book *The Music Lesson,* Victor discusses the spiritual and mental aspects of musicianship.

He explains how there are certain mental tricks and techniques you can use to improve your speed and coordination in unbelievable ways, without extra practice. No matter how much some of the book might possibly appear as "spiritual mumbo-jumbo" to some at first, Victor is absolutely dead-on with the claims that he makes in the stories he tells. This stuff really works. Not enough guitar players pursue and utilize the powers of their mind to accomplish better results with less effort.

I wrote a must-read blog post in the past about how those meditation techniques boosted my picking technique, speed, and coordination in ways I could not imagine. I think you will love the following story.

https://www.zotzinguitarlessons.com/blog/inspiring-story-about-practicing-without-practice-effort/

The post explains in great detail what to do and how and why it works. If you do this every day, as explained in this blog, in only two or three months you will be amazed and surprised at how much faster you can play and how much cleaner it all sounds.

Conclusion

Ideally, you want to combine these four different practice techniques. You could spend 60% of your technique practice time with the metronome, 20% using John Petrucci's approach, 10% Shawn Lane's approach, and 10% meditation and visualization. If you can only practice technique for ten minutes, I would suggest you prioritize the meditation and visualization approach.

One thing is for sure: when you combine these four approaches and practice this on a daily basis, you will see stellar results in your speed and guitar technique in no time.

Have fun! While we're at it talking about technique, this following chapter will do wonders for your accuracy and dexterity.

CHAPTER 31: ALL TWENTY-FOUR FINGER-COMBINATIONS

The fingers of the fretting hand are numbered:

1 = pointer finger
2 = middle finger
3 = ring finger
4 = pinky

When you place your fingers on four adjacent frets, and you play every note only once, then you have twenty-four possible finger combinations.

1234	**2134**	**3124**	**4123**
1243	**2143**	**3142**	**4132**
1324	**2314**	**3214**	**4213**
1342	**2341**	**3241**	**4231**
1423	**2413**	**3412**	**4312**
1432	**2431**	**3421**	**4321**

These twenty-four combinations serve as great dexterity exercises.

There are two important guitar technique skills you can improve with these twenty-four finger combinations. You can practice the combinations as (1) an accuracy exercise or (2) a dexterity exercise.

1. Accuracy Drill

1. Alternate pick everything.

2. Play the four-note finger combination of your choice, on the low E string, starting on the first fret.

3. Move only one finger at a time. Force your other fingers to stay completely still and very close to the fret board.

4. After you have played a note, gently lift that finger up again. Keep it close to the fret board. Play the next note, and so on.

5. Play slowly. After you have played all four notes/fingers, move on to the A string, and play the same combination, then again on the D string, and so on, without any pause. Try to make all notes perfectly even in length, loudness, and sound quality.

6. After you have played the four-note combination all the way up to the high E string, move up one fret, and play it again on the high E string. *(But now one fret higher).*

7. From there on, keep doing the same finger combination, on the B string, G string, etc. (now moving back to the low E string, one string at a time, with no pause between string changes).

8. When you reach the low E string, play the pattern, move up a fret, then start over again from there.

9. Keep going up and down the strings, always moving up a fret when you get to either E string.

10. Move your fingers in a very slow and controlled fashion.

11. Keep your whole focus and concentration on keeping **all** your fingers as close as possible to the fret board.

12. Your focus is **not** on the finger you're moving, but on forcing the fingers that are not moving to stay in place without any motion.

13. If one of your fingers that was not supposed to move does, then you need to slow down. You're playing too fast and/or lost control of your fingers.

14. This is about complete control and accuracy.

15. Do this for a week: one-and-a-half minutes per exercise, twelve exercises a day.

16. The next day, do the next twelve finger combinations. If you have time and you want to push the boundaries, do all of them every day, maybe broken up in two sessions of twelve exercises.

Drill time:
1.5min./exercise, 12 exercises/day
= **an 18-minute daily drill**

In the second or third week of doing these drills, you can start practicing the combinations with a metronome—very slowly, playing one note per beat.

Again, focus with all your might on keeping the fingers completely still that are not supposed to move.

When you can do so effortlessly, then go up a maximum three or four bpm at a time on the metronome. When you get to a speed where one of your fingers wants to move more, focus harder on keeping that finger as close as possible.

When you don't seem to be able to manage to keep the rebelling finger close by, slow the metronome down twenty beats, and work the tempo up again, in small increments of three to four bpm at a time.

2. Dexterity Drill

This is a completely different drill, using the same twenty-four finger combinations. You will be amazed at how well this drill will improve your dexterity.

1. Alternate pick everything.

2. Stay on one string, one position. I recommend 7th position on the high E string **(B C C♯ D)**.

3. Don't change strings, don't change frets: stay on the same four notes.

4. Pick any of the twenty-four finger combinations. (For example, **3421**.)

5. Play that finger combination with a metronome as fast as you can.

6. You will notice that your brain might choke after a couple of repetitions. Meaning: you might only be able to play the combination two or three times in a row and then your fingers and brain will just get confused and shut off.

7. In that case, slow down your metronome a lot. If the same happens at the slower speed, slow it down more.

8. Once you find a metronome speed that allows you to comfortably play that combination for a longer period of time without the fingers choking on it, gradually speed up from there in small increments of three to four bpm at a time

9. Practice any given finger combination for as long as you feel like. You can move on to another finger combination whenever you want to. You don't have to go in order.

You can use the following page to track your results. Whenever you feel like moving on to another combination, write down your best metronome setting before it got sloppy.

These are killer exercises. You will love what they will do for your playing.

Guitar Essentials

1234

1243

1324

1342

1423

1432

2341

2431

3241

3421

4231

4321

3412

4312

2413

4213

2314

3214

4123

3124

4132

2134

3142

2143

Chapter 32: Short Scalar Speed Drills

Here are a couple more short one-bar technique exercises.

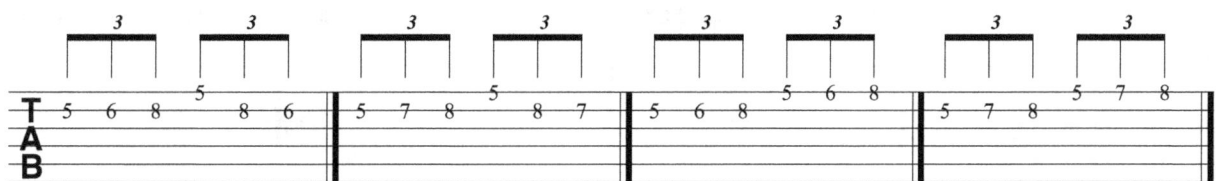

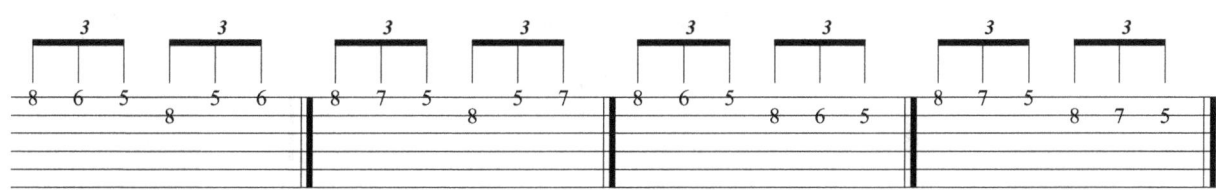

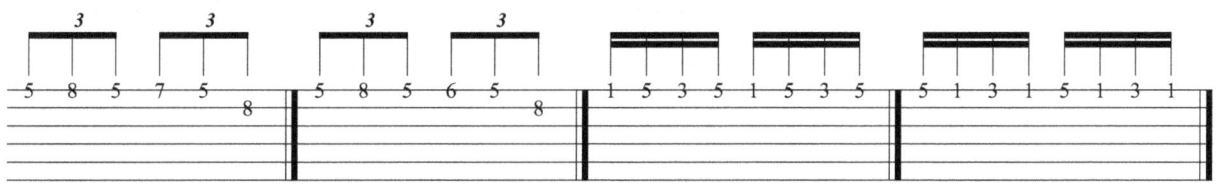

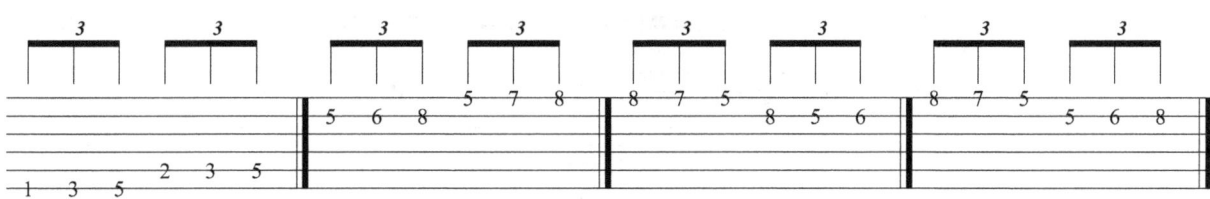

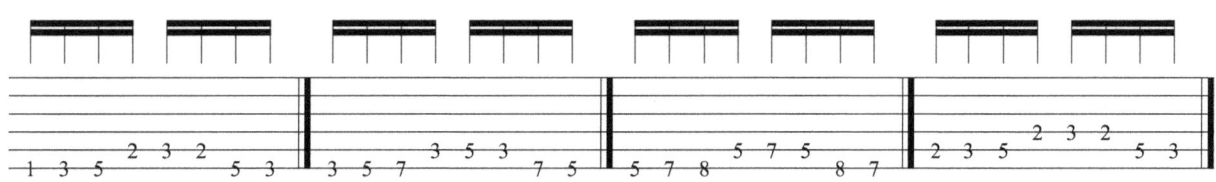

Guitar Essentials

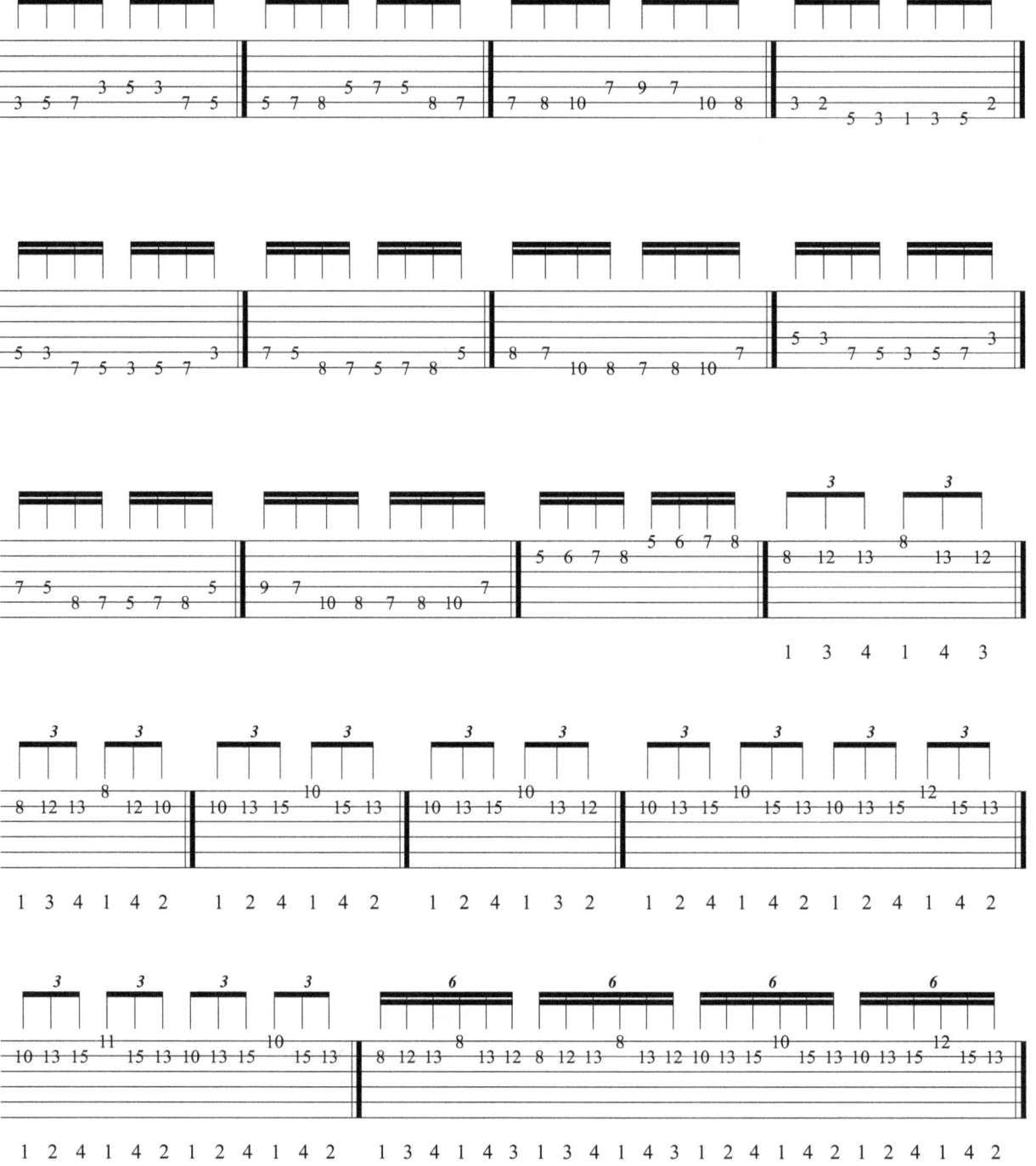

136

Short Scalar Speed Drills

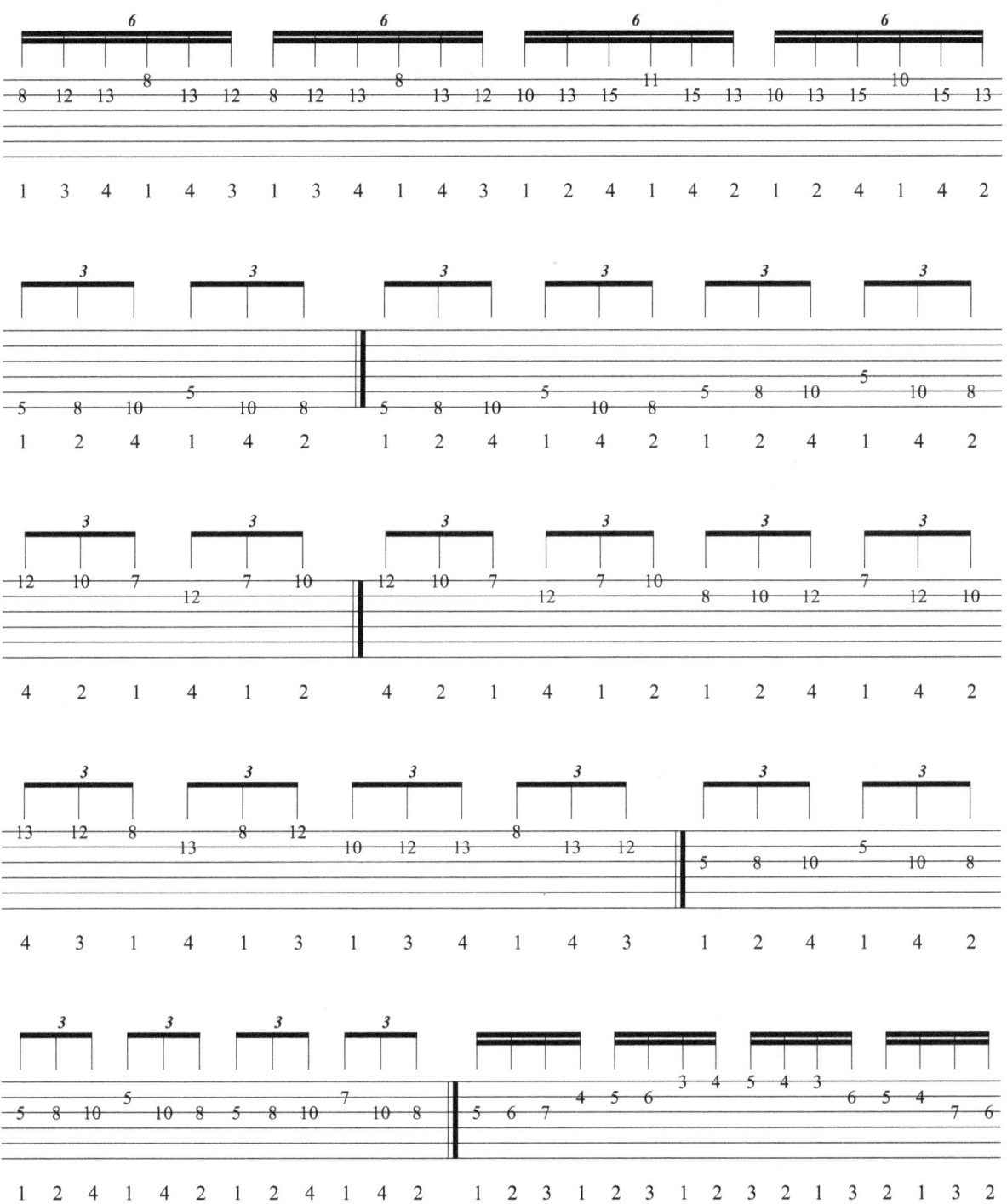

CHAPTER 33: COMPING WITH GUIDE TONES

What is Comping and What Are Guide Tones?

Comping is a term used by jazz musicians.

It's short for accompanying. It's the name given to jazz-style rhythm playing, as played on guitar or piano.

The term **guide tones** refers to the 3^{rds} and 7^{ths} of chords. These are the most important notes in a chord. The 3rd is the note that gives a chord its major or minor chord quality, while the 7th adds the "spice" to the chord.

If you were to leave the root or 5th out of a chord, and only keep the 3rd and 7th, it would still sound like that chord. The root and the 5th in other words, don't contribute as much to the overall sound, personality, or color of the chord.

The reason for this is explained in the study of intervals.

The chord's root has the same sonic character akin to the unison or octave. Unisons and octaves are called perfect intervals in the study of harmony. The 5th is a perfect interval as well. If one were to describe the sound and character of perfect intervals (unison, 4th, 5th, octave), one would use words like: **hollow, transparent, colorless,** or even descriptions like **lacking personality.**

The 3^{rds} and 7^{ths}, however, have a lot of personality.

- 3^{rds} sound sweet, pleasant, kind, like honey, also called **consonant.**
- 7^{ths} sound like vinegar, anger, pepper, spicy, also called **dissonant.**

If you're interested to learn more about the physics of sound, I recommend this intense but interesting read on ZOTZinGuitarLessons.com:

https://www.zotzinguitarlessons.com/blog/the-harmonic-series-and-its-implications-on-composition/

In case you want to learn more about intervals on guitar, here's a ton of free lessons explaining everything about intervals in great detail:

https://www.zotzinguitarlessons.com/blog/the-study-of-musical-intervals-part-8-the-octave/

Comping With 3^{rds} and 7^{ths}

So, to get back on topic: When you comp with guide tones, you are basically playing rhythm guitar only using the 3^{rds} and 7^{ths} of chords. A couple of traits of this rhythm playing style:

1. You get an uncluttered, more open sound.

2. You leave more space for the improviser, who has more improvisational freedom soloing over chords that are stripped down to their most basic form.

3. You're not stepping on the bass player's or pianist's toes since you're leaving the chord roots to them.

4. The stripped-down parts you play tend to sit better in the overall band mix.

5. This comping style works really well in larger ensembles with lots of musicians.

6. It's easier to voice lead these types of stripped-down harmonies. ("Voice leading" refers to a way of connecting the chords with the least amount of motion between chord tones). Voice leading makes it sound like you're composing on the spot, creating a tapestry of connected harmonies.

Comping With Guide Tones in Blues

Blues is played with the 1st, 4th, and 5th chord of a scale. These are labeled with Roman numerals: I IV V. In the key of G, those chords are G, C, and D.

C is a 4th above G (G A B C = four letters). That is why C is IV in the key of G.
D is a 5th above G (G A B C D = five letters). That is why D is V in the key of G.

One of the stylistic elements of blues is that in major keys, the I, IV, and V are played as dominant 7th chords: **G7, C7, and D7**. It wouldn't sound like blues if you played those chords as maj7 chords or any other type of 7th chords *(other than m7 chords in a minor blues)*.

You can comp through blues with guide tones. This is a really cool sounding, driven blues rhythm guitar style. This rhythm style is most commonly used in jazz, jazzed-up blues, or larger blues band ensembles.

The guide tones in the **G7 chord are F and B**

- ▶ **B is the 3rd** (G to B is a 3rd interval)
- ▶ **F is the ♭7th** (it takes seven letters to count from the letter G to the letter F)

The guide tones in the **C7 chord are E and B♭**

- ▶ **E is the 3rd** (C to E is a 3rd interval)
- ▶ **B♭ is the ♭7th** (It takes seven letters to count from the letter C to the letter B♭)

The guide tones in the **D7 chord are F♯ and C**

- ▶ **F♯ is the 3rd** (D to F♯ is a 3rd interval)
- ▶ **C is the ♭7th** (D to C is a ♭7th interval)

Those are the notes you'll be playing for each chord.

Now for the rhythm:

- ▶ Strum the guide tones with down stroke hits only.
- ▶ In quarter notes, one note per beat.

- ▶ Strum with big, strong arm motions.
- ▶ Squeeze the fingered notes on the G and D string with the fretting hand every time you hit the strings, and...
- ▶ Lift the fingers up right after, to make the chords short. Lift up the fretting hand fingers just enough for the strings to move away from the frets, but keep the fingers touching the D and G strings throughout.
- ▶ "Big strong arm motions" means: don't just hit the D and G strings. That's picking. We're not picking, but strumming the strings. Hit **all** strings on the down strum, and hit them fairly hard.
- ▶ **Mute all neighboring strings** by touching them with your fretting hand fingers. Grab over with your thumb to mute the low E string.
- ▶ To **accentuate the swing feel**, hit the occasional muted upstroke.

Remember: any upstrokes will sound muted because your fretting hand fingers only press down the strings on the down strokes and then immediately lift up. You are squeezing upon the down strokes and lifting up the fingers during the upswing in the strum arm.

Check out the following example of how to play a major blues with guide tones in G.

Now, here's something fun...

When you move the above fingerings up six frets, the same notes repeat but flip.

In the above accompaniment, the two guide tones from low to high for the G chord are F and B. Moving the exact same fingering up six frets on the same two strings, you get the same notes flipped around: B (9th fret) and F (10th fret). Pretty cool, right?

That means that you can play the exact same thing up three whole steps (six frets), as shown in following example:

For extra practice, also play all this on the A and the D strings, and on the low E and A strings.

Good news: All fingerings are exactly the same as above on all these string sets.

All that said, this rhythm style is usually played on the D and G strings as notated above.

CHAPTER 34: OVER EIGHTY WAYS TO MAKE GUITAR SOLOS BETTER

This is a random list of:

- ▶ All-too-common mistakes I've seen improvisation students make.
- ▶ Composition techniques that help build or structure a solo.
- ▶ Tricks and techniques you might not know about yet.
- ▶ Ideas to make your guitar solos more expressive and colorful.

1. Repeat a note x number of times in a row.

Don't play every note only once in a phrase. This is an incredibly common "mistake." A guitar solo sounds like it's meandering about without really saying anything if you don't play the occasional note x number of times in a row. I'm not talking here about playing a note again that you played a couple of notes ago in the same phrase. This is about playing a note x number of times in a row.

When you play a note x number of times in a row in a phrase, it makes that phrase sound like a statement. Your melody sounds like you meant to say it. You want that, because that is what makes your phrases stand out as more memorable.

2. Also, repeat phrases.

Repetition is an important part of communication. After you have played a melody line, you don't necessarily have to play an entirely new phrase again right after. You can totally repeat what you just played, and then build further from there. There are three major benefits to doing this:

- **a.** You relieve yourself from constantly having to come up with new stuff. The time this buys you to replenish your inspiration, makes that your phrases overall sound stronger.

- **b.** Your listeners end up liking your solo better. That's not only the case because your phrases are of higher quality, but also because you give your listeners time to enjoy what you're playing, without overloading their brain processing with constant new phrases. In addition, repetition breeds familiarity. Familiarity makes it easier for listeners to like your solos.

- **c.** Repetition is an effective tool in building and structuring a solo. This is not unlike regular communication. We don't speak in stand-alone sentences. Think about it, we always talk in paragraphs. You would never engage in a conversation like this: "Grandma just moved in with us. Our dog passed away last week. Jenny just took up tennis. I can't believe how cold it is. Man, playing guitar is so much fun." Nobody talks that way. "Grandma just moved in with us" would normally be followed with a couple more sentences about that topic before segueing into another topic.

3. Be aware of what the notes are that you're playing while playing them.

Of course, that is only possible when you know the locations of all the notes on the guitar neck really well. There are a ton of major benefits to knowing your fret board so well that you are aware of every note that you're playing while playing it. Some of the benefits include:

- ▶ You make fewer mistakes.
- ▶ You are more in control.
- ▶ You see more connections.
- ▶ You feel and sound much more confident. You sound like you know what you're doing.
- ▶ You're not dependent upon shapes and patterns anymore.

It pays off big time to train and get in the habit of thinking notes.

4. Play more behind the beat.

This item made the list here because of the vast number of guitar players who tend to rush their phrases and note placement in relationship to the beat. The lazier note placement makes you sounds more confident. People who are confident do things in their own time, whenever *they* feel like. That is how and what you sound like when you play a bit behind the beat.

5. Play interesting rhythmic patterns with the notes.

The title for this could have been: "Don't play all your notes with equal length and equal spacing." The importance of not playing too many rhythmically even-length notes might seem obvious, yet it is amazing how very often I hear guitar players (or students) who aren't very rhythmically creative. It's all too common in guitar lessons to hear solos where too many phrases in a row consist of nothing but perfectly even eighth notes or quarter notes. This sounds unnatural because no-bo-dy-e-ver-talks-like-that. Keep in mind: You're telling a story when you solo. Soloing is communication.

Instead, play random combinations of eighths, sixteenths, triplet, tied notes, syncopations, etc. This will make your solo sound more like regular speech. You don't want to play constant eighth notes, or constant quarter notes. Be rhythmically creative! Combine any type of division (quarters, eighths, sixteenths, triplets, etc.), speed up, slow down, place some notes ahead of the beat and other notes behind the beat, have notes that you cut short and other ones that you sustain.

6. Focus on playing shorter phrases.

Overplaying very much seems to be a guitar player thing. You don't have to play all the time, and you don't need a whole lot of notes to make a really strong statement.

7. Play (one-note) rhythmic phrases every couple of phrases.

There are two types of phrases:

    a. Melodic phrases: the phrase mainly consists of melody, a series of notes spaced at certain intervals.

    b. Rhythmic phrases: a phrase consisting of rhythmic patterns.

Pink Floyd's David Gilmour is a good example of someone who very effectively uses rhythmic phrases in his solos. Listen to the "Another Brick in the Wall, Pt. 2" solo. You'll hear great examples of rhythmic phrases in:

- ▶ The second bar of the solo at 2:12min.
- ▶ The fifth and sixth bar of the solo at 2:21min.
- ▶ The very rhythmic nature to the melodic sequence at 2:39.

You can also hear cool rhythmic phrases in the "Hotel California" solo at 4:38 (the two mutes) and at 5:21.

Most guitar players focus on constantly playing melodies, and in doing so, miss out on the great expressiveness, feel, drive, and energy that rhythmic phrases add to a solo.

8. Use double stops.

You play a double stop when you hit two notes simultaneously. In guitar player language, a double stop is more often than not a 4th interval. A great example is the intro to Johnny B. Goode. Chuck Berry hits a series of double stops after the first three notes of the intro.

Double stops add more sounds and colors to play around with in your solos. I like to think of each note in a scale as a color. When you combine two colors, you get another new color. For example, blue and yellow create green. You don't want to limit your sonic color palette to the five or seven notes provided by the scale. Mix some of these notes together to add more sounds in your solos.

9. Use phrase-by-phrase dynamics.

You want to make your guitar playing more dynamic. Dynamics means how quiet or loud you play. It's like voice-inflection in storytelling. Imagine how very boring stories would be if the storyteller had a monotonous, even voice quality with every word spoken at equal volume level. Good storytellers don't do that! They whisper, they scream when Grandma is about to be eaten by the wolf—the dynamics add emotion, drama, and a visual experience to the story. You can practically see Grandma being eaten in front of your eyes.

Do you see then how much expressiveness and feel you miss out on when you don't use dynamics in your guitar solos?

    a. Mix loud phrases and quiet phrases.

    b. Let your guitar whisper quietly, and scream super loudly, and everything in between.

    c. Exaggerate: play notes that nobody can hear—they are important too.

10. **Use individual note dynamics.**

    While the previous point covers dynamics on a phrase-by-phrase basis, the application of dynamics adds even more feel to a solo when applied to each individual note rather than to groups of notes.

    a. Make every individual note count by giving every note its own volume and intensity.

    b. Accent certain random notes in phrases.

    c. This is the next level of picking hand awareness and sensitivity. You are no longer just playing a couple of notes loud, a couple of notes soft—you are giving every single note its own dynamic, expression, and personality.

    d. One great example is the main melody to Andy Timmons' "Ghost of You." Every note is picked with its own intensity, making the melody very expressive with lots of personality.

    e. This leads to the next point: "It's not about which notes you play; it's about how you play them."

11. **"What" you play is less important than *how* you play it.**

    I could have named this: "Don't play notes, play emotions." This is so important that it deserves its own place in this list: "**It's not about which notes you play... it's about how you play them.**" Another way of saying this is that you should focus as much (if not more) on the **"how"** as you focus on the **"which/what"** notes to play. So many guitar students get so wrapped up in thinking shapes or playing series of notes that they forget the most important part: expressing emotion with those notes. Musical notes are nothing but a tool—expression is what it's all about. You're telling a story, not just reciting notes in a scale.

    There is no such thing as a bad or boring melody; there are only melodies you played in a boring way.

    It helps to keep the following questions in mind:

    a. What do you want to say with the notes? What do you want to communicate?

    b. How do you want to say it?

    c. What emotion are you trying to evoke?

    d. What do you want your listeners to feel?

    In other words, how are you going to express these notes you choose to play? Techniques to be more expressive include: bends, slides, hammer-ons, tremolo picking, playing loud, screaming, whispering, playing behind the beat, rush notes, and so on.

12. **Pick notes on different locations on the string.**

    This creates different timbres. Go nuts on this as a fun experiment. Pick the notes in a phrase right next to the bridge, only to pick the next phrase in the middle of the guitar neck. Go even more nuts: pick **each note** on a completely different string location. This is way too underused. You will love how much expression this adds to a solo.

13. Start every new phrase you play with the ending of the previous phrase.

This topic ties in a bit to one of the previous points about repetition. You will love how this great improvisation trick will give your solos structure and direction. This is not something you "have to do," but one of many improvisation techniques that you can apply at will. When you apply this technique, though, you need to be really diligent in its application. Meaning, play the very exact same three or four ending notes you ended your previous melody line with, exactly the same way, followed by a couple of new notes. Remember the explanation earlier about "talking in paragraphs." This is it! Every time you apply this technique, your phrases connect really well, adding a sense of structure and flow to the storytelling.

14. Go beyond pentatonics.

Pentatonic scales are cool but... it's really only five notes, isn't it? Some of the notes that add a lot of melodic feel, the half steps, are left out. I know many guitar players who get stuck in their pentatonics for years. Time to break out to other green pastures. You miss out if you never play those cool-sounding half steps in your solos. If you're one of those guitarists, go study the in-position major scale fingerings right now.

15. Try chicken picking.

I've always thought this is a hysterical name for a guitar technique.

Rest the middle finger of your picking hand on a string to mute that string, then pick a note on that muted string in a down stroke with your pick. This creates a muted sound cause you're muting that string with the tip of your middle finger. Right after you pick the muted string, pluck that fingered note with your middle finger. Pluck it pretty hard. This creates a snappy note. You can hear Jimmy Page play this technique in "Living Loving Maid (She's Just a Woman)" at 1:36.

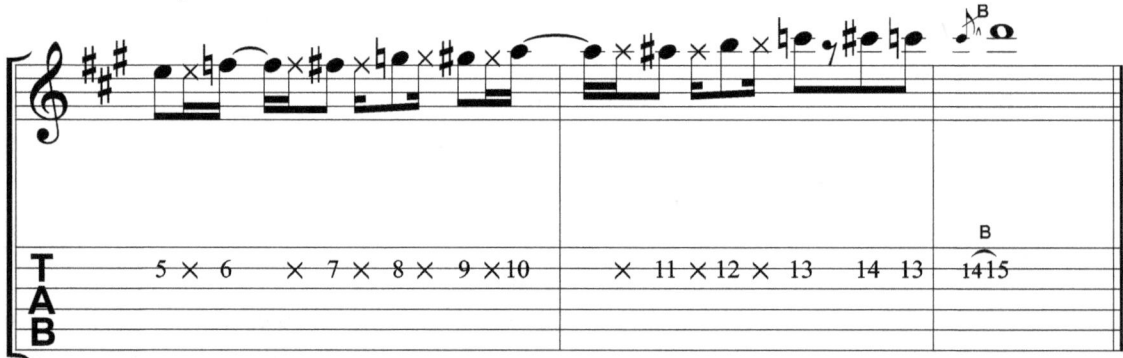

16. Use the whammy bar.

Steve Vai and Jeff Beck are two guitarists that come to mind who use the whammy bar very creatively. Check out Jeff Beck's "Where Were You" to hear him play entire melody lines out of one note with his whammy bar. Out of one picked note, he produces the rest of the melody notes by pressing down or pulling up on his whammy bar.

17. Remember: space and silence are important.

As mentioned earlier, overplaying seems to be a common guitar player's "disease."

   a. Experiment with having longer silences between phrases.

   b. Also experiment with leaving more silences between phrases (which means: play shorter phrases).

   c. Play less.

   d. Let your music breathe.

   e. This allows you the time to think before you play, which improves the quality of the melodic phrases you'll come up with.

   f. You give your listeners the time and space to enjoy what you're saying with your guitar.

   g. Think of it as Yin and Yang: you're constantly balancing silence with sound. Silence is the canvas against which you paint your story.

18. Have the occasional intervallic leap within your phrases.

Avoid playing in stepwise, scalar motion too much. The occasional wider intervallic leap in melody lines adds excitement and interest to melodies.

19. Try string skip soloing.

String skip soloing is what you do when you consistently solo linearly on two non-adjacent strings. It's a technique that creates really fun, interesting intervallic lines.

Important tip: Don't just play a phrase on one string, then pause, then play another phrase on the other string. The idea is that you incorporate both strings within each melodic phrase.

Here's an example:

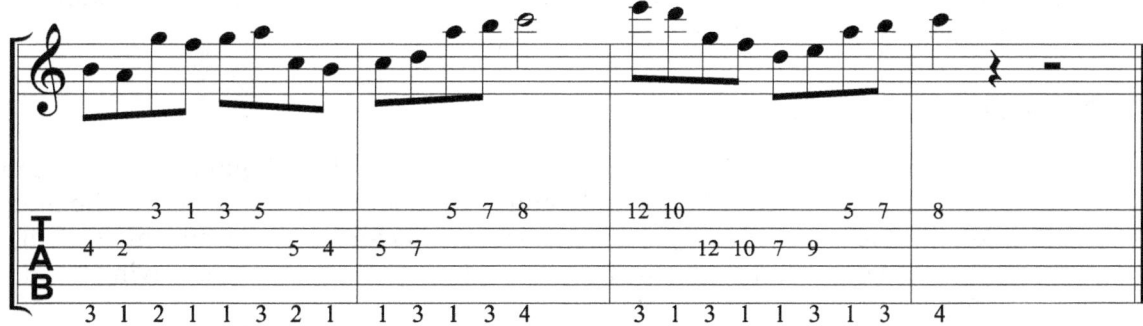

20. Use mutes.

Percussive hits can add a lot of drive, energy, passion, and feel to a solo. You can hear examples of mutes in David Gilmour's "Another Brick in the Wall" solo at 2:08 (right on the drum hit), 2:19, 2:24, and 2:33. The two percussive mutes at 4:41 in the "Hotel California" solo add energy and rhythmic flow to the solo.

Hit the occasional mute. It's a really effective tool you don't want to overlook in your own soloing.

21. Try pedal point.

Pedal point is a technique you can use in your soloing to add structure and cohesion to your solo. The name "pedal point" comes from classical baroque music. Organists play bass notes with pedals, and play moving melodies or harmonies on top of those bass notes with the hands. The way this is applied in improvisation: you simulate the feel of a constant pedal note by constantly repeating a note, which you alternate with another scale note. For example, the notes: A B A C A D A E A F A E etc.

That A note in this example is the pedal point. Here's what pedal point looks like:

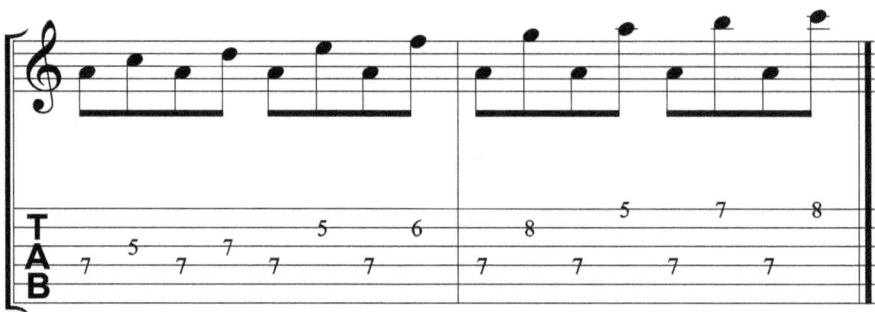

22. Use palm muting.

I always thought palm muting is a bit of a misnomer. Since the word "mute" in guitar playing is used to describe the sound of a dry, percussive attack, I always felt that palm muting should probably be called palm dampening. When you use this technique, you're dampening the string vibrations a bit, by resting the side of your picking hand slightly on the edge of the bridge, slightly touching the strings where they meet the bridge. This dampens the string vibrations, producing dampened notes.

23. Have open string fun.

One thing that sets top world-class guitarists apart from lesser guitarists is the number of tricks and techniques they draw from and remember using in the heat of the moment. It's interesting to note how, very often, guitar students forget to take advantage of the cool things one can do with the open strings, when I put them on the spot saying: "You, solo! Key of E!"

You can create fun open string pedal point melodies like Alex Lifeson, for example, does in the "YYZ" solo at 2:29 and at the end of the solo at 2:48.

Other examples that come to mind are AC/DC's "Thunderstruck" or Joe Satriani's ending solo in "Crystal Planet."

24. Play melodies linearly on one string, hitting a neighboring open string.

You can also play cool open string double stops as Eddie Van Halen does in "Ain't Talking 'Bout Love" at 1:22. In that solo, Eddie plays melodies on the B string, doubling every melody note on the B string with an open E string.

25. Use chromatic passing notes.

Chromatic = moving by half step.

Passing note = a note that you pass by when moving from a chord tone (or scale note) to another successive chord tone (or scale note).

For example:

- ▶ In the key of C, for the melody **C C♯ D**. The C and D are scale notes, and C♯ is a chromatic passing note.
- ▶ Here's a passing note example that is not a chromatic passing note but a scalar one. Over a C chord, the melody **E F G**. The E and G are chord tones, while the F note is a passing note (passing by from E to G).

Chromatic passing notes create strong forward momentum in melodies. They create a sense of urgency, purpose, and direction, as if leading the listener by the hand.

26. Use chromatic approach notes.

With chromatic approach notes, you're not passing by, but rather deliberately preceding a scale or chord note with a note a half step below or above, that you play before hitting the targeted scale or chord note.

Examples:

- ▶ Over a C chord you can play the melody: **B** C **E♭** E **G♭** G.

    C, E, and G are the chord tones. The bold B, E♭ and G♭ are approach notes approaching the notes of the C chord from a half step below.

    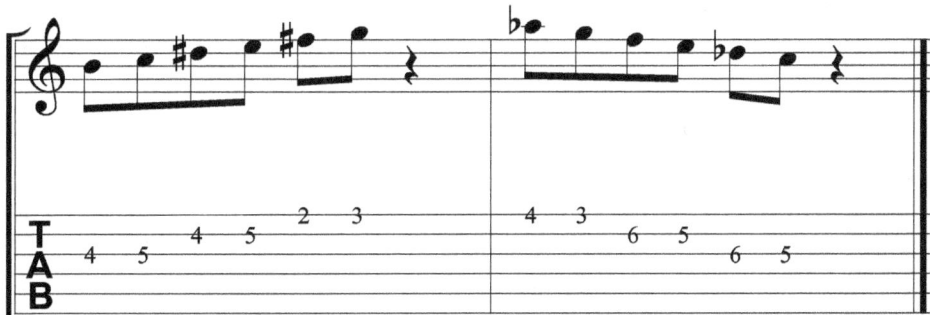

- ▶ In the A minor pentatonic scale root shape fingering, for example, on the top three strings, try this out:
    - ▷ Hit B on the fourth fret on the G string followed by C on the fifth fret
    - ▷ Immediately followed by E♭ on the fourth fret on the B string followed by E on the fifth fret

▷ Immediately followed by A♭ on the fourth fret on the E string followed by A on the fifth fret.

The notes you played on the fourth fret are approach notes approaching the A minor pentatonic scale notes on the fifth fret.

Check it out here:

In addition to approaching a target scale or chord note from a half step below or above, you can also double approach it:

▷ ½ step above – ½ step below – hit target note
▷ ½ step below – ½ step above – hit target note

Here's what "½ step above – ½ step below" looks like:

27. Use chromatic passing double stops.

This is the same as passing notes but with double stops instead of single notes.

28. Use chromatic approach double stops.

This is the same as chromatic approach notes but with double stops.

29. Incorporate triad arpeggios.

In the first couple of years of improvisation study, most guitar students tend to sound **linear or horizontal**, scalar. You can also adopt a more vertical approach to soloing.

The words "vertical" and "linear or horizontal" refer to how a solo looks when notated on a music staff. Melodies move horizontally on a staff, while chords look vertical. All notes in a chord are written on top of one another.

Imagine drawing a line through all the note heads of a melody that is notated on a staff. The motion of that line is called a **melodic curve**. As it turns out, the more a melodic curve moves, the more people tend to be moved (or emotionally touched) by that melody.

To say this differently...

Melodies get all the more melodic when you add a bit more vertical movement. What does that mean? How do you do that? The answer to both these questions is the same: chord arpeggios. Instead of only using scales and scale fingerings to build melodies, throw the occasional arpeggiated triad *(check the "Triads" chapter)* into your phrases. Since you're playing one note per string when arpeggiating the notes in a chord shape, this creates more verticality in the melodies. On a side note, you want to make sure you lift up your finger after every note, so you don't get overlap between the notes. Remember that you want it to sound like a single-note solo, without making it obvious that you're using a chord shape to create melodies.

One of my all-time favorite solos you definitely want to hear is Eric Johnson's solo in "Venus Isle." This solo shows how the use of arpeggios can add a lot of melody to a solo.

30. Arpeggio substitution.

We covered triad substitution in a previous chapter. This is really the same thing, but using arpeggios instead of hitting all the notes simultaneously as a chord. As an example, over a G7 groove you can solo by arpeggiating the notes of a D♭ triad. Try it out! You'll love the interesting, cool colors.

31. Pentatonic substitution.

Check the pentatonic substitution chapter to learn more.

32. Make your note placement (time) more elastic.

Drag notes behind the beat or push notes ahead of the beat.

Don't get locked in the grid provided by the rhythm section. Speak your phrases freely over the rhythmic grid the rhythm section provides. You can speak and lay down your notes and phrases wherever you feel like over that grid.

33. Incorporate odd divisions.

Combine even rhythmic divisions with the occasional triplet or even quintuplet. You find this all over the place in the solos of Shawn Lane, Joe Satriani, and Steve Vai, to name a few. It makes solos more interesting when you throw in the occasional triplet, quintuplet, or more complex beat divisions.

This is one of the ways you can really set yourself apart from the majority of the guitar players who can't get beyond using quarter, eighth, and sixteenth notes in their solos.

34. Use rhythmic displacement of a phrase.

All the greatest improvisers use this technique. What it comes down to is that you play a short melody line, and then keep repeating that exact same line, but now starting it from the second beat, or from the "and" (second eighth) of the second beat, or from the third beat or the "and" of the third beat, and so on. This makes for really interesting lines.

You can hear examples of this displacement in Aerosmith's "Walk This Way" riff. The four-note chromatic melody starts on the first beat, then repeats right after starting on the second sixteenth of the next beat.

Jimmy Page uses the same compositional device to great effect in "Black Dog" at 0:41.

35. Listen to your band.

Listen to the people you play with. If you're too much in your head, and not musically communicating (which requires "listening") with your band members, you will miss really cool things they are doing, which you could feed off of with your solo. The more you feed off of the cool rhythmic and harmonic information they are giving you, the more interesting your solo will sound.

When you use the musical cues and ideas you hear your band members come up with as a source of inspiration to build your solo from, you're relieved from constantly having to reinvent the wheel. Listen to the people you jam with. Don't miss the cool things they do. It's the people you play with who make soloing fun.

You want to play melodies that tell a cool story along with their chord progressions.

36. Rely more on your ear when you improvise.

    a. Really focus on crafting great, moving, interesting melodies on the spot.

    b. Avoid just playing visual patterns and stock phrases that are merely inspired by scale shapes.

    c. Avoid basing your phrases on riffs, fills, and other preconceived, or prefabricated lines, neurologically programmed finger motions, or clichés you're used to playing. There is nothing wrong with having the occasional phrase where your eyes (familiar shapes or patterns) were leading your fingers. This only becomes an issue if that is the only thing you're doing.

    d. Avoid the temptation to want to play something fast just for the sake of it, or to try to do anything just for the sake of it. Focus on your ear, and try to have your ear guide your fingers to cool melody lines. Focus on melodies, not on fingerings. Let your ear guide and decide the melodies, not your fingers.

    e. Step away from visual… into aural.

37. Move around more.

Avoid staying in the same range too long for too many notes in a row. It's freeing to move all over the place on the guitar neck.

38. Use octave jumps.

It's always fun to learn a soloing trick that instantly makes your solos sound amazing, without having to learn complicated concepts or a ton of new stuff.

Here's one of these improvisation techniques you might underuse or not know about yet.

Play a melodic phrase in one of the lower positions, then jump up twelve frets and play exactly the same thing there. The root position minor pentatonic fingering works really well for this. Play a cool soloing line in the key of A minor using the root minor pentatonic fingering on the fifth fret, then jump up an octave to the seventeenth fret and repeat exactly what you played on the fifth fret. Keep moving back and forth between the fifth and seventeenth fret. Make it rapid fire: Don't always leave a pause between the phrase on the fifth fret and its repetition up an octave. Play around with the rhythmic spacing between the phrases. When you make the octave jumps more rapid fire, it will make the solo more energetic and exciting.

39. Avoid playing too many phrases in a row in the bass range.

This made the list because it's so surprisingly common. It might seem redundant after I already made the point that you should "move around more," but I just wanted to make sure the point is clear that you should not play too long in the bass range.

40. Only play the occasional two-note phrase.

Being more melodic means you should not play too many two-note phrases. Melodies require more than two notes to tell a story or say something of value. There's nothing wrong with the occasional two-note phrase. We have the occasional two or three-word sentence too: "Hey!" "What's up?" "You good?" "What's wrong?" "It's hot!"

However, you would never have a whole conversation like that. The same holds true in the language of music. Playing a bunch of two-note phrases in a row is like trying to have a conversation only talking in two-word sentences.

41. Play more three- and four-note phrases.

This ties in to the above point. As it turns out, when you look at the bulk of the phrases that make up great melodies, more often than not those phrases consist of three, maximum four notes.

42. Use vibrato.

Vibrato makes your notes come to life. Key words for a good vibrato are **slow** and **small**. You don't want to quickly quiver the note, and you also don't want big motions that make the note sound out of tune. Gently and slowly move the fingered note up or down. Think of is as massaging your sound. A good vibrato is very subtle. It adds a lot of life to the sound without being distracting. While I could give entire explanations here about how to perform vibrato, the how doesn't really matter—all that matters is that you do it. The how takes care of itself over time as you keep getting better at it just by doing it.

There are as many ways of playing vibrato as there are guitarists. BB King likes shaking his whole hand with his thumb removed from the back of the guitar neck. Steve Vai likes making big circular motions with the finger fretting the note. Steve Morse likes a faster vibrato. Classical guitarists and violin players create vibrato through a sideways left-to-right motion of the fretting finger onto the string, instead of the up-and-down motion of rock guitarists. The technique of how you do it doesn't matter, as long as you get the sound you want.

43. Use octave lines.

While you could of course harmonize any melody with any interval, octaves deserve their own spot here. Melodies doubled in octaves stand out really well in the mix. The octave doubling makes melodies sound much bigger and fuller.

You can hear this to great effect in Jimi Hendrix's "Third Stone from the Sun" at 0:42, or in his intro of "Fire." Wes Montgomery made soloing in octave lines one of his signature style elements. Also, check out the epic intro to Dream Theater's "Under a Glass Moon."

I strongly recommend you practice soloing in octaves. It's a great tool to make certain phrases you want to emphasize stand out with a bigger, fuller sound.

On a different note, check out Led Zeppelin's "Immigrant Song" intro for an entirely different creative use of octaves.

44. Alternate pick.

It pays off to practice and get better at alternate picking. For one, you can play faster than is physically possible with only down strokes. Not that you need to become a shredder, but speed is one of the tools you can use to build up excitement and climax in a solo.

Alternate-picked notes also tend to stand out with more "character." It gives the notes more definition. To hear a great example of what I mean by that, check out Steve Morse's "Tumeni Notes." The melodies in the first two song sections consist of arpeggiated chords for the most part. Hear how very defined every note sounds. Most, if not all, guitar players would sweep pick this (sweeping over the strings in consecutive down or up strokes from string to string). Steve alternate picks every note, even when the notes in the melody are vertically arranged in actual chord shapes. This gives every note better definition, because down-stroked notes have a different timbre than up stroked notes. Down strokes always sound warmer, bigger, and fuller, while up-stroked notes sound a bit thinner and snappier. This alternating between those two timbres is what makes every note stand out as more defined within the flow of notes that make up a melody.

There is also a strong point to be made about the improved rhythmic flow that naturally occurs when one alternate picks. Notes in a melody that fall in between the downbeats (on the "and" in eighth-note melodies or on either the "ee", "and" or "duh" in sixteenth-note melodies) always naturally want to sound weaker than notes that fall right on the downbeats. When you consistently alternate pick, you are much less likely to accidentally give the notes on downbeats the weaker upstroke sound and the notes in between the beats the stronger down stroke sound, which makes the melodic flow sound a bit awkward, not unlike clapping on one and three.

Conclusion: There's only so much you can do with down strokes alone. The only times you would play a melody with solely down strokes would be if:

1. The melody consisted of quarter notes only. (Every note falls on a beat.)
2. You wanted to give the notes in the melody weight (fullness, strength), which would be the case if the melody were an important musical statement you wanted to give some emphasis to.
3. The melody was a bass line, and you wanted it to sound big and full.

Use the technique exercises in the technique chapters to train your alternate picking skills and consistency.

45. Tapping.

Tapping is the technique where you produce notes by hammering (tapping) on the strings with a finger of your picking hand. In tapping solos, the fretting hand usually produces notes with a series of hammer-ons and pull-offs while the picking hand taps the notes higher up the string.

The guitarist who usually comes to mind in lessons about tapping is Eddie Van Halen.

Eddie wasn't the first guitarist to use the technique, but we associate tapping with him because he made it such an integral part of this high-octane soloing style, using it in really well-written rock songs with vocals, which usually have a wider audience appeal than instrumental guitar music.

Here are some examples:

- ▶ Eddie Van Halen: "Eruption," "Beat It" solo (Michael Jackson)
- ▶ Joe Satriani: "Satch Boogie"
- ▶ Greg Howe: "Unlocked" (intro)
- ▶ Steve Vai: "Greasy Kid's Stuff" (2:10)

Then there are the guitarists who push this technique to the maximum, using what is called **eight-finger tapping** or **two-handed playing**. Some of those guitarists who use all four fingers of both hands are Jeff Watson (Night Ranger), Steve Lynch (Autograph), Joel Hoekstra, Don Lappin, Stanley Jordan, and Jennifer Batten.

Here are some examples to check out:

- ▶ Jeff Watson: "Mountain Cathedral"
- ▶ Steve Lynch: "Hammerhead"
- ▶ Jennifer Batten: "Flight of the Bumblebee"
- ▶ Stanley Jordan. Stanley taps everything. Check out his renditions of "Eleanor Rigby" or "Autumn Leaves."

Joe Satriani also uses tapping in compositional ways. Check out "The Forgotten (Part 1)," "Midnight," and "A Day at the Beach" to hear songs entirely played using the tapping technique.

46. Use one-note tapping.

Other than playing extended soloing sections with tapping, you can also use the technique to just play one note in a melodic phrase.

Some of the reasons why you would want to do this:

> ▶ When you run out of fretting hand fingers in fast shredding lines on one string.
>
> ▶ To play a note that is out of reach higher up the string.
>
> ▶ As an effect. A note that is tapped has a different sound and feel than notes that are played the more conventional ways with the fretting hand.
>
> ▶ As a performance thing, because it visually looks cool. As an example, Joe Satriani oftentimes taps the ending A bass note in "Tears in the Rain" when he performs the song live. He could simply hit an open A string instead, but that doesn't look as cool live.

You can hear an example of one-note tapping used to great effect in Steve Vai's "The Attitude Song" at 0:17. Steve bends a note, then taps higher up that string and releases the bend with his tapping finger still on that higher note. Jennifer Batten oftentimes uses that technique too of tapping into bends. Shredders very often tap a single note that is out of reach higher up that string in their fast, legato lines.

47. Finger pick solos.

It might seem silly this made the list, but if you've never soloed while finger picking the notes, you should really try it out. You will find out that you will solo differently. You will play different types of phrases, and will like the really cool sound you get when soloing with just fingers. Getting into finger picking techniques here would be beyond the scope of this book. The gist of it is that you want to experiment and find what works for you.

What works for me, and I think this is also the finger picking technique that most guitar players adhere to for soloing, is to work in two-string sections with thumb and index/middle fingers. For instance, when soloing on the D and G strings, my thumb plays the notes on the D string and my index and middle fingers the G string notes. When changing strings, I move my thumb and fingers down to the next string set.

48. Use hybrid picking.

Hybrid picking is the name of the technique where you combine a pick and fingers. Country pickers use the technique all the time in country rhythm guitar. The technique is also used in improvisation, to make certain harder-to-pick note combinations or more intervallic lines easier to play. You definitely want to check out Brett Garsed, who adopted hybrid picking as a major part of his soloing technique. Notice when you check out videos of his playing how much he switches between pick and middle finger.

Other notable guitarists who use this technique in their guitar solos are Guthrie Govan, Carl Verheyen, Wayne Krantz, Tommy Emmanuel, and Danny Gatton.

Stevie Ray Vaughan plays a magnificent hybrid picked chordal phrase in "Mary Had a Little Lamb" at 1:23.

49. Try slide guitar.

It's a testament to how amazing and versatile guitar is that you can even play the instrument sliding a bottleneck or metal tube over the strings. Some notable slide players to check out: Duane Allman, Bonnie Raitt, Sonny Landreth and Derek Trucks.

One of my favorite slide guitarists and slide solos is Chris Rea and the fiery solo he plays in "Road to Hell".

One of the ways I really like slide being used is when it is used not to play the whole solo, but as part of a solo, as Jimi Hendrix did in "All Along the Watchtower" at 1:59.

For some impressive, creative, advanced slide guitar, listen to Jeff Beck's "Angel Footsteps." Jeff plays a melody with a slide way up past the range of the guitar neck.

50. Switch pickups more often.

Top guitarists like Steve Vai, Steve Morse, Guthrie Govan or Joe Satriani switch pickups often during live performances. Most guitar players get so wrapped up in the minutia of notes, and fingerings, and patterns, and so on, that they forget to take advantage of all the sounds they have readily available at the flick of the pickup selector switch. Why would you want to play a whole solo with exactly the same pickup sound, if you could make your solo much more expressive by switching sounds for different solo sections or phrases? Steve Morse and Eric Johnson are especially known to be really attentive to switching pickups during solos as a means to create different textures and moods.

Even Stevie and Jimi creatively switch pickups to enhance their solos. Stevie Ray Vaughan switches from neck to bridge pickup at 0:59 in "I Wanna Testify," then again at 1:16 and then again two bars later. And for a really creative use, listen to Jimi Hendrix's "Voodoo Child (Slight Return)" at 4:55, where he switches back and forth between pickups while slowly releasing a bend.

51. Use harmonics.

Harmonics are the pure sine-wave sounds you get when you get the string to only vibrate around a node. Not to get too much into the physics of it all, let's instead focus on how harmonics can be creatively used in solos.

There are, broadly speaking, five ways to produce harmonics.

- a. **Natural harmonics**
    - i. These are harmonics that naturally pop out when you pick a string, which you lightly touch right on top of the fifth, seventh, ninth, twelfth, seventeenth, nineteenth, or twenty-forth fret. These are not the only locations where you can find natural harmonics. Some other locations include the fourth fret, the third fret, and in between the second and third fret.
    - ii. Examples:
        - ▶ Eddie Van Halen in "Ain't Talking 'Bout Love" at 2:05
        - ▶ Joe Satriani's intro in "Up In The Sky"
        - ▶ Jeff Beck does an exceptional job in "Two Rivers," in which he plays almost the entire melody with natural harmonics.

b. Pinch harmonics (also called "artificial harmonics")

    i. These harmonics are produced when you pick a string while lightly touching the string with the side of your thumb a fraction after the pick attack. This produces a squealing note. You want to play with distortion for this to work well. It's also easier to get the pinched harmonics to come out on thicker strings, which is why this technique is probably more often used on bass strings.

    ii. Two guitarists who incorporate this technique as a major part of their style are Zakk Wylde who played with Ozzy and his band Black Label Society, and Diamond Darrell from Pantera. Swedish guitarist Matthias Eklundh is another who uses pinch harmonics very regularly.

    iii. Examples:

- The squealing notes in Steve Vai's "The Attitude Song" intro
- Zakk Wylde in Ozzy's "No More Tears" at 0:41 (the ending note on the heavy riff after the first vocal line). Zakk plays numerous pinch harmonics throughout the song.
- Dimebag Darrell at 0:14 and every couple of notes thereafter in the "Cemetery Gates" intro

c. Tapped harmonics

    i. These harmonics are the result of quickly tapping right onto the fret that is exactly five, seven, or twelve frets above a fingered note.

    ii. Examples

- Eddie Van Halen at the beginning of the "Poundcake" solo *(check the official music video to see Eddie tap the harmonic.)*
- Eddie Van Halen: the first melody line and ending of "Spanish Fly"

d. Picked harmonics

    i. I've also seen these called "touch harmonics." You produce these harmonics when you pick a string, holding the pick between thumb and middle finger, while lightly touching the string with the tip of the picking hand's pointer finger, twelve frets above a note fingered with the fretting hand.

    ii. Example:

- Steve Morse with Deep Purple in the song "Sometimes I Feel Like Screaming" at 1:15. He plays all notes in the main guitar melody with picked harmonics. Check out a live performance of this song on YouTube so you see how to do this.

e. Harp harmonics

  i. These are a bit like picked harmonics, but you mix the harmonics up with non-harmonics notes that you let ring together, or pick multiple harmonics that you let ring within a fingered chord. This creates a harp-like sound.

  ii. Examples:

  ▶ Steve Morse in the first melody of one of my favorite Steve Morse songs, "Country Colors".

  ▶ Lenny Breau used harp harmonics very often.

52. Use scale cascades.

I don't think I've ever heard this used in any other style than country music.

Here's an example:

You want to ring out all notes as much as possible. Only lift up a finger when you have to. By the time you hit the last note, you will hear a full G chord ringing.

53. Mix up the note lengths, spaces, and durations.

"Rhythm" in soloing isn't only about where you place things or about beat divisions. It's also about how long or how short you make the notes. Do you let notes sustain into one another or do you leave spaces between notes? All that said, you want to mix things up. Avoid playing too many long, sustained notes.

In addition, avoid cutting every note short. Let the notes breathe and sing. Avoid (unintentionally) leaving spaces between all the notes. This is what happens when you lift up your finger off a note a bit too early before you hit the next note. It makes the melodies sound choppy, frantic, and usually also less memorable as a result.

On the other hand, melodies with too many long, sustained notes tend to sound boring. If you're still in the stage of figuring out how to keep a better balance: keep soloing. Record yourself or really listen to yourself when you solo. Over time, you will find a better balance between shorter and longer sustained notes.

54. Incorporate staccato.

We talked in the previous point about cutting all notes short. That is exactly what staccato is. The Italian word "staccato" means "detached" or "separate." It's very much the opposite of "legato." In legato, all notes fluently flow from one into the next through a series of slides, hammer-ons, and pull-offs.

Staccato examples:

- ▶ Richie Blackmore's "Smoke on the Water" riff, with every note but four long ones played staccato
- ▶ Paul Gilbert's "Get Out of My Yard," starting at 00:11. The combination of palm muting with heavy distortion creates a staccato feel to the fast notes.
- ▶ Steppenwolf's "Screaming Night Hog." The short staccato notes add a lot of character and spunk to the opening riff.
- ▶ Lenny Kravitz's "Always on the Run" riff has a bit of staccato attitude to it also.

55. Harmonize melody lines with different intervals.

You can harmonize melodies with 3rds, 4ths, 5ths... any interval really. You can learn more about this in the chapters on intervals and 3rds.

Some fun examples:

- ▶ Van Morrison's "Brown Eyed Girl" intro is played with 3rds.
- ▶ In "Dreaming #11," Joe Satriani alternates in the intro between 2nds and 3rds.
- ▶ In "Memories," at 00:52, you can hear Joe Satriani play a cool line in 5ths.
- ▶ Bon Jovi's "Dead or Alive" intro melody is harmonized in 6ths.
- ▶ Sam and Dave's "Soul Man" intro is played in 6th intervals.

56. Solo with chords.

Besides intervals or single notes, you can also solo with full chords.

You would think that chord soloing is very much a jazz guitarist thing, but it works equally well in blues, rock, or pop.

For a great example, listen to Stevie Ray Vaughan in "Love Struck Baby" at 1:11 – 1:23. More examples:

- ▶ From the same Stevie album, listen to "Dirty Pool" for amazing chordal work. The solo starts at 2:55.
- ▶ Jimi Hendrix in "Come On (Part 1)" at 2:11
- ▶ Jimi's "Little Wing" intro pretty much stands as a solo guitar piece composed of all great chordal work.
- ▶ Mark Knopfler plays a ton of tasty chordal phrases in "Once Upon a Time in the West" (the live "Alchemy" album) at 4:37 and 7:19.

You can also see a transcribed example of how to do this in the Triad Substitution chapter. It shows how to solo with Dm and Em chord shapes over a G chord groove.

57. Use unisons.

You play a unison when you hit two different versions of the same note on different strings. The intro to Jimi Hendrix's "Hey Joe" starts with a unison. So does Stevie Ray Vaughan's "Pride and Joy." Unisons have a characteristic sound that can sound a bit scream-y, especially when you play them with overdrive. They can add character and attitude to solos.

58. Play a whole solo with only three or four notes.

That's something that especially blues guys are very good at. This pretty much sums up most of B.B. King's career.

There is a lot to learn from practicing the discipline to try to say a whole lot with very few notes. I strongly recommend you deliberately practice on this. Pick three notes, then play a ten-minute solo with only these three notes.

In the beginning, you will probably think it sounds boring. As you get more experienced at this, you will find ways to make it more and more interesting. Some of the things that help:

- Play less: make the phrases short.
- Heavily focus on the use of dynamics.
- Leave longer silences between phrases.
- Be more rhythmic and rhythmically more creative with the note placements and durations.

59. Use interval fingerings to create interesting melody lines.

As you know, you can play intervals either harmonically or melodically.

When you play the two notes in an interval fingering melodically, you get a two-note melody. There are two options here. You can either play the highest note first followed by lowest note, or vice versa.

In addition, you can move that interval fingering through the scale. This is where things get interesting.

1. You can move horizontal staying on the same string set. This gives you four options. You can move:
    - Scalar ascending moving up the string to the next note
    - Scalar descending to the next note down
    - Intervallic leap (larger than a 2nd interval) up the scale
    - Intervallic leap (larger than a 2nd interval) down the scale

2. You can move the interval fingerings vertically over the six strings instead of horizontally over the same two strings. This creates wider intervallic soloing lines.

Imagine combining all of the above! Pick an interval—let's say 3rds. And let's pick the key of C.

Play a backing track in C major to solo over. Solo on one string set, moving up and down that string set with 3rd-interval fingerings, scalar by step or by leap in bigger horizontal motions on that string set, sometimes hitting the higher note first and sometimes the lower note first in the fingerings.

Once this gets easier, see if you can stay in one position, playing 3rd intervals melodically, while moving vertically across the six string sets.

Try to do both motions at the same time. For example, hit the notes A and C on the low E and A strings, then on the same two strings hit B and D, then move down a string set. Hit C and E on the A and D strings, move up horizontally on the same string set and hit the notes D and F, then move down vertically again to the same string set. Hit F and A on the D and G strings followed by the notes G and B on the same two strings, then move down a string set again. Hit B and D on the G and B strings followed by C and E on the same two strings, then move down to the lowest string set and play two 3rd intervals there. The following example shows how this works.

You can literally move in any direction horizontally, skip string sets vertically, and make big sideways, horizontal leaps while moving vertically up or down string sets. The sky is the limit.

You can even switch intervals, where you for example alternate between 3rds and 4ths, or any interval combination.

As if this were not enough yet, you can make the lines all the more intervallic and interesting sounding when you pick the occasional open string note in between.

For example, right before you hit the 3rd interval notes G and B on the D string (5th fret) and G string (4th fret), you can hit an open D string right before hitting the G note on the D string, or the open G string right before hitting the B note on the G string.

This creates really interesting melodies when you move vertically over string sets.

Here's an example that you can play in the key of C or Am:

Here's an example showing more switches between open strings and with some extra randomness, which makes the line more interesting sounding.

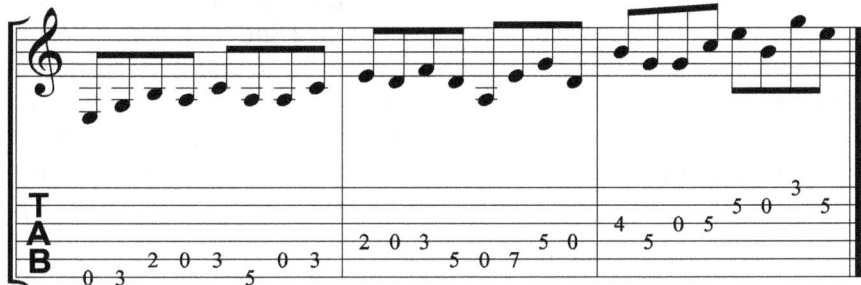

Those are all just examples with 3rd intervals. Experiment with any intervals and any interval combinations. Not only that, experiment being rhythmically more creative than in the given examples, which all show melodies with only eighth notes. If you think this all sounds really cool, wait till you hear yourself play these types of intervallic melodies while combining more diverse rhythmic combinations. There is so much more you can do with this improvisation technique—much more than this book can cover.

All of this will give you a good head start from which you can experiment and take this further.

This improvisation approach should open up whole new worlds of new melodic ideas. Given how cool this sounds, I'm surprised more guitar players don't use this soloing technique.

60. Use rakes.

A rake is a technique where you sweep-pick downward over a couple of muted strings, with the pick ending the down-stroked sweep on a non-muted note. Raking vertically over muted strings creates a percussive sound preceding the note you want to ring.

You can mute the neighboring strings you rake over, by touching them with the picking hand lying on those strings, or with the fretting hand fingers lying over those strings.

Hear how cool this sounds in Pink Floyd's "Another Brick in The Wall, pt. 2" at 2:27, where David Gilmour rakes into a note he bends right after.

It's one of the tools we have to make solos more expressive and give melodies more character.

Here's an exercise:

Play a C major scale on the B string, raking into every note.

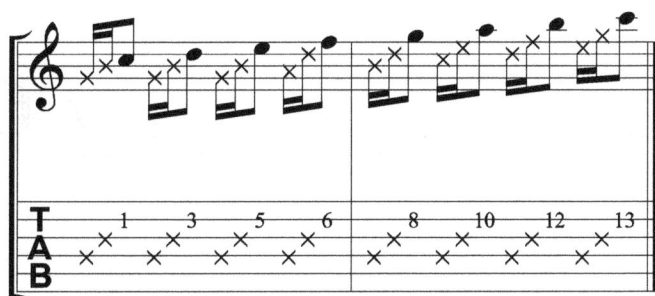

61. Use whammy flutter.

You can only produce this effect when your guitar has a floating tremolo style bridge. "Floating" means that the bridge can be pushed forward and pulled back from its neutral, at-rest point. Bridges can float when the wood is carved away under the bridge, allowing the bridge to be pulled up in pitch, which is what you do when you pull on the whammy bar. With these type of bridge setups, you get a chirpy cricket type of sound when you hit the whammy bar hard. You can hear this effect in Steve Vai's "Greasy Kid's Stuff" at 2:20.

62. Experiment with different picks.

It probably might seem odd that this item made this list. As turns out, the pick you use will affect how fast you can play. It will also affect your sound, and to some extent even the phrasing and so on. Experiment with a vast number of different picks. For some years, I played 4mm thick picks. I still love them. Gypsies play crazy fast, technical lines with a big full sound, using really thick picks. Experiment also with picks made of organic or unusual materials. For a number of years now, I have been in love with picks made of bone. There's a certain unique, relaxed feel that you get from picks that are made of organic materials. Hard to explain it. You have to experience it. Before that, I used picks from Red Bear Trading Company for a couple of years—expensive, but their picks feel like they're made of tortoise shell. Experiment!

63. Try Hendrix-y hammered double stops.

This is a very pianistic approach to guitar playing, that Jimi brought to an entirely new level. You can hear a ton of great examples of this technique in the instrumental intro to "Little Wing."

The way to perform this: Play two or three notes that you hit simultaneously, usually barred with one finger, then hammer onto a higher note on one of those two strings without muting the other note(s)/string(s) that are still ringing.

Try it out! In the key of A minor, press down the 5th fret on the D and G strings with your pointer finger. That's a G and a C note. Then hammer onto the 7th fret of the D string, producing an A note with your ring finger, without touching the G string with that ring finger so that that C note on the G string keeps sustaining.

Here's how to play this and two more examples.

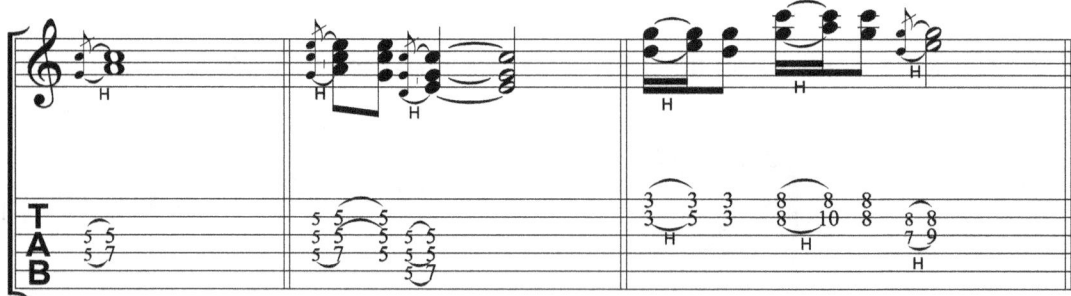

64. Use the harmonics gimmick.

I couldn't really think of a name for this, but it's such a cool thing to know about, it had to make this list. This is something you would see Steve Vai or Joe Satriani do.

First off, make sure you have a fair amount of distortion on. Second, it helps to be on the bridge pickup, so you have more shimmery high frequencies.

So, here are two ways to do this:

1. Tremolo-pick as fast as you can on an open bass string. It works best on one of the three bass strings. Meanwhile, very lightly touch that string with one of your fretting hand fingers without pressing on the string, and slide your finger horizontally over the string with a very light touch. This creates a plethora of cool harmonics as you slide over the string.

2. With one of your stronger fretting hand fingers, play a fast thrill on the second fret of one of the bass strings. It doesn't have to be the second fret. This would also work with a thrill on the first, third, or fourth fret, as long as you stay on one of the lower frets. Meanwhile, very lightly touch that string with one of your picking hand fingertips somewhere above the pickups. Slide that picking hand finger horizontally over that string while touching it very lightly. If you do this right, you should hear a really cool series of harmonics that keep rapidly changing according to how quickly you slide your finger across the string.

It's a cool, fun little gimmick you can throw in in a solo. Especially during live shows, it's one of these things that easily impresses people.

65. Try the constant structure phrase.

In the "Pentatonic Substitution" chapter, you learned that there are four different minor pentatonic scales you can play over a C chord. (A, B, D and E minor). This leads to a very interesting, advanced sounding improvisation technique that you will absolutely love knowing about. I call this "constant structure phrase soloing" because you repeat the exact intervallic structure of a phrase, across different minor pentatonic scales.

The concept is this:

- ▶ Over a C chord groove, play a **short** three- or four-note phrase in the A (or B or D or E) minor pentatonic root shape. The word "short" is an important word here. This improvisation concept doesn't work with long phrases with too many notes.

- ▶ Then, play exactly **the very same** line, same fingering, same rhythm, on the same strings, same everything, in the B minor, D minor, and E minor pentatonic (or A minor) scale root shape fingerings. You basically repeat the same phrase across any of those four minor pentatonic scales over a C chord.

As an example, let's say that you play the following phrase in the A minor pentatonic root shape.

The idea is that you play exactly the same phrase shape over a C chord, in the B, D, and E minor pentatonic scale root shapes, which looks like this:

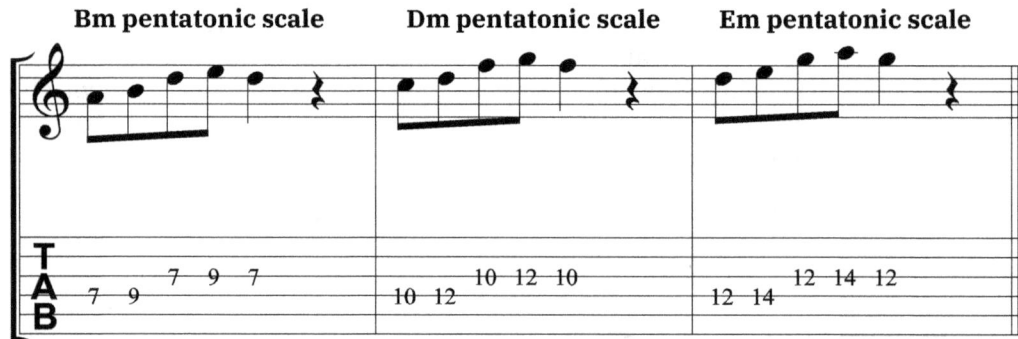

Not to beat a dead horse, but notice how the finger pattern is exactly the same every single time? I'm reiterating this over and again to hit the message home: Play the same thing across the different minor pentatonic scales that work over a C chord. Don't just play a phrase followed by an entirely different phrase right after in one of the other three minor pentatonic locations. You'll just end up sounding like you're playing a scale.

It's the phrase symmetry and consistent repetition across four different pentatonic keys over a static chord that creates this unique improvisation sound.

Also notice how the rhythm is very consistent across the repetitions in the four pentatonic scales. That consistency is what makes this sound so cool.

In a way, it sounds like you're soloing with four scales simultaneously over one chord. But at the same time, you're not, because the A, D, and E minor pentatonic scales all consist of naturals only, which makes them all partial C major scales.

Whatever phrase you come up with, keep in mind that you don't have to go in order from A to B to D to E minor pentatonic. Mix up the scale order. Start a phrase in any of those four minor pentatonic scales. You don't have to (and you don't want to) always start a new phrase in the A minor pentatonic position. Also, make sure to be rhythmically creative with the starting point of the phrase repetitions. You don't have to start every phrase repetition from the same beat in every bar. That would sound too predictable. Moreover, you can speed up (rush) or slow down the notes. You just want to keep the rhythmic division of the notes in relationship to one another relatively similar.

After three or four repetitions of the same phrase, come up with a new short phrase, which you'll then repeat exactly the same way through one or more of the remaining minor pentatonic scales.

Above all, experiment! That is how you will get better at this.

Given how special and interesting this sounds, it always amazes me that more guitar players don't know about this or use this. But now you do, and that makes me happy.

66. Use oblique bends.

Oblique bends are what you play when you pick two notes simultaneously, then bend one of those two notes. This creates what is called **oblique motion** between the notes. It's usually the lower of the two notes that is bent. Oblique bends are heavily used in country soloing. You can hear Mark Knopfler play oblique bends in "Sultans of Swing" at 1:38, 2:02, 2:55, and 3:41.

67. Use unison bends.

Pick two notes that are a minor or major 2nd interval apart on two adjacent strings. Bend the lower note up in pitch till both notes sound together like a unison. Listen to Jimi Hendrix playing a melody using unison bends in "Manic Depression" at 1:18. Steve Vai plays unison bends in "Greasy Kid's Stuff" at 0:14, 1:50, and 2:22.

68. Play double bends.

You can bend two notes simultaneously. It creates a really cool wailing sound. This is different from oblique bends where only one of the two notes is bent.

This double bend is usually played with the ring finger pressing down the G and B strings on the same fret, then bending both notes up.

You can hear Jimi Hendrix play this:

- ▶ Under the word "Dagger" in the song "Dolly Dagger"
- ▶ In "51st Anniversary" (one of my favorite Hendrix songs) at 1:30
- ▶ In "Spanish Castle Magic" at 1:24

69. Try the bend one string and pre-bend/release another string technique.

There isn't really a name for this. You can hear this technique in the Eagles' "Hotel California" solo at 5:02. What this comes down to is:

- ▶ Play a note and bend it.
- ▶ While bending that string up, grab the neighboring string underneath your fretting/bending finger, so that string gets bend up a bit too.

- ▶ Strike that neighboring string, which is now underneath your finger and hence fretted, with your pick.
- ▶ Release the bend.

This creates the cool effect of a note bending up in pitch, only to stop and immediately be followed by a lower pre-bent note, releasing down in pitch right after.

70. Use legato.

Legato is the technique whereby you only pick the occasional note, and produce most of the notes in your melody lines with series of hammer-ons, pull-offs and slides. Joe Satriani, Steve Vai, Allen Holdsworth, and Guthrie Govan are only some examples of guitarists who love legato. Because few notes are picked, the melody lines sound very fluent. The legato technique also makes it easier to play really fast lines even if you don't have good picking technique.

71. Be all about expression.

Here's a quick list of some other things you can do to make a solo more expressive.

i. Slides from the scale note below

ii. Slides from far below

iii. Slides from the scale note above

iv. Slides from far above

v. Wide bends (David Gilmour often plays wide bends.)

vi. Bends from the note below

vii. Pre bends (bend first, then pick the note, then release the bend.)

viii. Release. This is what you do when you release the pull on a bent string back from tension to neutral string position. The pitch, raised when you bend a string, drops to a lower note when you release the bend.

ix. Hammer-ons

x. Pull-offs

xi. Thrill (a series of consecutive hammer-ons and pull-offs)

xii. Pick tapping (Use the edge of the pick to tap notes. Listen to Joe Satriani's "Satch Boogie" at 1:55.)

xiii. Tremolo Picking. This is what you do when you repetitively pick one note as fast as you can. Check out Stevie Ray Vaughan's "Dirty Pool", and Eddie Van Halen at the end of the "Beat It" solo.

xiv. Micro bends (bends smaller than a half step)

xv. Pick scratches. Scrape the edge of your pick over the bass strings, either from head stock to guitar body or vice versa. Pick scratches sound all the cooler when you're playing through a distortion pedal or overdriven amp.

xvi. Pressing the strings behind the nut. This is a way for guitar players who play guitars with fixed bridges to reproduce the sound of a whammy bar pulling up a pitch. The effect this creates sounds quite different from bending.

72. Sing your lines along while playing.

This is something you often hear jazz musicians do. Singing your melodies while playing them can improve your solos because it makes them more speech-like. You're also not as apt to overplay when you only play what you can sing.

73. Remember: there are no wrong notes.

You never have to worry about playing a wrong note. There is no such thing. Every note you play that you didn't mean to play is an open opportunity to take it somewhere interesting. Repeat the "wrong" note so it sounds like you meant to play it, then resolve it somewhere. This leads to the important lesson to be learned: "There are no wrong notes, there are only notes you don't resolve."

As a matter of fact, as a fun exercise: Deliberately hit any random wrong note and see if you can turn it into an opportunity to create really cool melody lines. See if you can find a way to not make it sound like a mistake.

Here's a hint: Moving up or down a half step will usually resolve any wrong notes. After all, most scales consist of whole and half steps. When you hit a "wrong" sounding note, you're almost certainly right between two scale notes a whole step apart.

74. Try the half step up gimmick.

As a comedic gimmick, deliberately hit a minor second interval up a half step from the root in your solo. It's a deliberate mistake that comes with a high comedic value because of how out-of-proportion dissonant it sounds. It sounds so bad that most people will think you almost certainly must have done it deliberately (but they can never really be sure).

75. Incorporate canned phrases/clichés.

I could have titled this: "Learn and memorize musical vocabulary."

Top improvisers don't constantly come up with new phrases on the spot. Experienced improvisers have a certain vocabulary of phrases memorized that are common to that style.

Here's an excerpt from a handout my guitar students get when we tackle the "Blues Clichés" lesson. The handout contains a vast collection of phrases that keep appearing all over blues and rock guitar solos. Students who want to improve their blues and rock soloing are always happily surprised to hear how vastly better their guitar solos instantly sound, just as result of using these phrases.

On a quick, fun side note: When teaching a student who loves country music, I tend to call these "country clichés." As turns out, these exact same phrases, when played over a country-style rhythm part, completely sound like a kick-ass country solo.

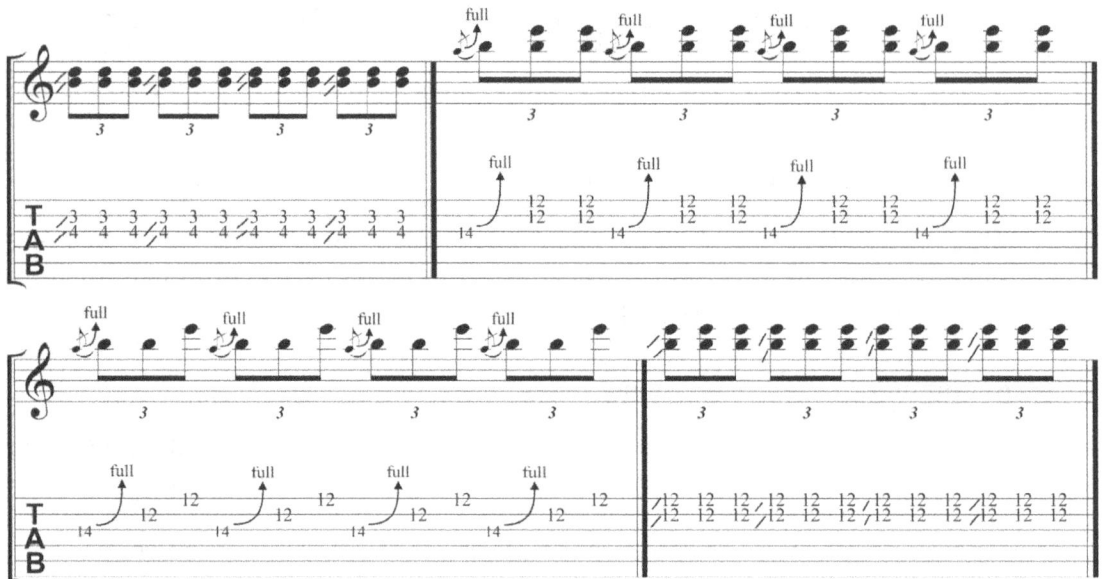

Spend time learning vocabulary. It is time well-spent. You might be amazed to find out how much better your solos sound and how much easier it is to come up with kick-ass melodies once you have amassed a good amount of vocabulary to throw in.

76. Incorporate the melody of a well-known song in your solo.

People absolutely love it when they suddenly hear "Frère Jacques" or "Twinkle Little Star" or the "Smoke on the Water" riff in the middle of your guitar solo. Practice this and use it live. It will help you attract and hold the attention of your audiences.

77. Incorporate parts taken from other solos.

This is to some extent similar to the idea of incorporating well-known melodies in your solo. You could throw in parts or phrases of other solos, like for example the "Stairway to Heaven," "Hotel California," or "Purple Haze" solo (or any solo for that matter).

78. Practice composed lines until they show up in your solo.

I cannot possibly overstate the importance of this technique.

To reiterate an earlier point made, the people who we think of very highly as the greatest masters of jazz improvisation, are not entirely improvising their solos.

When you study the solos of Charlie Parker or John Coltrane, who we consider geniuses of jazz improvisation, you will find that part of their solos consists of constantly repeating phrases that keep reappearing in all their solos. I was incredibly surprised myself many years ago, when I transcribed Charlie Parker and John Coltrane solos, to find out that the same phrases kept reoccurring over and over again in *all* their improvisations, on albums they recorded many years apart.

What does that tell you? It tells you that they composed and then practiced those phrases until those melody lines started showing up in their solos. Only part of the often long improvisations are actually improvised.

79. Use triad pairs over a given chord.

Check the chapter "Triad Substitution" to learn more about this.

80. Use volume swells.

This is how you make a guitar sound like a violin or cello or a string pad. You can either use a volume pedal or the volume knob on your guitar. From Jeff Beck, to Allan Holdsworth in his chordal playing, to Steve Morse, every guitar player probably has a song where they use volume swells.

Deep Purple's Richie Blackmore loved this. You can hear him use this in the song "Fools" from the *Fireball* album, at 4:12.

Zakk Wylde uses them in the intro of Black Label Society's "In This River."

81. Incorporate melodic sequences.

A melodic sequence is a repetition of the melodic curve or intervallic pattern of a short phrase, repeated starting on different starting notes in the scale. Melodic sequences help build structure and melodic cohesiveness into a solo.

For example:

- ▶ C D E | D E F | E F G | F G A | etc.
- ▶ C D E C | D E F D | E F G E | F G A F | etc.

Do you see the pattern in each example? If not, play the notes and you might be able to hear the constantly repeating melodic pattern climbing up the scale.

Here's a melodic sequence played on the B string in the key of C.

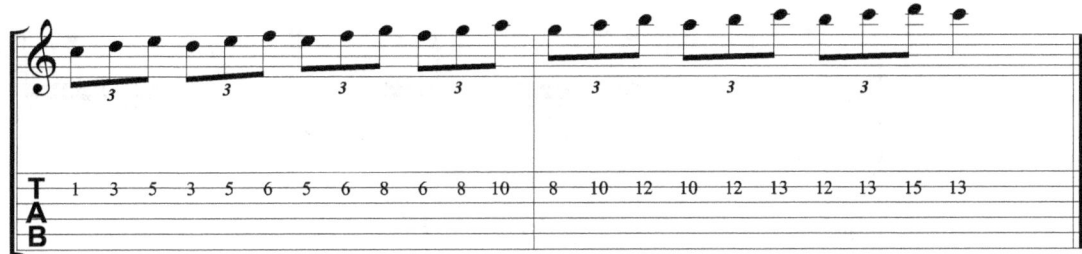

This following one is a six-note sequence.

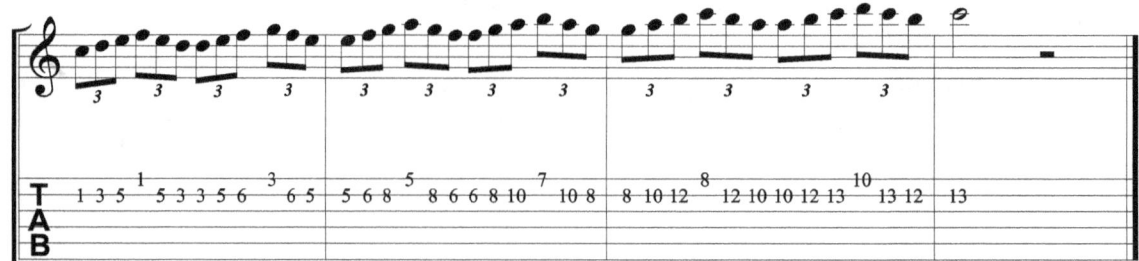

This one is on the bass strings.

Here's a melodic sequence in-position.

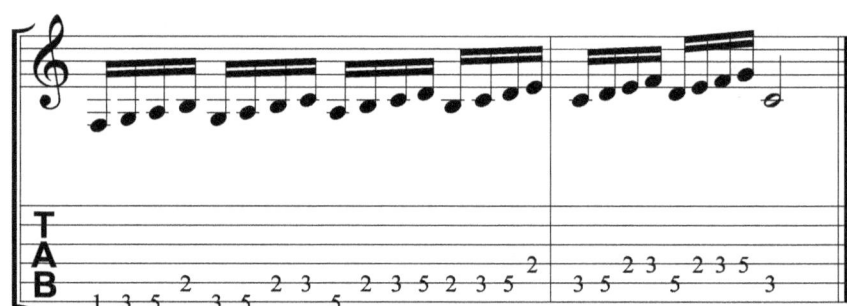

Here's one that moves down a 3rd up a 2nd.

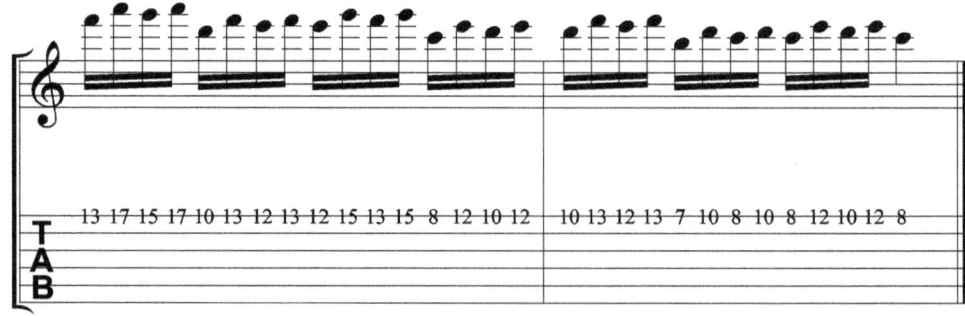

Melodic sequences are heavily used in the guitar work of neo-classical shredders like Yngwie Malmsteen, Jason Becker, Vinnie Moore, and Patrick Rondat.

Examples
- Yngwie Malmsteen's intro in "Far Beyond the Sun"
- In "Far Beyond the Sun," the main melody at 0:23 consists of a two-note sequence that climbs up the scale.
- Yngwie Malmsteen in "Rising Force"—the melody at 2:11
- Patrick Rondat's "Rape of the Earth" at 3:01

82. Use scale patterns.

You might think to yourself: "Aren't scale patterns the same as melodic sequences?"

In a musical and theoretical sense, melodic sequences are scale patterns, and scale patterns are melodic sequences. Though some of the differences might be a matter of semantics, they do exist.

1. **Melodic sequences**
   a. The term "melodic sequence" describes a type of melody that is formed when you repeat a short melodic phrase starting on various notes in a scale, those starting points being spaced in a repetitive interval pattern, like for example down three letters up one letter.
   b. You think more like a composer when you use melodic sequences.
   c. They sound composed. You can see why when you study the above examples. There is a lot of structure created by a pattern of motion through the scale that is strictly adhered to.
   d. The short melodic phrases move predictably through the scale in repetitive intervals. In the first four examples above, the melodic phrase consistently moves up its repetition to the next scale note. In the last example, the melodic phrase consistently moves down a 3rd and up a 2nd.
   e. It involves consistent, strict repetition of the melodic phrase's rhythm pattern. The note placement is strictly adhered to across every repetition of the melodic phrase.

2. **Scale patterns**
   a. With scale patterns, the thought processes lean a bit more toward the mindset of an improviser and a bit less that of a composer. The focus tends to be a bit more on the construction of melodies through shapes and visual patterns that you move around the neck.
   b. One of the big differences is that scale patterns don't have to move in predictable ways, while melodic sequences always do. A great example of this is the constant structure phrase soloing technique discussed in point number **65** in this list. Just by the fact that you are repeating a phrase in different locations, you are dealing with a scale pattern, but it doesn't sound like a melodic sequence, because you're not repeating it moving in a repetitive, predictable fashion. You can start your phrase in B minor pentatonic, move up to D minor

pentatonic, move back to B minor pentatonic, or instead move to E minor pentatonic, then A minor pentatonic. The diligent repetition of the phrase in different locations makes it sound like a scale pattern, but the lack of a defined, predictable motion through the scale is why it doesn't sound like a sequence.

c. You can perform the melodic phrase with minor rhythmic variations or alterations during consecutive repetitions, and it will still sound like that scale pattern.

83. Solo with randomly moving 2^{nds}.

Here's another improvisation idea that uses a scale pattern without being a melodic sequence.

The idea is simple: Randomly play nothing but 2nd intervals all over the neck, for an extended period of time.

The more (randomly) you jump all across and around the neck, the cooler it sounds.

It's the combination of random large interval leaps across the neck or across the strings, with the symmetry of a repetitive two-note interval pattern that constantly repeats, that gives this improvisation technique such a unique, interesting sound.

In addition to that, play around with any rhythmic grouping combinations.

Just to give you an idea of what that may look or sound like:

I love how this sounds. This is again one of these phrasing and melodic techniques where I wonder: "Why do I not hear more guitar players use this?"

84. Use a kill-switch

When I had one of my Suhr guitars custom built, one of the things on my wish list for that guitar was a kill-switch. It's a switch *(or button)* that you can install on your guitar, and it interrupts the signal flow when you press it, abruptly stopping the sound coming from your instrument. I loved the idea of being able to create all these cool rhythmic effects that you hear Rage Against The Machine's Tom Morello or Buckethead produce with their kill-switch set-up guitars.

John Suhr advised against installing the switch, because, if I remember well, of something having to do with it affecting the guitar's overall sound quality. The switch didn't make it onto my guitar, but luckily, it exists in pedal form. Murder One is a company that makes kill-switch pedals.

If you play a Les Paul or any guitar that has separate volume controls for each pickup, then you can get the kill-switch effect by turning one pickup volume control completely down and the other one completely up, and switching back and forth between the two pickups.

85. Out-of-key soloing

This is another cool concept you'll have a ton of fun with.

Have you ever heard solos where it seems like the improviser is playing notes that belong to an entirely different scale or key than what the band is playing, feeling intrigued as to why those notes don't sound wrong?

This is usually something you're more likely to hear in jazz rock, fusion, jazz, or even some R&B solos. One of the reasons why the notes don't sound wrong is that the improviser resolves the "wrong" notes back into the right key.

This is an application of one of the previously shared tidbits of musical wisdom: "There are no wrong notes, there are only notes you don't resolve."

There is a fun, fairly easy way you can already pull this off, using a scale you already know really well. All we need for you to rock out of key is the minor pentatonic scale.

Here's how you do this:

Over an Am groove, solo for a couple of beats with the A minor root shape, then without pausing the flow of notes, swiftly move up a half step, continuing your melody with notes of the B♭ minor pentatonic root shape, then resolve your melody back down a half step, ending it with notes of the A minor pentatonic.

This half step up trick creates the out-of-key sound against the Am groove. The B♭ minor scale doesn't sound "wrong," because you resolved those notes when you moved back down a half step into the "right" scale.

Here are a couple of tricks that will give you a head start:

1. Try to only play the out-of-key notes toward the end of a measure. A bar in music is a cycle that starts strong on the downbeat, and then weakens toward its end. Wrong notes sound less wrong when they're played toward the end of a bar. It is for that same reason that you want to resolve back into the A minor scale on (or before) the downbeat. You want to avoid hitting wrong notes where they are most noticeable, which is at the beginning of the bar.

2. Notice how, in the below example, the melody moves back and forth between the two scales by stepwise motion. The subtle, small, stepwise motion makes it less noticeable to the ear that you moved into another scale. By the time the ear catches on and hears the notes as wrong, you're already back in the right scale.

CHAPTER 35: SECONDARY DOMINANTS

The V chord in a major scale is called the dominant. It wants to resolve to the first chord of the scale. While I have never seen the V7 in a major scale being called the "primary dominant," there is a concept in music theory called **secondary dominants**.

Secondary dominants are dominants that resolve to any of the other six chords in the scale.

For example, you could precede the IIm chord in the scale by its dominant chord, or the IIIm by its dominant chord, and so on.

Songwriters and composers use secondary dominants to create stronger forward motion and momentum in songs. You will find them in the higher-level songs by, for example The Beatles, David Bowie, and ABBA, just to name a few.

When you do song and chord analysis in music schools, you label secondary dominants as:

"**V7** slash *scale degree (of the chord that V7 resolves to)*."

An example of a secondary dominant is V7/V, which is how you label a dominant chord that resolves down a 5th to chord number V in the scale.

V7/II means: dominant chord of chord number II in the scale. In the key of C, the V7/II is A7. Here's how you figure this out:

First off, you figure out which chord II is. In the key of C, II is Dm.

Then, you figure out what the dominant (V7) chord is that wants to resolve down a 5th to Dm. In other words: you need a dominant chord that is up five letters from D.

The V7 chord that wants to resolve to Dm is A7.

V7/II is pronounced as "V7 to II" (or, in other words: the V7 that resolves to II in the scale.)

Here come all the secondary dominant chords in the key of C. *(The secondary dominants are in bold typeface.)* Play the below chord progressions and notice how every secondary dominant creates strong forward momentum into the resolution chord that follows it.

- ▶ **V7/II** ➡ The V7 of Dm

    Cmaj7 | **A7** | Dm | G7

- ▶ **V7/III** ➡ The V7 of Em

    Cmaj7 | **B7** | Em | G7

176

- **V7/IV ➡ The V7 of F**

  Cmaj7 | **C7** | Fmaj7 | G7 ||

- **V7/V ➡ The V7 of G**

  Cmaj7 | Am | **D7** | G7

- **V7/VI ➡ The V7 of Am**

  Cmaj7 | **E7** | Am | Dm G7 ||

Lastly, there isn't really a secondary dominant for VII in a major scale. There are two problems preventing **V7/VII** from sounding like a secondary dominant.

1. VII in a major scale is an unstable-sounding chord. In the key of C, that chord is Bdim *(triad)* or Bm7♭5 *(7th chord)*. The scale built on that chord is the Locrian scale. When you play a Locrian scale, you can hear that that scale is not very suitable to write songs with. Because of its structure with the ♭2 and ♭5, the Locrian scale doesn't lend itself really well to create stories. The melodies sound kind a weird, there is no sense of tension or resolution, and the melodies don't feel like they're going anywhere or saying anything. The Bm7♭5 chord also feels like it's not exactly a chord you can resolve to.

2. The Bm7♭5 chord has so many notes in common with the V chord G7 that it just sounds like a G7 chord minus the G root.

   - Bm7♭5 = **B D F** A
   - G7 = G **B D F**

   The V dominant chord is such a strong-sounding chord in the major scale that the VIIm7♭5 chord, having so many notes in common with V, automatically always ends up sounding like a V chord. You can hear this really well in the following chord progression where the Bm7♭5 chord is preceded by its dominant chord, F♯7.

Cmaj7 | Fmaj7 | **F♯7** | Bm7♭5

Compare the sound of this F♯7 secondary dominant in this chord progression with the sound of the other five secondary dominants in the chord progressions above. Do you notice a difference in sound or feel?

To my ear, the F♯7 sounds more like a passing chord, not like a secondary dominant chord. The chord progression sounds and feels like Cmaj7 Fmaj7 F♯7 **G** (instead of Bm7♭5).

The point being made:

The F♯7 doesn't sound like it resolved down a 5th, but like it moved up a half step.

You might think to yourself, "Well yeah, of course it would sound like a passing chord when you have it preceded by an F chord." You get F F♯ G (remember: Bm7♭5 sounds like a G7 chord).

However, it doesn't really matter what chord you play before the F♯7. It's never going to sound like a secondary dominant resolving down a 5th to Bm7♭5.

Play the following chord progression: **Cmaj7 Dm7 F♯7 Bm7♭5**. Notice how the F♯7 now sounds like an approach chord. It still sounds like it moved up a half step to a chord that sounds like a G chord.

Conclusion:

There is no **V7/VII** because it doesn't sound like a secondary dominant.

There are only five secondary dominants:

1. V7/II
2. V7/III
3. V7/IV
4. V7/V
5. V7/VI

V7/I is the (primary) dominant we already have in the scale, and V7/VII is not an option because it doesn't sound like a secondary dominant.

Play the above chord progressions a couple of times every day. You ideally want to memorize them. Once you have those mastered and memorized, practice each of those five chord progressions in all twelve keys.

In addition, when you write songs, see if you can find ways to incorporate secondary dominants, preceding one of the chords (that is not the I chord) by its dominant chord.

Above all, have fun and be creative with it all.

Lastly, when jamming with friends or playing their songs, see if you can occasionally interject a secondary dominant that resolves to a target chord of your choosing in their song. You will see their eyes light up marveling at your genius.

Jazz musicians do this all the time, btw. A large part of what they do when they comp is finding ways to throw in extra II V progressions throughout a song. In a song in the key of C for example, a jazz musician oftentimes will throw in a Bm7 E7 progression, if there is space to do so, in the bar preceding an Am chord, even when those chords are not in the song.

CHAPTER 36: HARMONY IN COMPOSITION & SONGWRITING

I, IV, V

You probably have heard of I IV V before in the study of music.

The 1st, 4th, and 5th chord in a scale are the main chords that help build and guide all storytelling in a song. While musicians and music theory books always refer to I IV V as **chords**, the role of I IV V and its importance in musical story-telling actually goes way beyond just "chords." They're not I IV V chords, but I IV V experiences, emotions, characters, qualities, sensations, vibes. We even gave them names.

I is called the **tonic**, IV is called the **sub-dominant**, and V is called the **dominant**.

Because each of these three chords possesses a specific, intrinsic quality that fulfills one of the fundamental prerequisites that lie at the foundation of storytelling in all art forms, I, IV, and V perform certain functions—tasks, so to speak—within a song.

Chord Functions Within a Major Scale

What are those prerequisites without which there can be no storytelling, which I, IV and V provide us?

Answer:
- ▷ Starting point of a journey (home base, familiarity)
- ▷ Development (travel, out and about, on the go, the story is evolving, uncertainty)
- ▷ Tension (a breaking point, a drastic turn of events, a sentence that ends halfway and leaves you hanging or confused)
- ▷ Resolution (coming full circle, back home, back at ease, acceptance, or victory)

I, IV, and V provide all that.

▶ The tonic (I)

When you think of a scale as a seven-note journey climbing up in pitch, then I (the tonic) can be thought of as the place where it all starts. The tonic feels peaceful. This is the chord a song typically starts and ends on. It feels like home base, a point of no tension. It's the place you start from and always eventually keep coming back to.

▶ **The sub-dominant (IV)**

IV feels like things are moving. It feels like this chord in the overall progression of the key a song is written in wants to go somewhere. There's a bit of a feel of uncertainty, though, which is also exciting. Is it going to go back to I? Is it going to move on to full tension?

It can go either way.

▶ **The dominant (V)**

The dominant chord is the chord that brings the tension in a chord progression. V always wants to resolve to I. For that reason, V typically occurs before I.

This creates strong forward momentum when its tension resolves.

As a fun experiment that will showcase the tension of the V chord, play the following chord progression:

C | C | F | G |

C | Am | F | G |

G | G ||

Doesn't that ending drive you nuts? It sounds as if someone is saying: "Woooaaaw man, yesterday I went to the story and..."

Only to leave or start talking about an entirely different topic right after.

The chord progression, just like the sentence, feels unfinished. It's leaving you hanging, and it gets on your nerves after a while. The G chord (V) feels like an unfinished statement that never came to a conclusion.

It feels like a question, and you're not getting the answer you're longing for. All that gets resolved when eventually a C chord is played. Aahhhh... relief!

Common Progressions

    a. 12-bar blues

    b. I | I | IV | V

    c. I | V | I | V | I | V

    d. I | IV | I | V (This progression always reminds me of the Ramones.)

Of course, these progressions would eventually all end on the I chord when the song ends.

Substitutions

Now you might think to yourself: What about the other four chords in the scale? Seems like a shame to not use the four extra chord colors that we could enrich our songs with.

As it turns out, II, III, VI and VII can be categorized as either a I, a IV, or a V feel chord. The way this works is that chords that share many the same notes are going to sound very similar, and hence share the same I, IV, or V feel.

That is why I, IV, and V can be substituted with the other chords in the scale.

1. Tonic feel: Imaj7 can be substituted by III-7 and VI-7

I, IIIm, and VIm share many of the same notes.

Here are those chords shown as 7th chords. Of course, you could just play them as triads C, Am, and Em, but seeing I, III, and VI as four-note chords shows even more notes overlapping.

Imaj7 = C E G B
III-7 = E G B **D**
VI-7 = **A** C E G

To further enhance the notion that these three chords all feel like a I chord, consider:

- ▶ When the bass player hits a C bass note while you strum an Em7 chord, your combined notes sound like a Cmaj9 chord.
- ▶ When the bass player hits a C bass note while you strum an Am7 chord, your combined notes sound like a C6 chord.

2. Sub-dominant feel: IVmaj7 can be substituted by II-7

IVmaj7 = F A C E

II-7 = **D** F A C ➡ creates an F6 sound when the bass player hits an F

3. Dominant feel: V7 can be substituted by VII-7♭5

V7 = G B D F

VII-7♭5 = B D F **A** ➡ creates a G9 sound when played over a G bass note.

Common Progressions

||: Cmaj7 | Am7 | Fmaj7 | G7 :||

||: Cmaj7 | Am7 | Dm7 | G7 :||

||: Cmaj7 | Em7 | Dm7 | G7 :||

||: Cmaj7 | Em7 | Fmaj7 | G7 :||

CHAPTER 37: MAJOR BLUES RHYTHM STYLES

Honky Tonk Style

This is **the** most common and most used major blues rhythm guitar style.

There is no musical name or term to describe this blues guitar accompaniment style. I like calling it "honky tonk style" because this rhythm style is reminiscent of the piano player's left hand (bass) part in honky tonk piano.

Major Blues Rhythm Styles

Blues Bass Lines

All the following bass lines are in the key of G.

Pick with down strokes only. You want bass lines to sound big and full.

Here are ten more blues bass lines like this, all one bar long. Unlike above, in the following ten bass line examples, I'm only giving the first measure. You need to play every bar twelve times, moving each one-bar exercise through a twelve-bar blues progression.

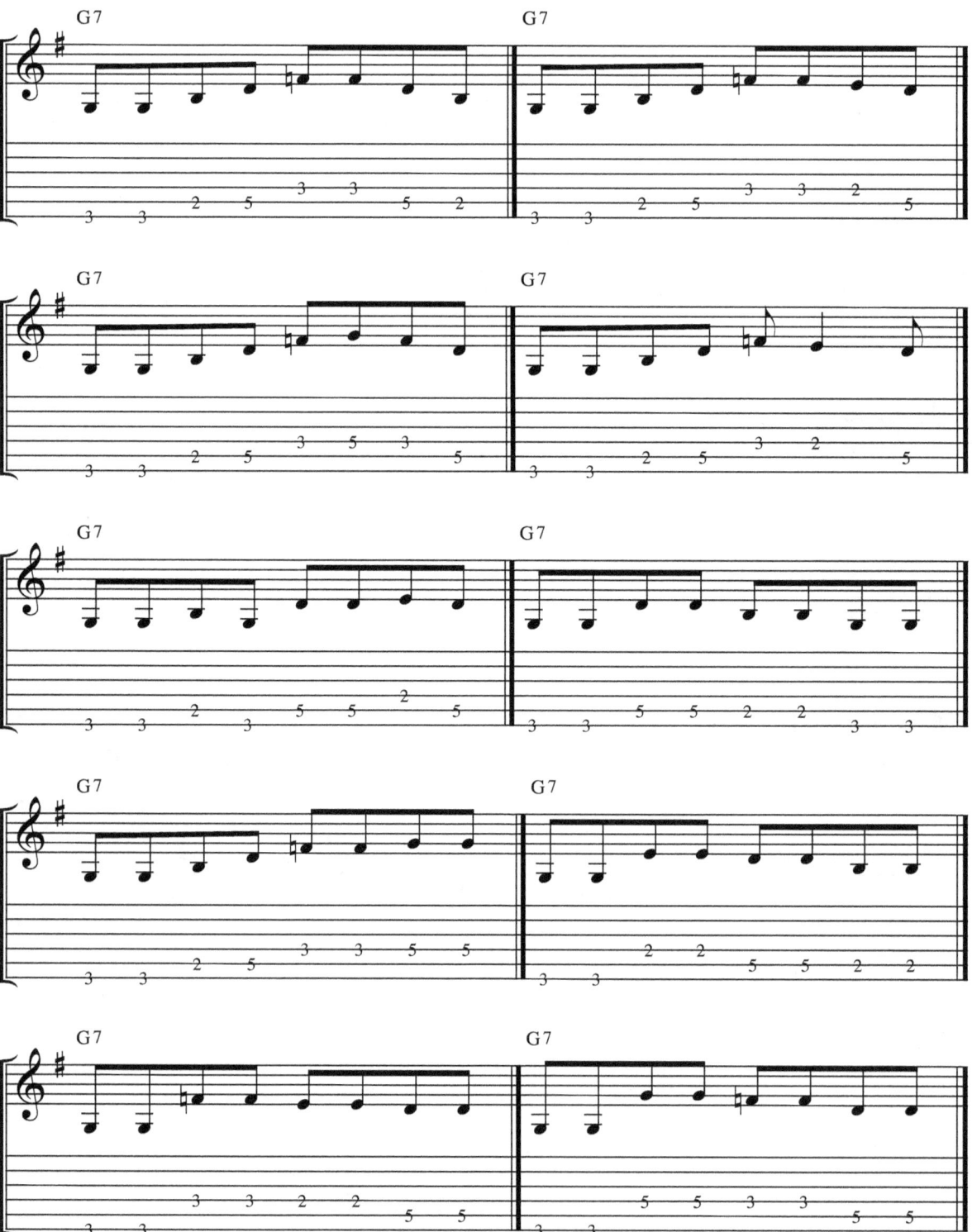

Blues With Approach Chords from Below

This is a very driven and swinging blues rhythm style. Here's how you play this:

- ▶ Play a dominant 7th chord as notated in the below chart. (Use middle, ring, pinky.)
- ▶ Strum down strokes only.
- ▶ Make every chord short—lift up your fingers right after every chord hit.
- ▶ Swing it. You do this by making your down strum longer than the up motion in the strum arm.
- ▶ Occasionally hit the strings in the upstroke to accentuate the swing. This will create a mute, since we are making the chords short, lifting up our fingers after every down stroke.
- ▶ Every time you move to another chord, approach that chord from a half step below. That is called an **approach chord.** You hit the approach chord on the last beat of the previous bar before the chord change. Study the following transcription for this to make more sense.

Blues With Approach Chords From Above

This is the same as above, but every chord is approached from a half step above.

Once you can comfortably play those two blues examples with the from-above and from-below approach chords, you're ready for the next level of fun: freely combining them.

As you probably can tell when you play the above, after a while the approach chords sound a bit predictable when you're always approaching from the same direction. It gets really fun and starts sounding really cool when you randomly decide on which direction you're going to approach each chord from. Ideally you want to aim for about 50-50. Approach half the chords from a half step below and the others from a half step above.

Blues With Sliding 9th Chords

This is a heavily used rhythm guitar style in major blues. The chord shape we're using for this is actually a m7♭5 chord shape. When you hit a Bm7♭5 over a G bass note, you get a G9 chord
➡ **G B D F A**

Hit the chord on the second beat of the bar. *(The bass player hits the root on the first beat.)* Then, slide up two frets, and on the same second beat quickly move back down two frets and hit the chord again while in its original starting position before the slide. Let the chord then sustain for the rest of the bar.

Here's how to play this.

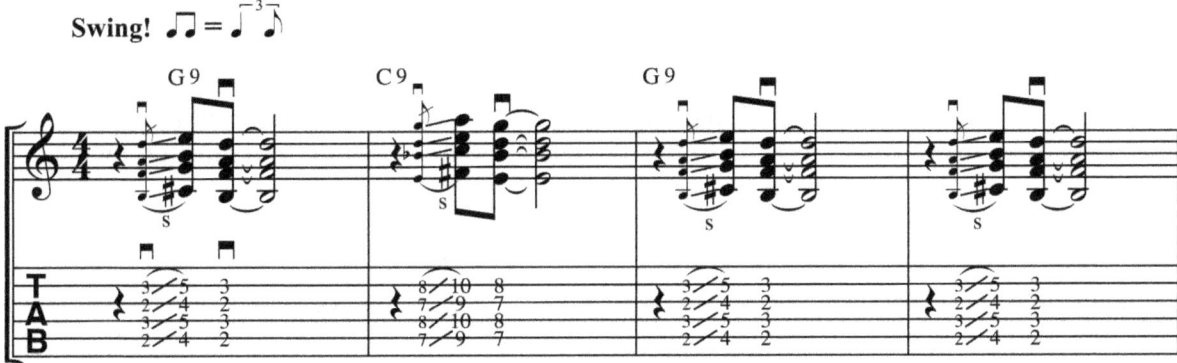

IN CLOSING

In closing, this is of course not a complete book on guitar or music theory. This book barely scratches the surface on music theory or the vast universe of things you can do with a guitar.

It should, however, give you enough material or new ideas to keep you going for a while.

Experiment with all the material covered, have fun with it, make it your own.

As you keep working on the lessons covered in this book, you will see yourself get better every day. You will also get more creative, with an enhanced sense of esteem and confidence.

That's exactly why I wrote this book. That, and bringing more musical joy into your life and your world. After all, music is not only a ton of fun, but it also gets all the more fun the better you keep getting at it.

I hope you enjoyed the book and learned a lot.

Hit me up anytime at **vreny@zotzinmusic.com** to share your thoughts or ideas, or if you have any questions. I would love to hear from you.

Thank you so much!

Vreny Van Elslande

VRENY & ZOT ZIN MUSIC

About Vreny

Vreny was born in Belgium in the early 1970s. He grew up listening to the Beatles, The Bee Gees, soul music, disco, and whatever else he heard on the radio that was constantly playing in his parents' house. He was almost seventeen when a high school classmate started playing guitar and got Vreny interested in playing. Around the same time, Vreny discovered Jimi Hendrix and was awestruck.

By the time he was twenty, Vreny was playing the songs of his idols—The Beatles, Queen, Jimi, Led Zeppelin, and all the great classic rock bands from the 1970s.

Vreny finished high school in 1989, and, after a year in the military in Germany, he returned to his hometown of Ypres in Belgium to attend the Academy for Music and Word (SAMW), where he studied classical guitar and composition.

Vreny finished SAMW's ten-year intense classical guitar program in about seven years, graduated with honors, and received special awards for outstanding achievement as a classical guitarist.

In 1998, Vreny left Belgium to go to Berklee College of Music in Boston, where he refined his guitar playing and compositional skills. He received scholarships and awards throughout his time at Berklee, and in 2002, Vreny graduated Summa Cum Laude from Berklee College of Music with two Bachelor's Degrees in (Jazz) Guitar Performance as well as Music Production & Engineering.

After many years of non-stop studying, teaching, and performing any style of music in numerous bands throughout the years, Vreny moved to Los Angeles in 2002.

Soon after arrival in LA, he restarted his guitar teaching business and produced demos from his home-based recording studio. He performed and co-wrote songs with various artists, including Leah King, whose dad is one of the founding members of the Commodores. Through the years, Vreny built a roster of many celebrity clients and famous musicians who hired him as a guitar coach and music teacher.

Vreny's songs and bands have played on the radio both in Europe and the US.

The single "Madland," released with his band, Automatik Eden, reached 12th place on the national Billboard charts.

About ZOT Zin Music & Guitar Lessons

ZOT Zin Music provides private one-on-one guitar and music lessons, as well as music recording and production services.

"**ZOT Zin**" is Flemish. (It's the language spoken in the northern part of Belgium.)

"**ZOT**" means "crazy," with all the same connotations as in the English language: crazy, unconventional, passionate, wild, but also "in love," and so on.

"**Zin**" means "to be."

To sum it all up: "**To be in love with music.**"

True to the company name, we have created a unique approach to guitar and music learning that has shown to create much better results than other guitar learning systems or schools.

Our students experience outstanding results because:

1. Each student gets a personalized guitar curriculum, customized to cater to each individual's learning styles, goals, and wishes.

2. That customized guitar plan is conveyed through a teaching approach that applies success principles of super-study, psychology, music pedagogy, time management, and neuroscience.

In other words, on the one hand there is the fact that the students get a completely personalized lesson plan to achieve their specific music goals with the least amount of effort in the least amount of time... and then there's also the way that lesson plan is taught. The teacher uses communication styles and methods that help the student get the best learning experience, and that maximizes the student's learning productivity in every lesson.

This leads to a unique approach to guitar education, which more than any approach really helps each student get the absolute maximum ROI out of their talent, focus skills, practice time, and lesson investment.

Lessons are fun and up-tempo, with lots of information and performance feedback conveyed in a very efficient and relaxed way.

Our students have weekly, well thought-of, fun exercises and timed drills for maximum impact and efficiency. Students see instant, fast, strong progress in their guitar playing, whatever level they are at, from complete beginner to intermediate to highly advanced.

That faster progress is also a huge money-saver, because students get more quality and more peace of mind knowing that they can do this, as well as better results for their money.

Pricing

I charge $75 an hour for guitar/music lessons

- ▶ **4 lessons** = $300
- ▶ **10 lessons** = $665 (you save $85)
- ▶ **20 lessons** = $1,199 (you save $301)
- ▶ **40 lessons** = $2,240 (you save $760)
- ▶ **50 lessons** = $2,700 (you save $1,050)
- ▶ **75 lessons** = $3,850 (you save $1,775)
- ▶ **100 lessons** = $4,900 (you save $2600)

Specialized twelve-week programs = $1,199

Specialized twelve-week programs include:

- ▶ Blues Guitar
- ▶ Fret Board Mastery
- ▶ Guitar Scales
- ▶ Master "Moving Pictures" (Rush Album)

There are payment plans available for larger packages.

You can check all rate info out here: **https://www.ZOTZinGuitarLessons.com/tuition/**

A Special Word of Thanks To:

Dr. Angela Blewitt for her much-needed help in reviewing, proofreading, and editing this book. I am so unbelievably grateful and happy we are such close friends. This book turned out all the better because of your expertise.

Dylan Garity for the amazing work he did getting my manuscript in shape, improving my language, wording, and so much more. I'm so happy to have you on my team.

Ani Boyadjian, my very dear friend and the Principal Librarian at Los Angeles Public Library, who helped me with the copyright page and guided me in improving this book. I can't begin to tell you how honored I feel that you contributed the copyright page in my book. Now we're even more connected for life, and I love that.

Ljiljana Pavkov for the fantastic job done on the inner page design and book design. I don't know what I would have done without your amazing expertise.

A big thank you to my graphic artist Andrey Poletskiy, for being able to realize my visions and for keeping up with my need to get it to look exactly right. I LOVE what you did with the cover.

My amazing best friends David Crocco and Cela Scott: You know how much I love you.

All my many music, guitar, songwriting, and composition teachers, who all shared their knowledge, skills, and insights with me. I am forever grateful.

My hundreds of colleague musicians I performed, jammed, or recorded with in the past thirty-plus years. It's been a blast. I can only imagine the many more fun music adventures that lie awaiting us.

My students who are making all this possible, and who keep propelling me forward to constantly keep improving things. I obviously could never have done any of this without you.

The over a thousand authors and researchers whose books I've read in past thirty years on psychology, pedagogy, music education, neuroscience, NLP, and learning styles.

Mum and Dad and my sister and her family: Thank you for always being there for me. I'm sure I sometimes must have driven you nuts with my loud guitar solos and the many hours of practicing every day.

Last but not least, the love of my life and extraordinary wife: Tiannah York Van Elslande. I'm so lucky and blessed I get to share my life with you. We'll keep laughing our butts off together for eternity, sweetie. And of course the other love of my life: Aiden, my lovely son, I love you. The last song about you has not been written yet.

Review

Before you go, I wanted to say thank you for purchasing this book.

You could have picked from hundreds of other guitar books, but you took a chance and chose this one.

So thank you for picking this one and studying it all the way to the end.

If you enjoyed this book and feel that you learned a lot, help me spread the word please by posting a review on Amazon. You'd be supporting an independent artist, and help other people find the value you found in this book. I'd be very grateful if you'd post a short review.

Your support really does make a difference because I read all reviews personally so I can get your feedback and make this book even better. This feedback also helps me continue to write the books that will help you get the results you want.

So if you enjoyed it, please let me know.

Thank you very much. It means a lot to me!

Contact Info

Website: https://www.ZOTZinGuitarLessons.com

Phone: 310-902-0993

Email: info@zotzinmusic.com

Facebook: https://www.facebook.com/ZOTZinMusic
Twitter: https://twitter.com/ZOTZinMusic
Yelp: https://www.yelp.com/biz/vrenys-guitar-lessons-los-angeles
Other: https://www.youtube.com/user/ZOTZin?feature=mhee

FREE BONUS GOODIES

Writing a book is not only an enormous endeavor—the writer also strives to give a ton of value to you, the reader, without making the book so big that it becomes super expensive. As a result, to keep the page count manageable, I had to omit some great information and some chapters I had initially planned to include. So it occurred to me, "Why not give this to you as a FREE bonus?"

To get your free bonus materials, head to my website:

https://ZOTZinGuitarLessons.com/guitaressentials/BONUS/

Here's what you get:

1. A collection of **over fifty backing tracks** you can download to practice the material covered in each chapter.
2. Extra lesson: "Minor pentatonic scale patterns" PDF
3. Single-String Extras: "Some Bonus Benefits You Get from Single-String Soloing" PDF
4. A results-tracking page for the "Twenty-Four Finger Combinations" chapter
5. Results-tracking pages for the whole book
6. Four FREE **Bonus Chapters:**
    a. The Solfeggio Note Names for Accidentals
    b. Country Rhythm Guitar Bass Transitions
    c. Ostinatos
    d. How to Figure Out Chords to Songs
7. **Instruction videos** showcasing how to perform some of the material covered in the book.
8. Links for every URL mentioned in the book, so you don't have to type lengthy URLs. You can just click them from the Guitar Essentials webpage.

As a matter of fact, go to the website right now and claim all your bonus materials first, so you have them available to help you learn and practice all the material you're about to tackle in this book.

www.ingramcontent.com/pod-product-compliance
Lightning Source LLC
Chambersburg PA
CBHW080919170426
43201CB00016B/2193